OCTOBER 1962
THE
'MISSILE' CRISIS
AS SEEN FROM
CUBA

OCTOBER 1962

THE 'MISSILE' CRISIS AS SEEN FROM CUBA

TOMÁS DIEZ ACOSTA

PATHFINDER

New York London Montreal Sydney

Edited by Steve Clark and Mary-Alice Waters

ISBN 0-87348-956-X
Library of Congress Control Number 2002110965
Manufactured in the United States of America

First edition, 2002

Cover photo: Fidel Castro visits artillery forces during October Crisis of 1962
(Verde Olivo).
Cover design: Eva Braiman.
Photo pages design: Eric Simpson.
Map preparation: Mike Shur and Eric Simpson.

Pathfinder
410 West Street, New York, NY 10014, U.S.A.
www.pathfinderpress.com
E-mail: pathfinderpress@compuserve.com
Fax: (212) 727-0150

PATHFINDER DISTRIBUTORS AROUND THE WORLD:
Australia (and Southeast Asia and the Pacific):
     Pathfinder, Level 1, 3/281-287 Beamish St., Campsie, NSW 2194
     Postal address: P.O. Box 164, Campsie, NSW 2194
Canada:
     Pathfinder, 2761 Dundas St. West, Toronto, ON, M6P 1Y4
Iceland:
     Pathfinder, Skolavordustig 6B, Reykjavík
     Postal address: P. Box 0233, IS 121 Reykjavík
New Zealand:
     Pathfinder, P.O. Box 3025, Auckland
Sweden:
     Pathfinder, Domargränd 16, S-129 47 Hägersten
United Kingdom (and Europe, Africa, Middle East, and South Asia):
     Pathfinder, 47 The Cut, London, SE1 8LL
United States (and Caribbean, Latin America, and East Asia):
     Pathfinder, 410 West Street, New York, NY 10014

"We possess moral long-range missiles
that cannot be dismantled
and will never be dismantled.
This is our strongest strategic weapon."

FIDEL CASTRO
NOVEMBER 1, 1962

＊

Contents

About the author   9

Preface to the English-language edition   11

Initials and abbreviations   21

Introduction   25

1. After the Bay of Pigs: The secret war continues   28

2. Cuba responds   59

3. Operation Mongoose and U.S. invasion plans   75

4. Top secret: Operation Anadyr   93

5. The secret and the deception   125

6. The crisis begins   135

7. The brilliant yet sad days of the crisis   155

8. In defense of principles   178

By way of an epilogue   199

Documents of the Cuban government

Draft agreement between Cuba and the USSR
on military cooperation and mutual defense
    August 1962   207

'The imperialists will find a people willing to defend
the nation house by house, inch by inch'
    Declaration by the Council of Ministers,
    September 29, 1962   213

'Anyone who tries to inspect Cuba
better come in full combat gear'
    Address by Fidel Castro, October 23, 1962   224

'Our five points are minimum conditions
to guarantee peace'
    Discussions with U Thant, October 30–31, 1962   256

'We have as little faith in Kennedy's words
as we have fear of his threats'
    Cuba's position on the Caribbean crisis,
    November 25, 1962   285

Notes   293

Glossary of individuals   309

Bibliography   317

Index   323

Map: Soviet missile placements in Cuba,
October 22, 1962   18

About the author

Born in Havana in 1946, Tomás Diez Acosta joined Cuba's Revolutionary Armed Forces (FAR) in 1961. During the 1962 October Crisis, he participated in the general mobilization in Cuba as a political instructor in Military Unit 2562 in the country's western region. From 1970 to 1986 he taught history at the General Máximo Gómez Academy of the FAR, and other higher military schools. In 1976 he graduated from the University of Havana with a degree in political science. He retired from active military service in 1998 with the rank of lieutenant colonel.

Since 1987 Diez has worked as a researcher at the Institute of Cuban History, where, among other responsibilities, he headed its Department of Military History. He has participated in the Cuba-Russia-U.S. tripartite international conferences on the October 1962 crisis in Moscow (1989), Antigua (1991), Havana (1992), and Moscow (1994). He also participated in "Girón: Forty Years Later," the Cuba-U.S. International Academic Conference on the Bay of Pigs invasion, held in Havana in 2001.

Published works by Diez include: *Peligros y principios* [Dangers and principles] (1992), which received honorable mention by the Cuban Academy of Sciences; *La guerra encubierta contra Cuba* [The covert war against Cuba] (1997); *La crisis de los misiles 1962. Una reflexión cubana* [The 1962 missile crisis: a Cuban view] (1997); and *La confrontación Cuba – Estados Unidos, a partir de la Primera Ley de Reforma Agraria* [The confrontation between Cuba and the United States beginning with the first agrarian reform law] (2002), which won a Concurso Julio award for books on social and political topics.

Preface to the English-language edition

In October 1962, during what is widely known as the Cuban Missile Crisis, Washington pushed the world to the precipice of nuclear war. Scores of books on the subject have been written by partisans of Washington and of Moscow. Here, for the first time, the story of that historic moment is told in full from the perspective of the central protagonist, the Cuban people and their revolutionary government.

The author, Tomás Diez Acosta, joined the ranks of the Revolutionary Armed Forces of Cuba in 1961 as a literacy worker, one of the three hundred thousand young Cubans who mobilized to the mountains, factories, fields, barrios, barracks, and fishing villages during Cuba's Year of Education to teach every Cuban how to read and write. He was fourteen years old. In the midst of an exploding revolutionary struggle there was no "minimum age" for combatants, Diez says with a laugh. When he retired from active military service thirty-seven years later he held the rank of lieutenant colonel. For the last fifteen years, as a researcher at the Institute of Cuban History, he has been assembling the material to tell the story that appears here, much of it in print for the first time.

Presenting a wealth of new information from Cuban archives and from interviews with direct participants, Diez details:

• the determination and readiness of Cuba's working people to defend the country's newly won sovereignty and the achievements of their unfolding socialist revolution against the increasingly aggressive designs of U.S. imperialism, including the full-scale bombing and invasion it was preparing during the October Crisis;

• the decision by Cuba's revolutionary leadership to allow

Soviet missiles to be stationed on the island, not because they thought such weapons were needed to defend Cuba from U.S. military assault, but as an act of international solidarity as the USSR was being ringed by U.S. strategic nuclear arms;

• the carrying out of Operation Anadyr, the code name for the eventual deployment of some 42,000 Soviet troops and missile units in Cuba between August and November 1962;

• the day-by-day unfolding of what Cuban revolutionary leader Ernesto Che Guevara called the "brilliant yet sad days" of the October Crisis, and the course followed by the revolutionary government as it worked simultaneously to defend Cuba's sovereignty and move Washington back from the brink.

Drawing on declassified White House, Central Intelligence Agency, and Pentagon files available largely to "specialists," the author makes the record of U.S. government policy accessible to the average reader. He documents Washington's plans for a massive military assault on Cuba in 1962, exposing the protestations of defenders of the administration of John F. Kennedy who have claimed the U.S. government had no such intentions.

On April 19, 1961, after fewer than seventy-two hours of hard-fought combat, the Cuban armed forces, national militias, revolutionary police, and fledgling air force had dealt a stunning defeat to a U.S.-trained, -organized, and -financed mercenary invasion force of some 1,500 at Playa Girón close by the Bay of Pigs on Cuba's southern coast. From that day on, as the pages that follow amply attest, U.S. policy makers at the highest levels acted on the conclusion that the revolutionary government of Cuba could be overthrown only by direct U.S. military action. And they marshaled seemingly limitless resources to prepare for that moment. Under the personal guidance of the president's brother, Attorney General Robert F. Kennedy, "Operation Mongoose," with its multifaceted plans for sabotage, subversion, and assassination of Cuba's revolutionary leaders, was unleashed to pave the way.

In October 1962, when U.S. spy planes photographed Soviet missile launch sites under construction in Cuba, the U.S. rulers recognized that the military and political costs of such an invasion were being qualitatively transformed, and they initiated the adventure detailed in these pages.

Most U.S. commentators treat the events of October 1962 as a Cold War showdown between the two superpowers, in which Cuba was at best a pawn, at worst a raging mute offstage. In that scenario the people of Cuba do not exist, nor in fact do the tens of thousands of Americans across the country who acted to oppose imperialist Washington's preparations for a military assault.

As Diez demonstrates in these pages, however, the roots of the crisis in the Caribbean lay not in Washington's Cold War with the Soviet Union, but in the drive by the U.S. government to overthrow the "first free territory of the Americas." Kennedy's acceptance of Khrushchev's offer to withdraw the missiles—an offer broadcast worldwide over Radio Moscow without even informing the Cuban government—was how the stand-down of the two strategic nuclear powers was announced. But it was the armed mobilization and political clarity of the Cuban people, and the capacities of their revolutionary leadership, that stayed Washington's hand, saving humanity from the consequences of a nuclear holocaust.

Divergent political courses pursued by the Cuban and Soviet governments marked each step. The Soviet leadership, seeking a way to enhance its strategic military position and to counter the Jupiter missiles the U.S. had recently installed in Turkey and Italy, insisted on secrecy and attempted deception. Cuba took the moral high ground, arguing from the beginning for the public announcement of the mutual assistance pact and the right of the Cuban people to defend themselves against U.S. aggression.

The defeat of the invasion force at the Bay of Pigs had bought precious time for Cuba to organize, train, and equip its Revolutionary Armed Forces. Even more decisive, the people of Cuba used that time to consolidate the agrarian reform; win the battle of the literacy campaign; build schools, homes, and hospitals;

extend electrification; advance social equality among Cuba's working people; and strengthen the worker-farmer alliance that was the bedrock of the revolution and of the respect Cuba had earned among the world's toilers. As they navigated the contradictory dialectic of the greatly appreciated aid they received from the USSR, the Cuban people were not only defending themselves against the Yankee predator. They stood *for* the future of humanity, as they stood *down* the power of U.S. imperialism.

And despite all odds they prevailed.

On October 26, at a decisive moment in the unfolding crisis, John F. Kennedy asked the Pentagon for an estimate of the U.S. casualties that would be incurred during the invasion they were weighing. He was informed that the Joint Chiefs of Staff expected 18,500 casualties in the first ten days alone—greater than the casualties U.S. troops would suffer in the entire first five years of fighting in Vietnam. And knowledgeable Cuban military personnel say U.S. casualties would have been far greater. From that moment on, Kennedy turned White House strategists away from their well-advanced plans to use U.S. military forces in an attempt to overthrow the revolution. The political price such body counts would entail continues to this day to hold off any direct U.S. military attack against Cuba.

As Cuba has proven not once but multiple times over the last forty-some years, the empire, despite its pretensions to hegemony, is in fact a tethered monster when a determined people, with a leadership worthy of it, does not flinch.

Inside the United States, a widely promoted myth has it that ordinary Americans everywhere were so consumed by panic over the danger of nuclear attack that they, too, were not a factor during these historic events. Those of us who lived through those days of crisis as active political people, however, know the extent of that lie.

The news clips of grocery stores swamped by semi-hysterical middle-class housewives buying up canned goods and flashlight batteries to stock their basement bomb shelters misrepresent the broader mood that prevailed. Most working people, aware of the heightened tensions, nonetheless went about their normal lives of work and family responsibilities.

Thousands of young people, meanwhile, as well as other partisans of the Cuban Revolution, took to the streets, determined to repudiate the course taken by a government that did not speak in our name. As the photographs in *October 1962* depict, some of these actions turned into violent confrontations when they were assaulted by ultraright-wing student organizations urged on by cops.

An October 24 demonstration on the steps of the student union on the Minneapolis campus of the University of Minnesota in which I took part came within a hairsbreadth of such an outcome. There were twenty of us perhaps, including members of the Student Peace Union, Fair Play for Cuba Committee, Socialist Workers Party, Communist Party, socialists and pacifists, and the chapters of the Young Socialist Alliance in Minneapolis and at nearby Carleton College where I was the newest member. With placards and bullhorns, we demanded an immediate lifting of the naval blockade and "U.S. Hands Off Cuba!" We held our ground as several thousand counterdemonstrators surrounded us, some hurling eggs and waving fraternity banners as they led a rhythmic chant of "War! War! War! War!"

Small though some of these protest actions were, we never felt isolated. To the contrary, we saw ourselves as part of the immense majority of humanity, starting with the workers, farmers, and young people of Cuba itself. We knew they would never go down on their knees before the nuclear blackmail of the Yankee colossus, and we were determined to stand with them. Justice and history were on our side. Far from any sense of panic or helplessness, we were conscious that our actions had weight, that minute by minute the men in the White House were calculating the political consequences of their potential moves. Each hour they postponed invading, each day they didn't launch a nuclear missile, was a victory. And each day our actions grew larger, and spread to more cities and towns across the United States.

They were a harbinger of what was to explode a few short years later in response to the Vietnam War, as Washington desperately tried—and again failed—to vanquish another people who would not flinch.

October 1962: The 'Missile' Crisis as Seen from Cuba makes the real dynamic of the October Crisis available for the first time. Therein lies its lasting merit.

❋

The Spanish-language original of this work was published in June 2002 in Havana by Editora Política, the publishing house of the Central Committee of the Communist Party of Cuba, under the title *Octubre de 1962: A un paso del holocausto: una mirada Cubana a la crisis de los misiles* [October 1962: One step from the holocaust: a Cuban look at the missile crisis]. Cuban editor Iraida Aguirrechu provided valuable assistance in preparing the English-language edition.

For the Pathfinder edition the author expanded and reorganized the structure of some chapters. Also included are translations of a number of major Cuban documents of the epoch, most of them never before published in English, or long unavailable. The September 29, 1962, declaration by Cuba's Council of Ministers appears here in English for the first time. The transcript of the October 30–31, 1962, meetings between United Nations Secretary-General U Thant and a Cuban leadership delegation headed by Prime Minister Fidel Castro has not previously been published in full in any language.

The original translation of the manuscript and integration of the English-language sources was the work of Ornán Batista Peña of the Institute of Cuban History.

A team of volunteers organized by John Riddell and George Rose, including Paul Coltrin, Robert Dees, Dan Dickeson, Mirta Vidal, and Matilde Zimmermann, edited the translation. They were supervised in this work by Pathfinder editor Michael Taber. George Rose undertook the considerable task of checking the sources.

Help in assembling the photo pages came from the author, as well as Delfín Xiqués of *Granma* and Manuel Martínez of *Bohemia*.

Finally, Pathfinder would like to express special appreciation to the Institute of Cuban History and to Tomás Diez Acosta. With competence and good humor the author devoted many days of work to reviewing the English-language manuscript, clarifying questions of translation and factual accuracy, and assuring that this edition would be accessible and understandable to readers outside Cuba, whether or not they lived through those historic days of October.

Mary-Alice Waters
AUGUST 2002

Soviet missile placements in Cuba, October 22, 1962

160 KILOMETERS
100 MILES

 Headquarters of Soviet Troop Force

 IL-28 bomber base

 MIG-21 fighter jet regiment

 Komar missile-carrying boat brigade

 Central nuclear warhead depot

 Motorized infantry regiment

 Coastal defense headquarters and Sopka missile launch center

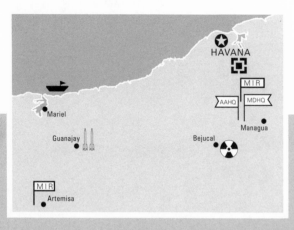

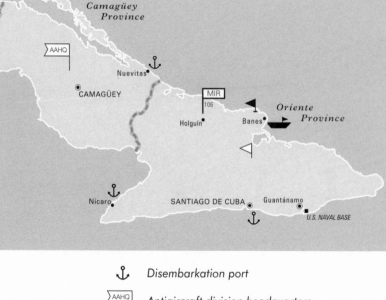

⚓	Disembarkation port
AAHQ	Antiaircraft division headquarters
◁	Cruise missile (FKR) regiment
MDHQ	Missile division headquarters
🚀	Emplacements of R-12 missiles (MRBM)
⚚	Planned emplacements of R-14 missiles (IRBM)

Initials and abbreviations

ANAP   National Association of Small Farmers (Asociación Nacional de Agricultores Pequeños), Cuba

BCBA   Central Office against Armed Bands (Buró Central contra Bandas Armadas), Cuba

CDR   Committees for the Defense of the Revolution (Comités de Defensa de la Revolución), Cuba

CIA   Central Intelligence Agency, U.S.

CID-FAR   Defense Information Center of the Revolutionary Armed Forces of Cuba (Centro de Información para la Defensa de las FAR)

CINCLANT   Commander in Chief of the Atlantic Command, U.S.

CPSU   Communist Party of the Soviet Union

CRC   Cuban Revolutionary Council, U.S.-based counterrevolutionary organization

CVA   Attack Aircraft Carrier, U.S. Navy

CVAN   Attack Aircraft Carrier (nuclear-powered), U.S. Navy

CVS   Anti-Submarine Carrier, U.S. Navy

DAA   Antiaircraft Defense (Defensa Antiaérea), Cuba

DAAFAR   Antiaircraft Defense and Revolutionary Air Force (Defensa Antiaérea y Fuerza Aérea Revolucionaria), Cuba

DEFCON   Defense Condition, U.S. military

DIA   Defense Intelligence Agency, U.S.

DP   People's Defense (Defensa Popular), Cuba

DSE	Department of State Security (Departamento de Seguridad del Estado), Cuba
EMG	General Staff (Estado Mayor General), Cuba
EXCOMM	Executive Committee of the National Security Council, U.S.
FAR	Revolutionary Armed Forces (Fuerzas Armadas Revolucionarias), Cuba
FKR	Soviet cruise missile
G2	Department of Information, investigative division of Cuban armed forces
IHC	Institute of Cuban History (Instituto de Historia de Cuba)
IL-28	Soviet medium-range bomber
JUCEI	Boards of Coordination, Implementation, and Inspection (Juntas de Coordinación, Ejecución e Inspección), Cuba
KOMAR	Class of Soviet missile-carrying boat (design 183R)
LCB	Lucha Contra Bandidos (Struggle against bandits), section of Cuba's armed forces
LUNA	(FROG—Free Rocket Over Ground), Soviet short-range rocket fired from mobile missile launcher
MGR	Revolutionary Navy (Marina de Guerra Revolucionaria), Cuba
MIG	Soviet fighter jet
MINFAR	Ministry of the Revolutionary Armed Forces (Ministerio de las Fuerzas Armadas Revolucionarias), Cuba
MININT	Ministry of the Interior (Ministerio del Interior), Cuba
MNR	Revolutionary National Militia (Milicias Nacionales Revolucionarias), Cuba
NATO	North Atlantic Treaty Organization

NSC   National Security Council, U.S.

OAS   Organization of American States

OMI   Military Industrial Organization (Organización Militar Industrial), reserve militia units, Cuba

ORI   Integrated Revolutionary Organizations (Organizaciones Revolucionarias Integradas), precursor of Communist Party of Cuba

R-12   Soviet medium-range ballistic missile (1,400 miles)

R-13   Soviet ballistic missile (340 miles), fired from submarines

R-14   Soviet intermediate-range ballistic missile (2,800 miles)

R-15   Soviet short-range ballistic missile (25 miles), fired from Komar-class missile boats

SA-75   Soviet surface-to-air missile

SAC   Strategic Air Command, U.S.

SLC   Second Logistic Command, U.S.

SOPKA   Soviet surface-to-sea missile

STF   Soviet Troop Force

TAC   Tactical Air Command, U.S.

TRT   Radio-Technical Troops (Tropas Radiotécnicas), Cuba

U-2   High-altitude U.S. spy plane

USIA   U.S. Information Agency

Introduction

More than forty years have passed since the revolutionary triumph of January 1, 1959. In countless events during those four decades, the Cuban people have been the main actors in defending their national independence against the stubborn, active hostility to the Cuban Revolution of successive U.S. administrations. Among these historic developments, the October Crisis—or "Cuban Missile Crisis"—of 1962 stands out for its character and its worldwide importance.

In the U.S. and western Europe, much has been written and published about the roles of the United States and the Soviet Union in this weighty and dangerous conflict, which brought humanity to the brink of nuclear war. But little has been said about the Cuban experience, perhaps due to the selective and discriminatory way that the powerful in today's world deal with the problems of small countries. The purpose of this book is therefore to help make known Cuba's position and the role it played, since Cuba was directly involved in the events and was the main scene of that confrontation between the two military superpowers in the era of the Cold War.

The immediate causes of the October Crisis are found in the political actions undertaken by the U.S. government after the defeat it suffered at the Bay of Pigs. It became clear to the Cuban government that after this failure the White House would consider, as its main military option, the use of its own armed forces in a direct intervention aimed at overthrowing the Cuban Revolution.

This estimate was confirmed in subsequent months by the increase in subversive actions within Cuba, organized and directed by Washington. The U.S. administration dedicated considerable financial, military, and technical resources to carrying out sabotage and terrorist acts in Cuba. This included preparing assassination attempts against key leaders of the Cuban Revolution; providing material support to armed counterrevolutionary bands that operated in various rural areas of the island; and unleashing intense ideological and psychological warfare against Cuba. In addition, Washington fully exercised its powerful influence to isolate Cuba diplomatically from the rest of Latin America and, among other actions, to implement a tightened economic blockade against the island.

This was the framework for developments over the second half of 1962, beginning with Cuba's acceptance of the Soviet proposal to deploy medium- and intermediate-range missiles in Cuba, and leading to the transfer of a contingent of some 42,000 Soviet troops with all their combat gear during Operation Anadyr. Subsequently, owing to the political mishandling of the secret operation by the Soviet leaders of the time, this deployment became the pretext used by the United States to justify a naval blockade of the island and to provoke the outbreak of the crisis on October 22, 1962.

For Cubans, the crisis was a lesson that confirmed and strengthened their conceptions of how to defend the country. At the same time, it proved to the world the ideological strength of the principles upheld by the Cuban Revolution, because in face of the actions of the two superpowers, Cuba defended, with dignity and courage, its self-determination and sovereignty. Cuba firmly confronted the U.S. policy of arrogance and force. And, basing its stance on justice and reason, Cuba discussed the disagreements that emerged with the Soviet Union in the midst of the crisis, due to the unilateral manner in which the USSR negotiated to end the conflict. In those "brilliant yet sad days," as Ernesto Che Guevara described them, Cuba's policy was distinguished by having the necessary flexibility to open the door to negotiations, without making any concessions of principle, despite the unceasing efforts of the U.S. government to exclude Cuba from the process.

This book thus aims to analyze and reflect on the origins, development, and outcome of this historic event, and the complex political decisions, the successes and mistakes, and the supreme confidence shown by the Cuban people at that time of great danger.

Tomás Diez Acosta
JUNE 2002

Chapter 1

After the Bay of Pigs:
The secret war continues

The defeat of the mercenary invasion at the Bay of Pigs in April 1961 was more than just a military failure for the U.S. government in its covert war against Cuba. It was a sharp political setback for the new Democratic administration and in particular for President John F. Kennedy, who had to publicly assume responsibility.

This setback also led to the dismantling of the whole apparatus created by the Republican administration of Dwight Eisenhower to overthrow the Cuban Revolution. The Kennedy administration then began to develop its own new anti-Cuba plan, in line with its approach to foreign policy and its political and military strategy of "flexible response." Its overall aim was to strengthen the role of the United States as the leader of the capitalist world in its Cold War confrontation with the Soviet Union and the socialist bloc countries.

In addition, the Bay of Pigs fiasco had become a constant concern—almost an obsession—for the Kennedy brothers, who inherited from their father the guiding principle: "Don't get mad.

Get even."[1]* For that reason, even before Cuban forces had captured the last mercenaries hiding in the mangroves and salt marshes of the Zapata Swamp, the president of the United States decided to create an Interagency Task Force of the National Security Council (NSC), whose mission was to come up with an immediate follow-up plan for Cuba. This group was initially headed by Paul H. Nitze, assistant secretary of defense for international security affairs, and consisted of representatives of the State, Defense, and Justice departments, as well as the Central Intelligence Agency (CIA) and U.S. Information Agency (USIA).

At the same time, Kennedy asked Gen. Maxwell Taylor to chair a working committee charged with evaluating the invasion's failure and providing new proposals for U.S. military and political action in situations like that of Cuba. The commission included Attorney General Robert Kennedy, CIA Director Allen Dulles, and Admiral Arleigh Burke, chief of naval operations.

The plans devised by the two groups marked the start of a new tide of aggression against Cuba, aimed at creating generalized unrest inside the country, which would lead to the overthrow of the revolutionary government and, if necessary, direct U.S. military intervention. Such aggression was considered fully justified in their eyes.

The Interagency Task Force plan

The urgent need for a new Cuba policy forced the Interagency Task Force to rapidly put together a set of proposals. On May 4, 1961—two weeks after the defeat—the plan was ready. The document, entitled "Cuba and Communism in the Hemisphere,"[2] was presented to the National Security Council for approval.

Under nine headings, the authors outlined why they believed the Cuban Revolution posed a threat to U.S. interests in Latin America. They proposed a series of possible actions, including

* Numbered endnotes begin on page 293.

political, economic, military, diplomatic, and subversive measures, as well as propaganda and psychological warfare.

The first section, entitled "The Nature of the Threat," argued "that Cuba is being used as a base for export of the communist-fidelista revolution."[3] The Cuban example must be wiped out, it said, because Castro "has provided a working example of a communist state in the Americas, successfully defying the United States. Thus he has appealed to widespread anti-American feeling, a feeling often shared by non-communists. His survival, in the face of persistent U.S. efforts to unseat him, has unquestionably lowered the prestige of the United States."[4]

The second section, "The Present Situation in Cuba," evaluated the combat capabilities of the Cuban armed forces and militias, and the control exerted by Cuba's national security forces. The report noted an increase in the kind of social and regional forces that could make up an internal opposition, while recognizing that this did not mean "an equal increase in willingness to act against the regime." Concerning the economic situation, the document acknowledged that, despite adversities, "basic needs for food and textiles are being met," and that the regime was making "strenuous efforts to expand agricultural production."[5]

The third part projected Cuba's political and economic situation five years afterwards if the United States did not intervene. The document predicted that "all effective opposition to the regime will probably have been eliminated" and that, with assistance from the Soviet bloc, "the combat effectiveness of the Cuban armed forces will substantially increase." The authors also expected the Cuban economy to recover, because "Cuba's natural resources and Bloc economic assistance will permit greater self-sufficiency and gradual economic growth."[6]

Based on these assumptions, the document said U.S. action should focus on what it called "Cuban Vulnerabilities," the heading of the fourth section. In the economic field, the "Trading with the Enemy Act" was to be used to impose a blockade on trade with Cuba, eliminating all commerce between the United States and the island and helping reduce Cuba's foreign trade. The plan also outlined "a campaign of limited sabotage against Cuba's industries and utilities" to aggravate these problems, while recognizing that such actions would not be sufficient, by themselves, "to jeopardize the regime's stability."[7]

Additional measures were therefore deemed necessary. In the political field, the authors evaluated the prospects for "Castro's elimination" from power, through actions designed to foment resentment and discontent among political leaders, military officers, civil servants, and the general populace; as well as measures to encourage desertions and acts of treason by the revolutionary figures who "exert control in Cuba." The plan also called for an increase in "guerrilla operations, effectively supported by the U.S." The authors concluded, however, *There is no sure way of overthrowing Castro short of U.S. military intervention.*[8] For that reason, direct U.S. military intervention received considerable attention in the task force document.

The fifth section looked at "The Decision to Intervene with U.S. Forces." In it the task force examined the consequences, advantages, and disadvantages of such a step, as well as its potential to gain international support and how military intervention would affect American foreign relations in general. The paper concluded, *The cost of eliminating Castro by military intervention would be substantial at the present time.*[9]

It is interesting to see what pretexts the authors considered sufficient to justify a step of this magnitude,* as well as how

---

* On this issue the document states: "A judgment whether to intervene will depend on many factors.

"(1) The degree of provocation offered by Cuba or the Soviet Union, and/or the growing intensity of the Cuba threat. Below are listed, in roughly ascending order of seriousness of provocation, a number of conceivable fact situations:

"(a) Present conditions, following the unsuccessful attempt of Cuban exiles to overthrow Castro, without any essentially new action on the part of Cuba;

"(b) Upon a unilateral finding by the United States that its own self-defense requires armed intervention in Cuba to terminate the hemispheric threat of Castro-Communism;

"(c) Direct Castro regime involvement in an attempt at subversive overthrow

they linked military intervention with the success Washington could achieve in implementing its so-called Alliance for Progress in Latin America—an additional way to reduce "the Castro-Communist threat." The document shamelessly called for contriving *"a new theory or doctrine of international law"* to justify armed intervention. Although the authors ended up not recommending military intervention, they insisted the U.S. government should "make no statements or take no action that would foreclose the possibility of military intervention in the future."[10]

in another Latin American Republic, the government of which requests United States assistance against Cuba;

"(d) Establishment of a Soviet military base on Cuban soil;

"(e) Indiscriminate and mass execution by the Castro regime of American citizens in Cuba, without regard to any prohibited activities or claimed offenses on their part;

"(f) Conditions of widespread unrest against the Castro regime produced not by United States covert operations but by popular Cuban hostility, with a general breakdown of law and order in Cuba, in which at least some local authorities requested United States intervention;

"(g) The event of the United States being asked for support by an anti-Castro provisional Cuban government which had succeeded on its own (without United States Government assistance) in establishing itself in control of a substantial part of Cuba, had maintained that control for a period of time, and had been recognized by the United States;

"(h) Systematic or large-scale attacks by the Cuban military establishment on shipping and aircraft of the American Republics on and over the high seas;

"(i) A decision by the members of the OAS under the Rio treaty to intervene, once that decision had received the United Nations endorsement or authorization required by the United Nations Charter;

"(j) A major and serious Cuban military effort to force the United States out of the Guantanamo base;

"(k) An armed attack by Cuba on the United States or another of the American Republics;

"(l) Retaliation against the Soviet Union for a Soviet action against the free world serious enough to warrant such retaliation.

"Under existing international law and our treaty obligations armed intervention would be justified only under (h), (i), (j), and (k)."

U.S. Department of State, *Foreign Relations of the United States, 1961–1963,* volume X, *Cuba, 1961–1962* (hereinafter *FRUS*) (Washington, D.C.: United States Government Printing Office, 1997), pp. 464–65.

The sixth section of the document dealt with policy toward Cuban exiles,[11] analyzing ways to make better use of them in the situation at that time and in the future. Parts seven and eight outlined a series of actions to isolate Cuba diplomatically and politically from other nations in the hemisphere, including using the Organization of American States (OAS) in a variety of ways. These sections also explained how the trade blockade would be implemented.[12] Using the outworn pretext of subversion and infiltration in other countries, the White House hoped to draw Caribbean and Central American nations into the organization of a multilateral punitive force that would operate in the Caribbean region under U.S. leadership. The document listed various political, diplomatic, economic, propagandistic, and psychological measures that could be used to achieve these goals.

The ninth and final section proposed the creation of two powerful new posts within the State Department—an assistant secretary for Latin American affairs and a Latin America regional director. In this way their great crusade against Cuba would benefit from "the centralization of greater authority."[13] Meanwhile, the Interagency Task Force was to continue its work of planning the counterrevolution.*

On May 5, the day following its submission, this proposal was discussed by the National Security Council, with President Kennedy in attendance.[14] The Bay of Pigs disaster and its international aftermath were uppermost in their minds. These concerns manifested themselves in different ways: some of those present favored immediate drastic actions; others approved of such actions but thought it necessary to do more groundwork to justify them; and several preferred a more moderate approach. Everyone agreed, however, with continuing the secret war already under way against Cuba.

---

* The document included five appendices, dealing with: (I) an intelligence appraisal; (II) considerations bearing on major intervention; (III) U.S. policy toward Cuban exiles; (IV) propaganda and psychological warfare; and (V) "Doctrine to Preserve the Independence of Latin America Revolution." Ibid., p. 459.

A draft of the document had been circulated to members of the NSC several days before the meeting. At the State Department, Theodore C. Achilles, special assistant to Secretary of State Dean Rusk, reviewed the plan and wrote a memorandum to Rusk expressing general agreement with the paper, because it "comes up with the right answer." Achilles felt, however, that while the document accurately presented the risks of a direct U.S. military intervention, it did not adequately recognize the dangers of allowing revolutionary power to continue in Cuba. According to a summary of Achilles' memo, the task force document gave "an impression of weakness or irresolution" concerning the Castro government. He therefore drafted two new points to add to the document:

"5) We should keep in mind (a) the possibility that if the Castro regime remains in power and succeeds all of Latin America may succumb to Soviet-dominated Communism within a relatively few years, and (b) that the measures recommended in this paper are highly unlikely to cause the regime's fall although they will both cause it difficulties and retard its influence elsewhere.

"6) It should also be borne in mind that as a result of the President's April 20 statement the U.S., Latin America and world opinion is looking to the Administration for strong and prudent leadership with respect to Cuba. We cannot afford weakness, irresponsibility or failure."[15]

Achilles was not the only one who thought the proposals were too weak. Admiral Burke, chief of naval operations, made the same argument[16] in discussions with Secretary of Defense Robert McNamara the night before the NSC meeting.

At the NSC meeting itself, given that all participants agreed that "U.S. policy toward Cuba should aim at the downfall of Castro," the debate began around the question of whether or not to undertake direct military action. The options considered were a naval blockade, air strikes, and an invasion with ground troops. In view of the dangers implied by all these steps, the NSC members ruled them out for the time being, while also stating the U.S. should do nothing "that would foreclose the possibility of a military intervention in the future."[17]

Based on the Interagency Task Force proposals, the NSC meeting, with the participation of President Kennedy, approved a Cuba policy designed to weaken the Cuban government and thereby lay the basis, inside and outside the country, for much stronger measures aimed at overthrowing the revolutionary government. They also agreed to review the policy later "with a view to further action."[18] The task force on Cuba was placed under the direction of Richard N. Goodwin, assistant special counsel to the president.

The Taylor Commission, its conclusions and recommendations

Shortly after the Bay of Pigs fiasco, on April 22, 1961, President Kennedy appointed retired Gen. Maxwell Taylor to chair a commission—the so-called Cuba Study Group—to analyze the reasons for the operation's failure. The U.S. president said Taylor needed "to take a close look at all our practices and programs in the areas of military and paramilitary, guerrilla and anti-guerrilla activities which fall short of outright war."[19]

Taylor had commanded paratroopers landing in Normandy during World War II, led U.S. occupation forces in Berlin, and then commanded the Eighth Army in Korea. Before he retired in 1959, he was army chief of staff for four years. In this last post he had argued for changes in the U.S. armed forces' strategy of relying almost exclusively on nuclear weapons.

This stance coincided with that of the new Democratic administration, particularly with the concerns of Kennedy and McNamara, who were anxious to strengthen U.S. conventional forces in preparation for local conflicts in various parts of the world. Taylor's 1960 book, *The Uncertain Trumpet*, which argued for this reorientation, made a profound impression on John Kennedy, who was still a U.S. senator at the time.[20]

The Bay of Pigs defeat undermined the president's relationship not only with the CIA but also with the Joint Chiefs of Staff.

While Kennedy believed that neither the CIA nor the Joint Chiefs had served him well, he placed most of the blame on the military body. In his view, the military's review of the CIA plan had been superficial at best.[21]

Admiral Burke, probably speaking for other members of the Joint Chiefs as well, blamed the defeat on the president's last-minute changes to the plan.[22] Burke and his colleagues felt that if they had been able to participate fully in the project from the beginning, and, above all, if air strikes had been carried out as set down in the original plan, then the outcome would have been different. This argument, which the CIA also used to justify its own failure, had no basis in fact, because it did not start from the material reality inside Cuba that made it possible for the revolution to defeat the mercenary invasion. Nevertheless, these differences of opinion do illustrate the real debate and divisions within ruling circles in the United States.

In order to introduce an independent analysis of the CIA's failed adventure in Cuba, Kennedy brought Taylor to the White House and positioned him as an authoritative and experienced figure "between himself and the Joint Chiefs of Staff."[23] Kennedy also raised the idea of a new top-level post, military representative to the president.[24]

Taylor's first responsibility was to chair the Cuba Study Group, which included Attorney General Robert Kennedy, the president's brother, as well as representatives of the agencies directly involved in the Bay of Pigs failure: CIA Director Dulles and Admiral Burke.

The Cuba Study Group questioned all the individuals and agencies directly or indirectly involved in the organization, preparation, and carrying out of the Bay of Pigs invasion. Its work culminated in the issuance of four memoranda on June 13, 1961: "Narrative of the Anti-Castro Cuban Operation Zapata"; "Immediate Causes of Failure of the Operation Zapata"; "Conclusions of the Cuban Study Group"; and "Recommendations of the Cuban Study Group."[25]

This document listed more than thirty conclusions and recommendations. It affirmed that the U.S. government could not live with Castro as a neighbor over the long term. Castro was called a dangerously effective proponent of Communism and anti-Americanism within the community of American states, someone who posed a real threat of being able to overthrow elected governments in any one or more of the weak republics of Latin America. The group recommended that the Cuban situation be reappraised in light of all known facts and that "new guidance be provided for political, military, economic and propaganda action against Castro."[26]

The document also urged the U.S. government to organize and carry out paramilitary operations, like the one attempted at the Bay of Pigs, using whatever agencies were best able to bring into play, "in addition to military and covert techniques, all other forces, political, economic, ideological, and intelligence, which can contribute to its success."[27]

In the same vein, the document concluded that one of the factors contributing to the failure of the Bay of Pigs invasion was the fact that the operation had been so large and difficult for the CIA to handle. It recommended that operations of such magnitude be placed under the control of the Pentagon, and that the CIA should henceforth limit itself to paramilitary operations that could be "plausibly disclaimed."[28] The Taylor Commission also suggested the creation of new rapid-response units within the U.S. armed forces that could be mobilized quickly for action anywhere in the world.

The conclusions and recommendations of the Taylor Commission guided the policy of the Kennedy administration toward Cuba, as well as any other underdeveloped country that might take the road of revolution. Concurring with the report, the president assigned the Pentagon a more active role in supporting, overseeing, and advising the various covert operations of the CIA. The new anti-Cuba plan, therefore, differed from its predecessors in assigning the Pentagon a leading role in the coordination and development of actions, even though the CIA continued to be largely responsible for carrying them out. Other government agencies were also to be integrated more effectively into the campaign against Cuba, including the departments of State, Treasury, and Commerce, as well as the U.S. Information Agency.

As a result of the Taylor Commission, the Joint Chiefs of Staff were expected to contribute more effectively to military and paramilitary aspects of the secret war against Cuba, through the appointment of officers with more dynamism and initiative. At the same time, the CIA was reminded of the principle that covert actions had to be kept secret and had to be deniable in the court of international public opinion.

New operations of the CIA

At the time of the Bay of Pigs landing, units of the Cuban security forces, acting with popular support, had arrested hundreds of individuals suspected of involvement in the counterrevolution.* This prevented the operational groups created for that situation by the CIA from functioning and broke up the actions planned by the fifth columnists. The counterrevolutionary organizations were thus shattered, and the CIA lost contact with most of its agents inside Cuba.

The heads of these groups both inside and outside the country, who had offered to serve as puppets to conceal direct U.S. involvement in the plans against Cuba, felt betrayed. Demoralization spread through their ranks. "The opposition has lost some of its strongest forces, its factionalism is greater, and its confidence in the United States has been shaken,"[29] stated a paper prepared by the CIA to assess the situation at that time.

Taking this reality as its starting point, the Central Intelligence Agency drew up an action program against Cuba, sub-

---

* Most of the people arrested were soon released. Many individuals active in counterrevolutionary organizations were able to escape revolutionary justice. Faced with the Bay of Pigs debacle, the majority chose to leave the country; others continued their underground activities. See Jesús Arboleya, *La contrarrevolución cubana* [The Cuban counterrevolution] (Havana: Editorial Ciencias Sociales, 1997), pp. 95–104.

mitted on May 19, 1961. According to C. Tracy Barnes, CIA assistant deputy director for covert action, this plan was a secret appendix to the paper that the Interagency Task Force drafted May 4 for the National Security Council.

In its authors' estimation, the new CIA program was aimed at "weakening the Castro regime." This did not mean that the Agency had renounced its goal of overthrowing the revolution. As the document stated, "This plan should be viewed only as the covert contribution to an overall national program designed to accelerate the moral and physical disintegration of the Castro government and to hasten the day when a combination of actions and circumstances will make possible its replacement."[30]

The objective for that period was to achieve the reorganization of the forces within Cuba—agent and saboteur networks, armed bands, and others—so as to create conditions that would make possible more decisive actions. For this reason, the program was limited to exploiting the so-called "economic, political and psychological vulnerabilities"[31] of the country, in order to create favorable conditions for new, longer-range plans. The CIA did not expect the internal situation to change over the next six months.

The first task of the CIA officials responsible for operations in Cuba was to reorganize clandestine activity inside the country. To do so, they sought more accurate data on the strength of the counterrevolutionary groups and their networks of agents. The directors of the "Cuba Project" hoped to use this information to relaunch and, if possible, step up subversive actions.

Many of these officials wanted to get quick revenge for the defeat they had suffered by carrying out operations that would bring immediate results, results going beyond the objectives approved for the program. One of their goals was to show President Kennedy that their estimates of the internal support that the invaders would receive had been correct and, at the same time, to force him into direct military action against Cuba. Thus was born one of the most dangerous operations organized by the CIA, which was given the code name Patty.[32]

This project called for actions throughout Cuban territory intended to spark a general uprising. The date chosen to begin the uprising was July 26, 1961, in order to take advantage of the celebrations organized across the country—particularly in Havana and Santiago de Cuba, where Fidel and Raúl Castro, respectively, were targeted for assassination.

The plan in Santiago was to occupy one of the houses next to the stadium, as close as possible to the platform from which Commander Raúl Castro was to speak. A .30-caliber machine gun was to be set up in the house to carry out the assassination. Four men armed with grenades were to cover the retreat. In the event that this action failed, the conspirators assumed that Raúl would immediately travel to Havana to report what had happened, and so they planned to set an ambush on the road to the airport, using six men armed with submachine guns.

The assassination of Raúl was to be synchronized with a mortar attack on the "Hermanos Díaz" oil refinery in Santiago de Cuba. The plan included carrying out, at the same time, an attack seemingly directed against themselves—an assault on the U.S. naval base at Guantánamo. To carry out this action, they were to station a group of men on the "El Cuero" farm—next to the U.S. enclave—where they would deploy seven mortars. Six of these were to fire thirty projectiles at the naval base, and the other was to fire on a Cuban military camp located nearby. This action was meant to provoke a confrontation, as both forces would consider themselves under attack.

The CIA was to prepare a story on these events, saying that "Cuban military commanders, blinded by the assassination that had taken the life of Raúl Castro, had gone to the extreme of attacking the naval base." This would provide the pretext the United States was seeking for direct military intervention. It must be borne in mind that the CIA had included in its plans for the Bay of Pigs invasion a similar provocation, which was to be carried out by a group of mercenaries commanded by the traitor Higinio Díaz. He did not dare to land, however.*

The authors of this plan also proposed to undertake the assassination of Prime Minister Fidel Castro during a mass rally to be held that day at the Plaza of the Revolution in Havana. For this action an 82-mm. mortar was to be hidden at a spot near the platform and fired, in an attempt to kill as many as possible of the revolutionary leaders gathered there.

At the same time, armed bands in Las Villas province (now Villa Clara) and Camagüey province were to carry out assassinations and attacks on public facilities, blow up bridges, and so on. These plans also included the possible elimination of key political leaders and civilian and military officials, so that within a few hours of the start of Operation Patty, chaos would reign across the nation.

The CIA was kept abreast of the progress of preparations by its agents in Cuba. In the final days of June, the agency approved the operation and provided precise instructions to the plotters with regard to the provisioning of arms and military supplies to all the groups operating in the country.

Cuban security forces were kept informed of the conspiracy's development by their agents who had infiltrated the ranks of the enemy. In mid-July, when the strands of this deadly operation's complex web were fully in place, Cuban authorities decided to put an end to it, placing the main plotters under arrest.

This action brought in a large haul of weapons, explosives, and war matériel. A month later, on August 12, 1961, the Cuban government publicly denounced the new conspiracy.[33]

Despite the setback suffered by Operation Patty, CIA officials assigned to the Cuba project prepared new subversive actions. In late July 1961, two new programs were outlined at the agency's headquarters in Langley, Virginia. The first was a covert program against Cuba; the second, a program of clandestine activity within the country. Both were discussed by the

---

* Among the factors cited in the May 4 Interagency Task Force report as justification for direct military intervention was point (j), which read: "A major and serious Cuban military effort to force the United States out of the Guantanamo base."

Cuba Task Force, chaired by Richard Goodwin, and also by the Special Group of the National Security Council.

According to Arthur Schlesinger, Jr., special assistant to the president, the covert action program was to be the key element in overall U.S. policy toward Cuba. It received backing at the highest level, and a multimillion-dollar budget was approved. This program included intelligence and counterintelligence, political action, propaganda, and paramilitary activities.

The clandestine action plan was not essentially different from the covert program. It aimed to reorient the CIA's work toward better supervision and control of counterrevolutionary organizations in Cuba. Increased support was to be provided to groups that showed more promise in carrying out clandestine actions. President Kennedy approved these two programs in early August.

The early drafts of both projects were strongly criticized by Schlesinger, who thought it wrong to believe that "clandestine activity can be carried out in a political vacuum."[34] These new plans, however, did express the CIA's doubts that some key counterrevolutionary figures were capable of leading clandestine actions. These doubts arose from the repeated failure of the groups they headed, caused in the main by the penetration of their ranks by Cuban counterintelligence officers.

Skepticism was also evident at top levels of the CIA about the prospects of the so-called Cuban Revolutionary Council (Consejo Revolucionario Cubano), chaired by José Miró Cardona. Miró Cardona had received Kennedy's backing[35] to put himself at the head of an opposition movement that would pull together the various counterrevolutionary groups, inside and outside Cuba—groups that were vying for the favors of the U.S. government and especially those of the CIA, the institution that sustained and used them.

After the failure at the Bay of Pigs, the highest circles of the U.S. government also made a critical evaluation of the incapacity of the CIA—especially its top leadership—to direct clandestine operations against Cuba in such a way that U.S. involvement remained completely covered up. This was expressed at the Special Group meeting when important changes were made to the CIA's proposed project, such as an agreement that "actual sabotage operations will be carried out only after policy approval by the Special Group."[36] The multimillion-dollar proposed budget was likewise questioned. Although the budget was approved, only 50 percent was authorized for current use, with the other 50 percent subject to further discussion.

In the end the CIA had to redesign both projects and present a single plan, which was signed off by the president in early August, after being discussed by the Special Group.[37]

"Washington, undated.

"*Recommendation*

"It is recommended that the Special Group approve the following covert action program against Cuba:

"*a) Intelligence and Counterintelligence.*

"Collection of intelligence on the internal Cuban situation and the attitude of the Cuban people, particularly with regard to opposition elements. Improved and expanded collection of operational intelligence on Castro's plans, intentions and capabilities. Penetration of Cuban security services and protection of Agency operations against action by these services.

"*b) Political Action*

"Foster support for U.S. national policies with respect to Cuba, throughout Latin America. Combat Castro's subversive efforts in that area. Assist in strengthening unified opposition to Castro among Cubans, inside and outside of Cuba. Identify and support, if found, any such groups or leaders with real potential for overthrowing and replacing the Castro government.

"*c) Propaganda*

"Continue to support propaganda assets, including magazines, newspapers, news letters and radio. Conduct continual review of the effectiveness of these media. Attempt to destroy the popular image of Castro in Cuba, and combat his propaganda efforts throughout Latin America.

"*d) Paramilitary*

"Expand present personnel and support aspects inside and outside of Cuba, for use in working with or through Cuban groups in developing an underground organization or organizations. Once such a secure organization is established, engage in infiltration and exfiltration of personnel, supplies and matériel, in intelligence collection and propaganda, and in a low key sabotage and resistance program. Large scale sabotage activities may be planned for, but will not be mounted until approved by the Special Group. Provide modest support, as approved by the Special Group, to those guerrilla elements that might arise in Cuba and which are believed worthy of support. Maintain a limited air capability largely through pilot training.

"*e) Support*

"Maintain necessary personnel, forward-operating base on U.S. territory, maritime base, operational or training sites and communications facilities.

"A maximum of $12,738,132 is authorized for funding of the above program. Only fifty percent of this total will be withdrawn initially from the Bureau of the Budget, with later withdrawals to be dependent on a review, within six months, of the operational progress made.

"Budget breakdown (for 12 months) is as follows:

"Intelligence and counterintelligence	739,132
"Political action	200,000
"Propaganda	4,204,000
"Paramilitary	3,570,000
"Support	4,025,000
	12,738,132"

After the failure of Operation Patty, the CIA undertook a new plan. It made initial arrangements with its agent José Pujals Mederos,* who was in the United States at the time. By late July, the CIA infiltrated Pujals into Cuba through the north coast of

---

* José Pujals Mederos had left Cuba in early July 1961, just days before Operation Candela by the Cuban security services (Departamento de Seguridad del

Havana province. He was quickly able to meet with the heads of counterrevolutionary groups and pass on to them the instructions he had received. This was the start for the new project, code-named Liborio.

The plan was to carry out a series of attacks and acts of sabotage in the city of Havana against electricity and transport facilities; to burn down big department stores and clothing warehouses such as Sears, J. Vallés, and La Época; and to assassinate leaders of the revolutionary organizations. The conspirators reckoned that such acts would provoke popular anger, and that, as on other such occasions, a mass rally would be held in front of the old Presidential Palace to repudiate the attacks. This could provide an opportunity to assassinate Prime Minister Fidel Castro and other leaders.

To carry out this action, the plotters were to make use of Antonio Veciana Blanch,[*] who had made a study of the location in early 1961 under CIA instructions. He had rented an apartment facing the northern terrace of the palace, the spot from which political figures addressed the populace. This apartment, in a building at 29 Avenida de las Misiones, was a mere fifty meters away from the planned target. Various weapons were brought into the apartment, including a bazooka for use in the assassination.[†]

The actions in Havana were to be coordinated with an ex-

Estado—DSE), which dismantled Operation Patty. He thus escaped arrest during the raid by Cuban counterintelligence.

[*] Antonio Veciana Blanch was a "public accountant, who had worked for the sugar magnate Julio Lobo during the final years of the Batista dictatorship. The Cuban Revolution spoiled his rising career in the world of high finance, and that gave CIA official David A. Phillips the opportunity to recruit him. During the final months of 1959 Veciana was being trained in the techniques of sabotage, terrorism, espionage, and psychological warfare. He was among the first individuals who joined the MRP (Movimiento Revolucionario del Pueblo—Revolutionary Movement of the People)." Fabián Escalante Font, *Cuba: La guerra secreta de la CIA, 1959–1962* [Cuba, the CIA's secret war, 1959–1962] (Havana: Editorial Capitán San Luis, 1993), pp. 119–20.

[†] An assassination attempt against Fidel Castro had been planned for that location during Operation Patty, in case the July 26 rally were to be moved there at the last minute instead of the Plaza of the Revolution.

tensive campaign of sabotage and terrorism all over the country. Acts of psychological warfare were also to be stepped up, in order to try to discredit the Cuban Revolution in the eyes of the population. A plan was devised, with the help of members of the Catholic church hierarchy in Cuba, to carry out provocative actions during various traditional religious festivities, in order to accuse the Cuban government of preventing and repressing the practice of religion.[*] The plotters also circulated a phony draft law taking away parents' custody rights over their underage children. The text of this fabrication was passed around secretly—especially in the Catholic churches run by priests who were part of the conspiracy—in order to frighten parents into sending their children to the United States. Thousands of children and teenagers emigrated, without their parents, only to face terrible experiences that deeply marked their lives forever.[38]

The CIA and the domestic counterrevolution hoped in this way to destabilize the country, creating an opening for their scheme to have Latin American governments, supposedly concerned about ongoing instability in Cuba, urge the OAS to support a joint intervention force headed by the United States.

But the forces of the revolution did not stand by with arms folded while these plans were set in motion. On August 4, 1961, the Cuban government shocked the counterrevolution by passing a new law on currency exchange that dealt a sharp blow to the financial power of the revolution's enemies.[39]

On August 8, 1961, Cuban security forces arrested Pujals Mederos and Octavio Barroso Gómez.[†] As a result of its interrogation, Cuban counterintelligence gained detailed knowledge

---

[*] A September 1961 report of the Ministry of the Interior exposed the provocative activities of the right-wing hierarchy of the church located on Manrique and San Nicolás Streets in central Havana. On September 8 these activities culminated in an armed counterrevolutionary street demonstration that was confronted by passersby chanting revolutionary slogans. After the counterrevolutionaries retreated back into the church, they opened fire, killing a seventeen-year-old worker. *Revolución*, September 12, 1961, (second edition), pp. 1, 12.

[†] The spy Octavio Barroso Gómez operated a CIA intelligence network that was

of the most important features of the conspiracies. While continuing its investigations, it called on the Cuban people to organize popular vigilance everywhere the counterrevolution was planning acts of aggression.

In mid-September, the printing plant where the fake "Parental Custody Act" had been prepared was raided.[40] Then, on September 29, a counterrevolutionary named Dalia Jorge Díaz was arrested while trying to plant a firebomb at the Sears department store. Her arrest became a decisive factor in frustrating the planned assassination of Fidel and other revolutionary leaders.

The date chosen for this attack was October 4. A rally had been called for that day in front of the Presidential Palace in Havana to welcome President Osvaldo Dorticós Torrado back from a trip to the Soviet Union. Antonio Veciana, together with Reynold González, alerted the men chosen for this action. Their plan was to fire on the speakers' platform with a bazooka and then hurl grenades into the crowd. In the resulting chaos, the attackers planned to escape disguised in militia uniforms.

But this was never carried out. Antonio Veciana, frightened by the arrest of Dalia Jorge, fled the country by boat on October 3, abandoning to their fate the men who were to carry out the attack. They in turn lost their nerve when they learned their chief had fled, and sought shelter in houses that they thought were not known to Cuban counterintelligence.

As these events were happening in Havana in early October 1961, in Washington U.S. officials were counting on success. Thomas A. Parrott, assistant to Maxwell Taylor, contacted Assistant Secretary of State Robert F. Woodward on instructions from Taylor. He asked Woodward to urgently prepare a political plan to respond to the prospect that Prime Minister Fidel Castro "would in some way or other be removed from the Cuban scene."[41] To underline the importance of the request, Parrott

carrying out espionage at the San Antonio de los Baños Air Base, a military facility that had recently received the first Soviet MIG-15 aircraft. *Playa Girón: La gran conjura* [Playa Girón: the great plot] (Havana: Editorial Capitán San Luis, 1991), p. 34.

said that it was of interest to the U.S. president, although he preferred this not be mentioned. Around the same time, the CIA assistant deputy director for covert actions, C. Tracy Barnes, sent a memorandum to Jacob D. Esterline, head of Branch 4 of the agency's Western Hemisphere Division, instructing Esterline to prepare "a contingency plan based on the assumption of the unexpected removal of Castro from power."[42]

But within days, all the Operation Liborio conspirators inside Cuba were arrested and their weapons seized. The facts of the counterrevolutionary plot were revealed and denounced in the Cuban news media.[43] Thus ended these schemes by which the CIA and the internal counterrevolution had hoped to overthrow the revolutionary government and make up for their humiliating defeat at the Bay of Pigs.

Diplomatic isolation and economic blockade

While the CIA was organizing its secret war, other U.S. government agencies also continued working to destabilize Cuba. Diplomatic isolation and economic siege were key weapons used by Washington to try to overthrow the Cuban government, with the departments of Treasury, Commerce, and State playing central roles.

This policy was nothing new—it had been used during the Eisenhower administration to pressure Cuba and try to punish it for daring to make a genuine revolution. But now Washington was trying to create a climate of discontent among the Cuban people that would promote internal subversion. Furthermore, Kennedy's political strategy was that direct aggression by the U.S. armed forces—if used—ought to have the cover of being a collective action of the Western Hemisphere, in the framework of the Inter-American Treaty of Reciprocal Assistance—also known as the Rio Treaty—in common struggle against communist penetration.* The Organization of American States was to be the vehicle.

---

* The Inter-American Treaty of Reciprocal Assistance was signed by twenty-one governments on September 2, 1947, in Rio de Janeiro. It declared that aggression

In this new phase, the U.S. government's most characteristic move against the revolution from the economic point of view was its implementation of the Alliance for Progress. The Alliance for Progress was announced by President Kennedy on March 13, 1961, during a meeting in Washington with Latin American diplomatic representatives. It was to be an "aid" program of $20 billion over a ten-year period for social and economic development.*

At the same time, Kennedy also requested a special meeting of the OAS. To that end, on May 8 the United States proposed to the OAS a working agenda to discuss the project at a special meeting of ministers of the Inter-American Economic and Social Council.

This was the first time in the history of hemispheric relations that a U.S. administration had pushed to hold an economic meeting of such magnitude. Traditionally, Washington had strongly resisted meetings of this kind, since the conflicting interests between the United States and the countries of the region are most obvious in the economic arena. In all such conferences, clashes had erupted over unequal trade relations— expressed in the constant decline of raw materials prices in comparison to those of industrial goods—and the instability of markets for Latin America's primary products. Even the countries most obedient to Washington's orders were heard to protest the practice of dumping U.S. agricultural surplus at the expense of Latin American exports.†

What caused this change of attitude? It was the Cuban Rev-

---

against any treaty member state would be considered an attack on all of them.

* The immediate predecessor of the Alliance for Progress was a project known as the U.S. Economic Plan for Aid to Latin America, announced by Eisenhower in mid-1960 in preparation for the OAS foreign ministers conference in Costa Rica. That plan was allocated $500 million.

† Dumping is the action of selling merchandise in foreign markets at prices that are often less than the cost of production. It is a capitalist business practice usually backed by the imperialist government of the offending company, designed to control the market, eliminate competitors, and get rid of surplus production.

olution, which had opened a new road to solving Latin America's serious problems. The impact of the Cuban Revolution was manifested not only among the peoples of the continent, but also by the conduct of various governments, which—encouraged by the Cuban example—began to follow policies more independent of the United States and to seek new markets and credits in the socialist countries.

Faced with this trend, Washington tried to follow the path of promises. Through the Alliance for Progress, it sought to prevent social explosions and new Cuba-style revolutions, as well as to enlist the majority of Latin American governments in its campaign against Cuba.

The special meeting of the Inter-American Economic and Social Conference was held August 5–17, 1961, at an exclusive resort in Punta del Este, Uruguay. The United States carefully prepared this meeting—President Kennedy declared it to be the most important debate since the start of his administration. A strong delegation headed by Treasury Secretary Douglas Dillon was sent to present the U.S. program. The delegation included an important group of advisers, among them the president's assistant for Latin American affairs, Richard Goodwin, who had been in charge of the Cuba Task Force since the previous May.

Commander Ernesto Che Guevara headed the Cuban delegation. Addressing a plenary session, he said, "This conference, and the special treatment that the delegations have received, and the credits that may be granted, all bear the name of Cuba, whether the beneficiaries like it or not, because a qualitative change has taken place in the Americas." Later he declared, "Cuba comes to condemn what is worthy of condemnation from the point of view of principles. But Cuba also comes to work harmoniously, if possible, in order to straighten out this thing that has been born so twisted."[44]

The Cuban delegation presented twenty-nine carefully drafted motions along these lines, acting calmly and correctly while presenting its viewpoint during conference sessions. As a result, many delegates considered Cuba's behavior reasonable, serious, and constructive. This stance did not, however, stop the Cuban delegation from firmly denouncing all the various attacks that Cuba had suffered. Despite offers of "aid," the United States succeeded neither in isolating Cuba nor in obtaining any agreement to condemn it. Goodwin reflected this in a memo to Kennedy, which stated that "any hope for OAS action . . . is dead. . . . It is my strong belief that the big countries (Brazil and Mexico especially) are not prepared to buy this, that they feel such action would be a meaningless gesture at great internal political cost to them."[45] Nevertheless, the Alliance for Progress provided the United States with a new mechanism with which to exert pressure on Latin American governments against Cuba.

The U.S. strategy, aimed at diplomatically isolating Cuba from the rest of Latin America and winning those governments over to U.S. policy, was also expressed in the attempt to conclude a joint agreement condemning Cuba by using OAS diplomatic and political mechanisms and the Inter-American Treaty of Reciprocal Assistance.

This policy was evident in the conduct of the Peruvian government,[*] which throughout 1961 demanded that a meeting of foreign ministers be called to put Cuba on trial for alleged interference by Cuban diplomats in the internal affairs of other countries. According to the Peruvian statement, Cuban diplomatic authorities "were carrying out communist infiltration in

---

[*] On December 30, 1960, the Peruvian Foreign Office informed Cuba of the decision of the Peruvian government to break diplomatic relations. An anti-Cuba press campaign was unleashed, headed by the newspaper *La Prensa*, which was owned by the Peruvian prime minister. The previous month, on November 8, five armed individuals had assaulted the Cuban embassy in Lima. In addition to destroying furniture and office equipment, they plundered the archives. Shortly afterwards a series of forged documents was printed in *La Prensa*, alleging interference by the Cuban embassy in internal Peruvian affairs. This maneuver was so crudely conceived that the documents included names of individuals who had died before the revolution triumphed. This was the case with the journalist Benito Montesino, who supposedly had received money from the Cuban consulate in Arequipa.

other countries of America."

Important Latin American nations, however, such as Mexico, Brazil, Bolivia, Chile, and Ecuador, expressed unwillingness to be a part of such schemes. There was also concern about the popular reaction this might trigger in the region.

Meanwhile, Colombia was competing with Peru in calling for a new conference. At the end of August 1961, the Colombian foreign minister, Julio César Turbay Ayala, toured the continent seeking backing for Bogotá's plan. According to the memoirs of Manuel Tello, former foreign minister of Mexico, this plan consisted of "laying a trap for Fidel Castro's government and hoping it would fall for it, thereby justifying collective military sanctions."[46] The Peruvian plan collapsed on October 30, 1961, during a meeting of the OAS general commission, whereas the Colombian proposal, presented on November 9, succeeded. Carlos Lechuga Hevía, the last Cuban representative in the OAS council, said of this: "The Colombian draft, in contrast to the Peruvian one, did not mention Cuba by name, although it had the same goal. That is why one failed while the other succeeded. In this peculiar way, OAS governments could attend the meeting with an easy conscience without siding with an explicitly anti-Cuban position paper."[47]

Discussions that took place between the U.S. president and important Latin American political figures are revealing. What follow are memoranda prepared by the State Department on conversations held between Kennedy and Juscelino Kubitschek de Oliveira, Brazilian senator and former president, and Arturo Frondizi, president of the Republic of Argentina. The conversations took place on September 15 and 26, 1961, respectively.

In conversation with Senator Kubitschek, who was visiting Washington as part of a tour of several countries, Kennedy voiced his concern over the Cuban situation. Kubitschek responded "that Cuba was a most serious problem for the entire Hemisphere." He warned, however, "that any act or even attitude on the part of the U.S. that could be construed as aggression would immediately bring about a strong anti-U.S. reaction from Latin American left-wing groups." The U.S. president described some of the actions planned against Cuba and pointed out the need to "undertake appropriate political and economic action that would circumvent the danger posed by the Castro regime to the entire Hemisphere."

Kubitschek, in turn, "mentioned in passing his talks with Prado of Peru and Frondizi of Argentina on the need for discreet action to isolate Cuba."* He also discussed the political situation in Brazil following the events that led to the resignation of President Jânio Quadros in August 1961, and the stance of the Goulart administration toward Cuba, which he characterized as "cautious."†

Kennedy's discussion with the Argentine president took place at the Hotel Carlyle in New York, when he and Frondizi were there for the opening session of the UN General Assembly. Kennedy said that "it was necessary to isolate Cuba and increase its economic problems, which were already serious. He said that it was important not to leave the impression of the United States, great imperialist power from the North, attacking poor, brave Cuba, which is the impression Castro wants to give."[48]

Later in the discussion, Kennedy asked Frondizi whether he saw any merit in the Colombian proposal to call a meeting of foreign ministers in order to declare Cuba a "Soviet satellite" and, under the terms of the Rio Treaty, exclude it from "the American family." He also asked whether Frondizi thought it possible to find some excuse for Argentina to break off relations with Cuba, and if it did so, whether this would cause domestic

---

* "Memorandum of Conversation between President Kennedy and Senator Kubitschek of Brazil. Washington, September 15, 1961," *FRUS*, vol. X, pp. 654–56. Manuel Prado Ugarteche (1889–1967) was president of the Republic of Peru from 1939 to 1945. He was reelected in 1956 and overthrown by the army in 1962. Frondizi was president of Argentina, 1958–62.

† João Goulart (1918–1976) was elected vice president of Brazil in 1961 and assumed the presidency when Quadros resigned. He was overthrown in a military coup in March 1964.

problems in Argentina. Kennedy requested Frondizi's support for any action the United States might take against Cuba.

These two meetings, along with others held by President Kennedy himself and other senior U.S. officials, typify the diplomatic pressures and maneuvers that the United States carried out in pursuit of its goals.

On December 4 the OAS Council met in special session to decide on the Colombian request to call a meeting of foreign ministers. Despite strong opposition from Cuba and Mexico, both of which pointed out that such a request was legally invalid, it was approved with fourteen votes in favor, two opposed, and five abstaining.*

The U.S. State Department and several countries quickly took on the task of finding a site for the foreign ministers' meeting. They excluded all locations that might be the scene of large popular protest demonstrations. The Uruguayan government was consulted, and it offered the resort at Punta del Este.[49]

The meeting was held January 22–31, 1962. It was no easy task, however, for the State Department officials to gather enough votes to condemn the Cuban government. On January 30, 1962, the resolution to "exclude the current government of Cuba from participation in the inter-American system" passed with fourteen votes in favor, one opposed, and six abstaining.† This action capped a lengthy period of attacks aimed at isolating Cuba from the regional body.

In this regard, Carlos Lechuga has written, "The decision that was imposed—to expel the Caribbean island from the OAS—had no legal basis. The organization's charter did not provide

---

* Countries voting in favor: El Salvador, Colombia, Costa Rica, the United States, Guatemala, Haiti, Honduras, Nicaragua, Panama, Paraguay, Peru, Dominican Republic, Uruguay, and Venezuela. Opposed: Cuba and Mexico. Abstaining: Argentina, Bolivia, Brazil, Chile, and Ecuador.

† The resolution received the support of Colombia, Costa Rica, Dominican Republic, El Salvador, Guatemala, Haiti, Honduras, Nicaragua, Panama, Paraguay, Peru, Uruguay, the United States, and Venezuela. Cuba voted against. Abstaining were Argentina, Bolivia, Brazil, Chile, Mexico, and Ecuador.

for such an action and thus could not legally be invoked. To provide an excuse, an idea was invented that a Marxist-Leninist regime was incompatible with the Inter-American System. This argument had little worth and drew its credibility solely from the irrational subversion of values imposed by the 'Cold War,' from the U.S. policy of disruption toward Cuba, and from the intimidation and subjugation of most governments represented in it."[50]

The counterrevolutionary leader José Miró Cardona commented on the outcome from another perspective. With that conference, he said, the United States had concluded "a long, complex, and difficult chapter—that of diplomatic negotiations—and ushered in a new one: that of military action."[51]

This assertion is borne out by other information as well. While the conference was taking place in Uruguay, for example, John F. Kennedy held a private luncheon in Washington with Aleksei Adzhubei, editor of the newspaper *Izvestia* and son-in-law of Nikita S. Khrushchev. The U.S. president told Adzhubei that Soviet influence in Cuba had altered the balance of power between East and West and thereby endangered U.S.-Soviet coexistence. He also reminded his guest that the United States had not interfered when the USSR intervened in Hungary in 1956.[52]

This reference is further proof that the United States was trying to use any means to justify its future intervention in Cuba, suggesting here that since the United States had accepted the actions of the Soviet government in Hungary, in Eastern Europe, the USSR should do likewise for U.S. action in Cuba.

These actions in the diplomatic arena were complemented by others of an economic nature. The United States continued its efforts to starve the Cuban Revolution into submission. After the U.S. defeat at the Bay of Pigs, the list of measures extending the economic blockade grew longer and longer. These included the suspension of purchases of tobacco, fruit, and molasses, and the prohibition of interstate transport of products from Cuba. Meanwhile, Washington increased its economic pressure against those Latin American countries that collaborated with Cuba—for example, threatening to withhold all aid from them.

It is interesting to note that the State Department was awaiting the outcome of the foreign ministers' meeting before implementing other measures against Cuba. On January 16, 1962, Robert A. Hurwitch—the officer in charge of Cuban affairs at the State Department—wrote that this meeting would have "a direct bearing on economic actions which the United States may undertake." He stated: "Assuming that as a minimum the Meeting results in agreement to condemn Cuba as an accomplice of the Sino-Soviet Bloc and in general adopts language to the effect that Cuba presents a threat to the peace and security of the Hemisphere, the Department of State would be prepared to recommend to the President that remaining trade between the United States and Cuba be barred."[53]

So it was that on February 3, 1962, three days after the end of the charade at Punta del Este, the president of the United States signed the 27th Federal Regulation 1085, entitled "Embargo on Cuban Trade." This regulation was put into effect by Presidential Decree No. 3447 on February 6. The document states the following:

"The Eighth Meeting of Consultation of Ministers of Foreign Affairs . . . in its Final Statement resolves that the Government of Cuba is incompatible with the principles and objectives of the Inter-American System; and, in light of the subversive offensive of Sino-Soviet Communism . . . urged the member states to take those steps that they may consider appropriate for their individual and collective self-defense;

". . . The Congress of the United States . . . has authorized the President to establish and maintain an embargo upon all trade between the United States and Cuba; . . .

". . . The United States, in accordance with its international obligations, is prepared to take all the necessary actions to promote national and hemispheric security by isolating the present Government of Cuba and therefore reducing the threat posed by its alignment with the communist powers:

"NOW, THEREFORE, I, JOHN F. KENNEDY, President of the United States of America, acting under the authority of Section 620 (a) of the Foreign Assistance Act of 1961 (75 stat. 445), as amended, do

"1. Hereby proclaim an embargo on trade between the United States and Cuba . . . ;

"2. Hereby prohibit . . . the importation into the United States of all goods of Cuban origin; of all products also imported from or through Cuba; and I hereby authorize and direct the Secretary of the Treasury to carry out such prohibition, to make such exceptions thereto, by license or otherwise, as he determines to be consistent with the effective operation of the embargo hereby proclaimed, and to promulgate such rules and regulations as may be necessary to perform such functions.

"3. AND FURTHER I do direct the Secretary of Commerce . . . to continue to carry out the prohibition of all exports from the United States to Cuba, and I hereby authorize him . . . to continue, make, modify, or revoke exceptions from such prohibitions."[54]

Through this order, the economic blockade officially came into effect. Euphemistically called a "trade embargo," it has in fact been an economic war waged against Cuba for decades, even after the Cold War and the USSR itself disappeared from the international stage. Over the years, the initial resolution was followed by measure after measure, leading up to the Torricelli Act and the Helms-Burton Act.*

---

* The Cuban Democracy Act, also called the Torricelli Act, after its sponsor New Jersey liberal Democratic congressman Robert Torricelli, was enacted by Washington in 1992. It provides for a two-pronged effort against Cuba. "Track one" refers to tightening the U.S. economic embargo, while "track two" calls for provisions that—in the guise of promoting the "free flow of ideas" between the United States and Cuba—aims to corrupt and buy off Cuban academics and professionals.

The "Cuban Liberty and Democratic Solidarity (Libertad) Act of 1996," usually called the Helms-Burton Act, includes a number of provisions that tighten the embargo, including one penalizing non-U.S. companies that invest in Cuban property expropriated from U.S. corporations in the early 1960s. Its spon-

Less than one month after the OAS meeting, the United States asked the NATO Council to take into account the measures adopted by the regional body of the Americas in formulating its policy on Cuba. The U.S. also asked its allies to voluntarily end trade in strategic matériel and, in general, to reduce trade with Cuba.

sors were North Carolina Senator Jesse Helms and Indiana congressman Dan Burton, both Republicans.

Chapter 2

Cuba responds

In Cuba, a high priority was assigned to social and economic development tasks, particularly the National Literacy Campaign. The revolutionary government declared 1961 "The Year of Education." The ambitious goal set by the government—to eliminate illiteracy before the end of that year—was questioned by many international figures and organizations, who doubted Cuba's ability to organize and mobilize to meet this commitment. About 100,000 high school students, most of them from the cities, volunteered to go and carry the light of knowledge to every corner of the country.* These young people were organized into the "Conrado Benítez" Brigades, in honor of the volunteer teacher who was murdered on January 5, 1961, by counterrevolutionary bands in the Escambray mountains.†

* Joining these students were more than 120,000 literacy workers and about 12,700 young workers organized into the "Patria o Muerte" brigades of the Central Organization of Cuban Workers (Central de Trabajadores de Cuba—CTC). In all, about 300,000 people were mobilized for this special effort.

† These bands also killed volunteer teacher Pedro Morejón Quintana on Febru-

After the defeat suffered by the U.S. government on the sands of Playa Girón, two roads were open for the new Democratic administration of President John F. Kennedy to follow in its policy toward Cuba: continuing the same hostile and aggressive course, trying to avoid failures like the Bay of Pigs; or changing the policy of hostility that had been developed up to that point and looking for forms of understanding and mutual respect with its Caribbean neighbor. Under these circumstances, the revolutionary government felt it appropriate to offer the White House gestures of good will that expressed Cuba's interest in negotiating a solution to the differences between the two countries.

One example was Cuba's initiative to exchange the mercenaries captured during the Bay of Pigs invasion for agricultural supplies and machinery. Even aside from the political developments of the time, this would have been a good reason to initiate talks between the two nations. This gesture, however, was rejected by Kennedy.*

---

ary 22, 1961, in Matanzas, and teacher Delfín Sen Cedré on October 3 at the Novoa farm in Quemado de Güines, Las Villas province. Later that year, on November 26, a literacy worker, Manuel Ascunce Domenech, and a peasant, Pedro Lantigua Ortega, were murdered as well.

* On May 17, 1961, Fidel Castro, speaking to the congress of the National Association of Small Farmers, publicly announced the Cuban government's proposal to exchange the mercenaries captured at Playa Girón who had not committed murders "for 500 bulldozers from imperialism, should they care to rescue them." (*Obra Revolucionaria*, no. 21, Havana, May 29, 1961, p. 21.)

The U.S. government, unable to duck its responsibility for the fate of these individuals, initially dealt with the matter in private and off the record, first through the so-called Tractors for Freedom Committee, made up of Eleanor Roosevelt, Milton Eisenhower, and Walter Reuther—whose efforts failed—and later through the Committee of Prisoners' Families, represented by lawyer James Donovan, who had been personally brought into the talks by Attorney General Robert Kennedy. Participating in negotiations were no fewer than fourteen U.S. government agencies, including the CIA. The talks were restarted in June 1962 but suspended because of the October Crisis. Resumed on December 18 of that year, they concluded on December 21, when representatives from both sides signed a memorandum whereby the U.S. government was to pay within a six-month period $62 million in food and medicine for children, while Cuba would release 1,113 imprisoned mercenaries.

Faced with criticism from his staunchest opponents, who were calling the government weak, Kennedy chose to continue the policies of Eisenhower's Republican administration. Severe hostility and hatred permeated the U.S. stance toward its closest neighbor in the Caribbean.

Cuba increases its defense capabilities

Faced with the likelihood of a direct military attack, the Cuban government was forced to adopt measures to ensure that the national security system could respond to the challenges posed by the enemy's aggressiveness. The country had to devote enormous human and material resources to this end, far beyond its economic potential. This was made possible, first of all, by the decisive support of the Cuban people and their firm will to defend the gains of the revolution, as shown by the tens of thousands of men who volunteered to join the armed forces and who resolutely accepted all the sacrifices involved in military service; and second, by the solidarity of the socialist camp, primarily the USSR, which was willing to provide the necessary arms, with the payment and credit plans needed to acquire them.

This made it possible to begin a process of organization, starting in early 1961, that would transform the Revolutionary Armed Forces (Fuerzas Armadas Revolucionarias—FAR) into a powerful regular force that, in the event of a direct U.S. military attack, would be able to put up stiff resistance and cost the enemy a high price in lives—a price that the U.S. politicians and strategists would not be ready to pay. This would have a significant deterrent effect.

Based on the strategy of establishing a strong antilanding defense, it was necessary to rapidly increase the regular forces and prepare them to carry out their combat missions. This was made possible by the integration of the Rebel Army and the Revolutionary National Militia (Milicias Nacionales Revolucionarias—MNR) into a single regular armed body. In this way, the number of troops on active duty rose sharply from 49,015 in mid-1960[1] to 138,132 in December 1961.[2]

The FAR experienced substantial changes as a result. The ground troops went from a battalion-company structure to a division (brigade)-army structure, which brought about a qualitative change in Cuban military organization.

Along these lines, starting in the second quarter of 1961, three armies were established—Central, Eastern, and Western—each given the responsibility of defending the area of the country assigned to it.

On April 4—just days before the battle at Playa Girón—the high command of the FAR decided to establish the Central Army, which would be responsible for defending an area that initially included the former provinces of Camagüey and Las Villas, as well as part of Matanzas. Commander Juan Almeida Bosque was assigned to head up this army, and Commander Raúl Menéndez Tomassevich was to be chief of staff. The process of organizing the main units took place from April to October 1961.

The units of the Tactical Combat Forces of the Rebel Army in the region and the battalions of the MNR were placed directly under the Central Army's command. Many of the Rebel Army and militia fighters had actively participated in combat against armed counterrevolutionary bands in the Escambray and at the battle of Playa Girón. Also, some of its militia battalions, such as the 339th in Cienfuegos, were the first to fight against the invading mercenaries, since its members were entrenched in the locations where the landing took place.

In late 1961 the Central Army was made up of thirteen infantry divisions, four independent battalions, and an independent antitank artillery group.* Also, there was a corps (5th Army Corps) for the command and direction of the military units deployed in Camagüey. The total forces included 18,693 troops on

---

* The infantry divisions included one regular division (the 4th), with all its units and personnel on active duty; two smaller divisions, made up of regular and reserve (militia) units and personnel; and ten wartime divisions, consisting of battalions made up of militia members. The independent battalions included two antilanding battalions, one for engineering and the other for communications.

active duty and about 29,000 reserve militia members.[3]

With the general mobilization of the country still in effect, in anticipation of a military response by the United States to the defeat of its mercenary forces on the sands of Girón, the Eastern Army was established on April 21, 1961. Its founder and first head was Commander Raúl Castro.* Working with him to establish this command were Commander Calixto García Martínez, second-in-command of the army, and Commander Belarmino Castilla Mas, chief of staff.

As in the central region, the units of the Eastern Army were initially made up of Rebel Army fighters who belonged to the Eastern Tactical Forces and members of the Revolutionary National Militia (MNR).

In fact, it was on April 21 when Commander Raúl Castro decided to establish the first regular division of the FAR (the 50th) out of combatants from the ten MNR battalions in Oriente province that had participated in the fight against bandits in the mountains of the central region from the beginning of the year until mid-March.[4] The task of setting up this division was assigned to Captain Senén Casas Regueiro.

It took until late 1961 to organize this army, which was made up of twelve infantry divisions, three antilanding battalions, one artillery brigade, and five mountain groups.† Later, in 1962, an army corps command was established to head up the military units located in the northern region of the former Oriente province. According to data collected in the approved personnel lists for this army, in early 1962 the number of regular troops rose

---

* Raúl Castro, in the early days of the Eastern Army, served both as minister of the FAR and as chief of that command.

† According to the FAR personnel summary for 1962, the twelve infantry divisions included one permanent division (the 50th), three smaller divisions (the 53rd, 56th, and 59th), and eight wartime divisions. The mountain groups were the territorial military organization that brought together the militia companies, poor peasants, and agricultural workers in the mountains of the eastern part of the country. These groups blocked the enemy's attempt to set up centers of counterrevolutionary guerrilla activity in these areas.

to 22,215, with reserve militia members estimated at about 55,000.[5]

As a part of the Eastern Army, the Border Battalion was formed on November 9, 1961. The goal of this special unit was to improve defenses along the perimeter of the area occupied by the U.S. naval base on Guantánamo Bay. This area, which was used for infiltrating and evacuating counterrevolutionary terrorist bands, was the site of constant dangerous provocations that threatened the country's security.

The Western Army was established on June 14, 1961, covering the provinces of Matanzas, Havana, and Pinar del Río. Appointed to head up this command was Commander Guillermo García Frías, and Commander Oscar Fernández Mell was named chief of staff.

As in the other regions of the country, its forces came from the Rebel Army and the MNR, most of them combatants who had participated in the fight against bandits in the Escambray, the battle at Playa Girón, and other important defense missions, such as the military reinforcement of the Isle of Pines (today called the Isle of Youth).

This larger unit included 26,164 regular troops and 85,000 reservists, and was made up of eighteen infantry divisions, five antilanding battalions, and five supply battalions, as well as an independent antitank artillery group.[*][6]

To defend the Isle of Pines, a military region was established on March 15, 1962, and placed under Commander William Gálvez Rodríguez. With 3,314 regular troops, this independent formation was equivalent to an infantry division.[7]

In the second half of 1961, two agreements between the Cuban and Soviet governments were signed,[8] under which the USSR pledged to supply military equipment and resources. The

---

[*] According to the FAR personnel summary for 1962, the eighteen infantry divisions included one permanent division (Military Unit 2350), five smaller divisions, and twenty-two wartime divisions. The supply battalions included two for security, one for engineering, one for communications, and one for transport.

first agreement, dated August 4, called for the delivery of matériel worth $48.5 million, of which Cuba would have to pay only
$6 million. The overall value of the supplies covered by the sec-
ond agreement, signed on September 30, totaled $149.55 mil-
lion, of which the Cuban government would have to pay $67.55
million. In both documents, it was agreed that the debts could
be paid off over a ten-year period, at an annual interest rate of
2 percent.

A third agreement was signed on July 13, 1962, during a visit
to Moscow by the minister of the FAR, Raúl Castro, to finalize
details for the deployment of Soviet missile forces in Cuba, as
called for in what was code-named Operation Anadyr.* The new
document canceled the debts incurred by Cuba under the previous agreements; it also provided for the delivery of weapons
and ammunition to Cuba, free of charge, over a two-year period.[9]

The treaties signed in 1961 covered weapons for ground
troops, such as light arms for infantry, artillery of various types
and calibers, tanks and armored vehicles, communications equipment, and radar stations. The air force was to receive MIG-15
fighter planes, IL-28 light bombers, MI-4 helicopters, transport
aircraft, and equipment needed for airfields.

The navy would be provided with torpedo boats and submarine chasers. Furthermore, the USSR would supply all necessary ammunition, and machinery for various repair shops for
weapons and matériel. The agreements also called for military
experts to be sent to Cuba, as well as for Cuban personnel to
study in the Soviet Union.[10]

The armies received the weapons and combat matériel covered in the agreements as soon as they arrived. This made it
necessary for the general staffs to learn how to operate the new
equipment and lead the combat training of their subordinate
units.

Antiaircraft defense troops, the air force, and the navy were

* See chapter 4 of this book.

also developed and modernized, along with various special military units.

On April 17, 1961, the Antiaircraft Defense and Revolutionary Air Force (Defensa Antiaérea y Fuerza Aérea Revolucionaria—DAAFAR) was created, unifying the command of the units of the country's Antiaircraft Defense (Defensa Antiaérea—DAA), Radio-Technical Troops (Tropas Radiotécnicas—TRT), and Revolutionary Air Force (Fuerza Aérea Revolucionaria).* All these troops were given new weaponry and equipment during the second half of 1961.

In 1962 the Revolutionary Navy (Marina de Guerra Revolucionaria—MGR), whose forces totalled 5,000 permanent combatants, started receiving the first Soviet torpedo boats and submarine chasers, which were sent to the eastern, central, and western naval districts. The new military equipment allowed the navy to carry out more complex combat missions, since it was now able to strike against enemy naval groupings, in cooperation with the air force and ground artillery.

In 1961 the FAR also had important ground artillery units and a tank brigade that were directly responsible to the Ministry of the Revolutionary Armed Forces (MINFAR) and the General Staff (Estado Mayor General—EMG). These units together formed the reserve of the High Command. In addition, three combat supply battalions were under the command of various leadership bodies of the General Staff.†

The People's Defense (Defensa Popular—DP) was formed in

---

* According to the FAR personnel summary for 1962, in late 1961 the DAAFAR had 5,464 permanent combatants. By early 1962 the DAA was made up of an independent group of 100-mm. antiaircraft artillery, as well as twenty-two additional batteries: nine 57-mm., seven 37-mm., and six 30-mm. batteries. At this early stage, the TRT was made up of two companies.

Shortly after Girón, according to the summary, the first MIG-15 and MIG-19 fighter jets, helicopters, and transport aircraft began arriving in Cuba from the USSR. In early 1962, the air force had four aircraft squadrons (three with fighter planes and one with L-60s), two helicopter squadrons, and one squadron of reconnaissance planes.

† According to the FAR personnel summary for 1962, the reserve units featured

mid-1962 as a branch of the MINFAR. Its missions were protection of the population, social and economic projects, and other civil defense tasks in the event of natural disasters or enemy attacks. This new armed institution came from militia units in the Military Industrial Organization (Organización Militar Industrial—OMI), which was made up of militia members who could not be spared from their jobs in manufacturing or services or who, due to their age or health, were not in the MNR, the primary reserve of regular units.

The MINFAR, as the central military structure, and the General Staff improved in step with the growth, development, and complexity of the missions assigned to them for defense of the country. By late 1961 there was a leadership and command structure in place to ensure the concentration of all operational and mobilizational work of the General Staff, as well as effective leadership in preparing the troops for combat.

The transformation of the FAR—with growing forces, more modern weaponry, and new missions—required raising the level of military professionalism and improving the knowledge of the command personnel. The training and retraining of officers to assume positions as commanders and specialists became a necessity.

In 1961 the FAR devised a plan to create new military schools to provide accelerated training courses for commanders, revolutionary instructors, and technical officers. Playing a large role in this endeavor was the experience gained in the courses for militia leaders, which were implemented with the founding in mid-1960 of the Ignacio Agramonte Officers School in Matanzas, devoted to the training of battalion and platoon chiefs in

two campaign artillery brigades and five independent groups, including three with rocket launchers and two with artillery. Furthermore, plans for the following year included establishing, as part of this reserve, one tank battalion, three groups of rocket launchers, five 120-mm. mortar groups, and forty antiaircraft artillery batteries, including nine 100-mm., nine 57-mm., and twenty-two 30-mm. batteries. The three combat supply battalions included one communications battalion, one for reconnaissance, and one for sappers.

six- and three-month courses, respectively.

Likewise, the rapid development of the artillery forces required a larger number of qualified specialists. This led to the founding of the Camilo Cienfuegos Artillery School of the FAR on September 11, 1961. Intensive courses were also organized for officers in communications, engineering, and other fields.

Along with military training, political and ideological education was an essential task of the armed forces. In order to train qualified personnel for this task, the first course at the Osvaldo Sánchez Cabrera School for Revolutionary Instructors was opened on May 8. The students for this course were selected from the militias and the Rebel Army.

Similarly, a number of other institutions were set up: for specialists; schools for squadron, platoon, and company leaders; as well as training and continuing education courses, corresponding to the needs of the armies, their weapons, and types of forces.

The FAR's plans for combat, operational, and mobilizational readiness were primarily oriented toward antilanding defense, with the aim of resisting and inflicting heavy losses on the enemy. From a strategic point of view, they also allowed for the possibility of using regular units to wage irregular warfare in the event that any part of the country were occupied by an invader.

On December 1, 1961, the commander in chief issued Order no. 1 for the 1962 instructional year. This order analyzed the development of the Revolutionary Armed Forces up to that point, highlighting some of the experiences gained by the senior officers of the units for planning and directing combat training. It also identified as a priority the continual enhancement of combat readiness, and ordered troops to pay special attention to tactical classes on antilanding defense and training exercises in night combat. Furthermore, emphasis was placed on training for protection against enemy air attacks and on defensive deployment in designated fortified areas.[11]

In a speech to troops on December 18, Commander in Chief Fidel Castro assessed the changes in the FAR. During 1961, he said, "the Cuban people had begun to forge a modern, victorious army, with a great fighting spirit, equipped with magnificent weaponry, under commanding officers who are tested, alert, and knowledgeable."[12]

In the first half of 1962, the regular troops and reservists greatly increased their combat capacity and readiness, and also achieved further gains in the organization and discipline of their units. Along with the successes, there were some leadership shortcomings in terms of combat readiness and in methodological and organizational questions. In response, Order no. 2 from the Minister of the FAR, issued on June 1, 1962, made an in-depth assessment of these issues and ordered measures aimed at eradicating the problems and consolidating the gains already made. This order called for organizing military exercises, such as division maneuvers of the various armies and one to be led by the General Staff during the second instructional period of 1962.[13]

As a part of enhancing the country's defense capabilities, the Council of Ministers passed a law on June 6, 1961, dissolving the former Home Ministry and establishing in its place the Ministry of the Interior (Ministerio del Interior—MININT). Designated as general offices in this new ministry were the Department of Information (G2), the Revolutionary National Police, and the Maritime Police, which until then had been under the MINFAR.

The bodies of the MININT, particularly the Department of State Security (Departamento de Seguridad del Estado—DSE), worked in close coordination with the FAR and with the support of the people, organized in the Committees for the Defense of the Revolution (Comités de Defensa de la Revolución—CDR). Together they waged a successful battle against the CIA's secret war and thwarted its plans to create a state of internal unrest that would have been used to justify a direct military attack against Cuba. The new structure adopted by the MININT helped to further improve the organization and methods of the intelligence and counterintelligence bodies of State Security, whose main missions continued to be to penetrate the ranks of the counterrevolution, as well as to support the military actions of the FAR with the necessary information.

These advances in preparing the country for defense show how the leadership of the Cuban Revolution was taking measures in 1961 and 1962 to confront foreign aggression with the power of a united, armed people.

Confronting the armed counterrevolutionary bands

In the military field, the FAR also sought to develop better methods and structures to fight the counterrevolutionary bandits, especially after the beginning of Operation Mongoose in 1962,* which saw a significant increase in the activities of harassment groups and armed bands throughout the country. In the Escambray alone, these actions increased from forty-two in March to seventy-nine in September. Over the course of 1962 there were ninety-seven CIA sea operations to transport agents and supplies for the armed counterrevolutionary groups inside Cuba.

As a result, improved methods of struggle against the armed bands were needed. It was necessary at one and the same time to develop social programs for education and health; meet the basic material needs of the population; keep up production and services; prepare the country for defense; and wage the struggle against armed groups within the country. All these efforts drew on the same forces: the working people and, in the first place, the youth.

Under these conditions it didn't make sense to continue mobilizations on the large scale of Operation Jaula [cage].† Experiments were carried out with new structures, which could achieve a greater specialization of troops in the tactics of fight-

---

* See chapter 3.

† Name of the first clean-up operation in the Escambray, completed shortly before the mercenary invasion at the Bay of Pigs. In it the leadership of the Cuban Revolution had to mobilize some 60,000 militia members—40,000 of them from the capital city—in order to completely surround and neutralize the armed bands operating there.

ing against the bandits.[14]

Although this idea had emerged in mid-1959 and had been implemented from late 1961 in the mountainous areas of Oriente province, it was now put forward in an improved form that could bring together:

• Adoption of a territorial structure, flexibly organized according to the characteristics of the theater of operations;

• Within each theater, establishment of three tactical levels: zone, sector, and subsector;

• Formation of companies and permanent special battalions, made up of young peasants and agricultural workers who—and this was a matter of principle—had joined the armed forces as volunteers;

• Intensive preparation of these units for counterinsurgency actions;

• Creation of reserve militia companies and battalions assigned to particular zones, sectors, and subsectors, to be used as reinforcements in large-scale operations.

Until August 1962, this process was undertaken in a somewhat different way in each army. By that time enough experience had been gained from the functioning of different fighting units to set up a uniform structure nationwide.

On August 31, 1962, Order 00023 from the FAR chief of staff gave instructions for the creation of the Lucha Contra Bandidos (LCB) [Struggle against bandits] and laid out its organization and structure. In late 1962 the LCB command of the MINFAR was established.

Likewise, on October 1, 1961, the Central Office against Armed Bands (Buró Central contra Bandas Armadas—BCBA) was established in the General Counterintelligence Command of the Department of State Security of the MININT. Similar bodies were established in the provincial and regional Counterintelligence Sections. As LCB sectors and subsectors were set up, each had a liaison officer from the respective Office against Armed Bands.[15]

From the second half of 1961 and through 1962, closer ties

were knit among the forces—military, intelligence, counterintelligence—that were fighting the counterrevolution in its various expressions. In this way a general system to fight the bands was brought together in practice.

In the political field, the Boards of Coordination, Implementation, and Inspection (Juntas de Coordinación, Ejecución e Inspección—JUCEI)* started to eradicate certain bureaucratic obstacles in the former municipal and provincial administrations. In provinces of major strategic importance, JUCEI was headed by historic leaders of the revolution, who also exercised military command in those territories. In this way, government management advanced in close interconnection with military actions against the internal enemy.

Likewise, the process of establishing the Integrated Revolutionary Organizations (ORI) brought revolutionary militants together in united political action against the resistance of the reactionary classes.† ORI leadership bodies at all levels facilitated the ideological and political work that Revolutionary Instructors of the FAR were developing, both with the troops and with the population living in the areas most affected by the counterrevolutionary bands.

In the social field, the establishment of the National Association of Small Farmers (Asociación Nacional de Agricultores Pequeños—ANAP) on May 17, 1961, contributed to neutralizing the political influence of capitalist farmers who, up until then, had dominated the leadership of the Association of Tenant Farmers, Landowners, and Others (Asociaciones de Colonos, Hacendados y Otras). ANAP carried out its work among the

---

* Local government bodies at the municipal and provincial levels that were set up beginning in 1962 to replace the old government agencies at those levels.

† In 1961 the July 26 Movement initiated a fusion with the Popular Socialist Party and the Revolutionary Directorate, to form the Integrated Revolutionary Organizations (ORI). All three had gone through a process of differentiation and clarification as the revolution deepened. In 1963 the ORI became the United Party of the Socialist Revolution; and in October 1965 the Communist Party of Cuba was formed, with Fidel Castro as first secretary of its Central Committee.

peasants on a democratic and revolutionary basis, which made it possible to mark out the dividing lines of struggle in Cuban rural society at that time. ANAP stood as a social and popular pole of attraction, counterposed to the wealthy farmers, who still survived in the Cuban countryside and who sided with the counterrevolution, making their lands available for training camps of the armed bands.

Changes in the economic field—strengthening the socialist sector by placing the sugarcane cooperatives under ownership of the entire people, and establishing state-run farms—increased the weight of the rural proletariat as the predominant social force in the revolutionary process in the Cuban countryside. Young workers from the countryside were the basis for bringing to full strength the military units that fought the counterrevolutionary bands during that period of the revolution.

The Cuban state also had to adopt important measures in the judicial field to impose strict revolutionary justice against counterrevolutionary terror. Already in January 1961, an amendment to the Fundamental Law* was introduced to allow the death penalty against those who carried out sabotage and crimes against the state.[16]

The escalation of attacks and assassinations in the second half of 1961, however, impelled the Council of Ministers on November 29, 1961, to pass Law 988 mandating the death penalty for members of armed counterrevolutionary bands organized inside or outside the country. Similar measures applied to all those who committed politically motivated sabotage or killings, whether or not they belonged to any group. This law also decreed the

---

* On February 7, 1959, the revolutionary government enacted the Fundamental Law of the Republic, which put into effect the main provisions of the 1940 constitution, except that the Council of Ministers was endowed with the powers of congress, and references to the Senate and House of Representatives were eliminated. Article 25 of the law stated, "The death penalty shall not be imposed," although there were several exceptions for crimes committed under the Batista dictatorship. See *Ley Fundamental de la República. Leyes de la Revolución II* [Fundamental Law of the Republic. Laws of the Revolution II.] (Special collection). Pamphlet (Havana: Editorial Lex, 1959).

confiscation of rural property and other assets of those individuals who collaborated with the counterrevolutionary bands, in addition to whatever other legal penalties these individuals might face for specific crimes.[17]

After the promulgation of Law 988, summary criminal trials of the type established in January 1961 were strictly carried out. Punishments were imposed with the full severity set by law. Numerous public trials were held in the same locales that had been the scene of criminal actions by the counterrevolution.

The bands were finally eradicated in 1965 when the last group active in the country—that of Juan Alberto Martínez Andrade—was captured on July 4. In subsequent months some other scattered bandits were captured as they tried to flee revolutionary justice. And so this phase of the dirty war imposed on the Cuban people by Yankee imperialism and the reactionary classes was brought to an end. The armed confrontation had spanned seven years and affected all six provinces that made up the country at that time.

In this dirty war encouraged and supported by the United States, 299 bands had been active in Cuban national territory between 1959 and 1965, with a total of 3,995 combatants. Counting casualties among regular Cuban troops, militia members, other participants in the operations, and victims of crimes carried out by the bands, 549 persons lost their lives and many others were disabled. Cuba had to spend some one billion pesos on this struggle, during years of great economic difficulty.[18]

The combination of military actions with ideological and political struggle was decisive in the victory over the bands. The defeat of the counterrevolutionary bands in Cuba proved that guerrilla warfare cannot be victorious against an armed people that is the protagonist of a genuine revolution.

Chapter 3

Operation Mongoose
and U.S. invasion plans

As the Cuban people undertook huge efforts to develop their country despite the campaign of subversion, new plans for aggression were being drawn up in the United States. A debate was under way in Washington over the most effective method of directing, applying, and controlling the many resources devoted to overthrowing the Cuban revolutionary government.

In view of ongoing blunders in the anti-Cuba plans carried out by different departments and agencies, top echelons of the Kennedy administration began looking in late October 1961 for new methods to eliminate the prevailing "disorganization and lack of coordination." Just as in their earlier analysis of the Bay of Pigs operation, failures were ascribed to operational problems. Once again Washington underestimated the capacity of the Cuban people and their revolutionary leadership to successfully confront the challenges that such a hostile policy posed for their country.

U.S. Attorney General Robert Kennedy proposed to President John F. Kennedy the establishment of an operational command to direct the various plans of action in a unified, coordinated, and organized fashion and merge them into a "single plan." In practice, this meant the preparation of a new covert operation, not merely by the CIA but by the entire U.S. government. The president asked Assistant Special Counsel Richard N. Goodwin for his opinion. Goodwin, who also headed the Interagency Task Force, replied in a memorandum, "The beauty of such an operation over the next few months is that we cannot lose. If the best happens we will unseat Castro. If not, then at least we will emerge with a stronger underground, better propaganda and a far clearer idea of the dimensions of the problems which affect us."[1]

Operation Mongoose takes shape

At a White House meeting on November 3, 1961, Kennedy authorized the development of a new program, much more sinister than its predecessors, designed to destroy the Cuban Revolution.* The project was code-named Operation Mongoose.

As a first step, several documents were prepared laying out the government's existing action plans and its options against Cuba. The CIA prepared a report on covert actions under way,† and the Interagency Task Force presented a "Plan for Cuba"—according to its authors, a study "to determine the courses of action which the U.S. would follow with reference to Cuba in

---

* In attendance at the meeting were Attorney General Robert Kennedy; George W. Ball, U. Alexis Johnson, Wymberley Coerr, and Robert Hurwitch for the State Department; Gen. Charles Cabell, Richard Bissell, Robert Amory, and Col. J.C. King for the CIA; and McGeorge Bundy and Goodwin of the White House staff. Also present were Defense Secretary Robert McNamara, Assistant Defense Secretary Paul Nitze, and Gen. Edward Lansdale.

† The CIA document had six points, including propaganda activities and psychological warfare (classified as nonsensitive); agent training; infiltration/exfiltration; creation of spy networks and counterrevolutionary organizations inside Cuba; encouragement of and material support to terrorist attacks and sabotage; and finally, air operations to support these subversive goals. "Paper Prepared in the Central Intelligence Agency: Types of Covert Action against the Castro Regime. Washington, November 8, 1961," *FRUS*, vol. X, pp. 675–77.

the event of Fidel Castro's death in order to insure the replacement of the Castro regime with a friendly government."[2]

Among the scenarios foreseen in this paper was that a general uprising would occur in Cuba as the result of a power struggle and massive reprisals against political opponents of the regime. In that situation, a devious plan would be implemented to prepare the ideological and political conditions for military intervention. The document stated: "Although the U.S. cannot defend this action as justified under international law, we can stress the morality of the action on the basis that a chaotic, near civil war situation exists off our shores where millions of Cubans are seeking freedom by throwing off the Communist yoke and have requested our assistance."[3]

As for the acceptability and feasibility of an invasion of Cuba, the document asserted, "American investments will suffer less in the long run than they would if Castro-Communism continued and spread throughout the hemisphere. The Alliance for Progress program will not encounter serious obstacles as a result of this action. If the operation is quickly and successfully accomplished, the political damage will be correspondingly reduced."[4] Analyzing the repercussions that such action might have in Latin America, the document stated, "Widespread organized Communist disturbances will occur immediately but the more quickly the Castro regime is crushed the greater the difficulty the Communists will encounter in maintaining existing disturbances and in mounting further disturbances. A successful invasion may strengthen the will of Latin American Governments to destroy the Communist menace in their own countries."[5] It concluded emphatically, "We can foresee no way other than invasion to accomplish the objective as stated in the problem."[6]

On November 20, 1961, President Kennedy called the incoming CIA director, John A. McCone, to inform him that a new program of action against Cuba was being studied. In a memorandum summarizing Kennedy's call, McCone noted that the proposal "would embody a variety of covert operations, propaganda, all possible actions that would create dissensions within Cuba and would discredit the Castro regime, and political action with members of the OAS in support of the action."[7] In addition, McCone recorded that the president told him that Brig. Gen. Edward Lansdale, an expert on guerrilla and antisubversive operations, would be in charge of designing the project, under the direct supervision of the attorney general. The president told McCone that he and his brother Robert wanted the plan to be ready in two weeks. To that end a committee was to be established, headed up by Lansdale—who would also represent the Defense Department—along with high-level representatives of the State Department, CIA, and USIA. So obsessed were the Kennedys with the problem of Cuba that they proposed this committee be able to "cut across" the command structure of other agencies. McCone opposed this course, explaining the difficulties that it might pose once the operation was under way.*

Ten days later, on November 30, 1961, President Kennedy

---

* Concerning this, McCone stated:

"a) That he observed that the Agency and indeed the Administration appeared to be in a condition of 'shock' as a result of the happenings in Cuba and, therefore, were doing very little. He supported dynamic action but emphasized that action should not be reckless.

"b) He supported the Lansdale committee concept.

"c) This committee should report to the '5412' group [see following footnote], which he stated was properly organized, met regularly, had senior representation, and was a proper unit to give political guidance to the Lansdale committee and also to evaluate action proposals of the committee.

"d) He proposed that the facilities of all Departments of Government and the CIA be made available to the extent needed, but these facilities be maintained 'in place' and that under no circumstances should an attempt be made to 'lift' elements of departments or agencies out of their 'in place' position and placed under the Lansdale group. He explained that the resources or assets of the departments and the CIA were most extensive and depended upon support, logistics, communications, etc. which were an integral part of the departments and agencies, and if an attempt was made to 'lift' certain activities, these activities could not properly function because of lack of support and communication." "Memorandum for the Record. Washington, November 22, 1961," *FRUS*, vol. X, p. 685.

officially communicated the key decisions made concerning the new operation in a presidential memorandum to the secretaries of state and defense, the director of the CIA, the attorney general, Richard Goodwin, and Generals Taylor and Lansdale.

The memorandum ordered the use of all "our available assets to . . . overthrow the communist regime" and designated General Lansdale as chief of operations, with the responsibility to lead the project through the appropriate government organizations and departments. It stipulated that "The NSC 5412 group* will be kept closely informed of activities and be available for advice and recommendation." Kennedy also directed the secretaries of state and defense and the director of the Central Intelligence Agency to appoint "senior officers of their department as personal representatives to assist the Chief of Operations as required. These senior officers should be able to exercise—either themselves or through the Secretaries and Director—effective operational control over all aspects of their Department's operations dealing with Cuba." Finally, Kennedy specified, "Knowledge of the existence of this operation should be restricted to the recipients of this memorandum, members of the 5412 group and the representatives appointed by the Secretaries and the Director."[8]

It was also decided to expand the 5412 group—made up of

* A 1975 U.S. Senate report described the NSC 5412 as follows: "Beginning in 1955, the responsibility for authorizing CIA covert action operations lay with the Special Group, a subcommittee of the National Security Council composed of the President's Assistant for National Security Affairs, the Director of Central Intelligence, the Deputy Secretary of Defense and the Under Secretary of State for Political Affairs. Today this group is known as the 40 Committee, and its membership has been expanded to include the Chairman of the Joint Chiefs of Staff. During 1962 another NSC subcommittee was established to oversee covert operations in Cuba. This subcommittee was the Special Group (Augmented); its membership included the Special Group, the Attorney General, and certain other high officials." *Alleged Assassination Plots Involving Foreign Leaders: An Interim Report of the Select Committee to Study Governmental Operations with Respect to Intelligence Activities* (also known as the Church Committee report). Washington, D.C: United States Government Printing Office, 1975.

McGeorge Bundy, U. Alexis Johnson, Roswell Gilpatric, John McCone, and Gen. Lyman Lemnitzer—by adding Robert Kennedy and Gen. Maxwell Taylor. Known as the Special Group (Augmented), it was responsible for overall control of the operation. Secretary of State Dean Rusk and Secretary of Defense Robert McNamara were occasionally present at its meetings but were not regular members. President Kennedy designated Taylor as chairman, although his brother Robert was the main figure and the informal direct link to the president.

The next day, December 1, the Special Group (Augmented) met for the first time. Robert Kennedy told the group about a series of meetings held recently "with higher authority," and of the decision "that higher priority should be given to Cuba." He also announced that General Lansdale had been designated chief of operations and explained what that position entailed. The meeting agreed that Lansdale should prepare a broad program to be reviewed and then submitted to the president.[9]

The 'Cuba Project' of Operation Mongoose

General Lansdale drafted a memorandum to the members of the 5412 group, dated December 7, 1961, which listed the concepts and general lines of action to be carried out in Operation Mongoose. This document can be considered the first draft of the Cuba Project aimed at overthrowing the revolution.

Utilizing his authority to employ all available means in the project, Lansdale openly spelled out the tasks of different agencies involved—tasks that had already been undertaken covertly but had not been put in writing in documents such as this. These included a proposal that the CIA undertake "bold new actions" and that it utilize the "potential of the underworld" and, in close cooperation with the FBI, "enlist the assistance of American links" to the Mafia in Cuba.[10]

This draft of Operation Mongoose was discussed and approved by Group 5412 without changing or amending any of the projected tasks.[11] Based on those projections, Lansdale and his operational group conducted studies and coordinated with the departments and agencies involved to finalize their project of secret war against Cuba.

On January 18, 1962, Lansdale submitted the Cuba Project to top government authorities and the Special Group (Augmented). It envisioned thirty-two tasks to be carried out by departments and agencies participating in Operation Mongoose. "The U.S. objective," the paper stated, "is to help the Cubans overthrow the Communist regime from within Cuba and institute a new government with which the United States can live in peace."[12]

The program included a variety of political, diplomatic, economic, psychological, propaganda, and espionage actions, different acts of terrorism and sabotage, as well as encouragement and logistical support to armed counterrevolutionary bands. In short, the operation was aimed at provoking a "revolt" of the Cuban people, which once begun would lay the basis for direct military intervention by the armed forces of the United States and its Latin American allies. The document asserted:

"The revolt requires a strongly motivated political action movement established within Cuba, to generate the revolt, to give it direction towards the object, and to capitalize on the climactic moment. The political actions will be assisted by economic warfare to induce failure of the Communist regime to supply Cuba's economic needs, psychological operations to turn the peoples' resentment increasingly against the regime, and military-type groups to give the popular movement an action arm for sabotage and armed resistance in support of political objectives."[13]

General Lansdale's mentality in drawing up the project was shown in a memorandum to members of the Operation Mongoose working group, in which he emphasized: "It is our job to put the American genius to work on this project, quickly and effectively."[14] The kind of genius the chief of operations had in mind was shown when he later added task thirty-three,* con-

---

* Declassified documents suggest that this task was conceived by Lansdale at the end of his January 19 meeting with Attorney General Robert Kennedy.

sisting of "a plan to disable Cuban sugar workers during the harvest by means of chemical weapons."[15]

A day later, in a meeting chaired by Robert Kennedy, all those present were called on to show absolute, resolute determination not to fail in carrying out their tasks. Kennedy stated that solving "the Cuban problem" was at that moment "the top priority in the United States Government—all else is secondary—no time, money, effort, or manpower is to be spared." He stressed that the president of the United States had told him that "the final chapter on Cuba has not been written" and that "it's got to be done and will be done."[16]

The Cuba Project was analyzed by the Special Group (Augmented) and subsequently sent to the relevant government departments and agencies for their opinions and proposals.

As already detailed in chapter 1, the Cuban government was expelled from the Organization of American States in late January 1962, during its Eighth Consultative Conference of Foreign Ministers in Punta del Este, Uruguay. On February 3 President Kennedy decreed the trade embargo, stepping up the economic blockade that had been carried out since 1959 to force the revolution to back down. But this time Kennedy was declaring not a simple "embargo," but the start of an economic war.

Proposals from departments and agencies were submitted by February 15, 1962, and used as the basis for a new document, also named the Cuba Project, presented February 20 by General Lansdale. It contained six specific plans for support and a six-step schedule—the Basic Action Plan inside Cuba—aimed at destroying the Cuban Revolution between March and October.

The target dates were set out as follows:

"Phase I, *Action*, March 1962. Start moving in.

"Phase II, *Build-up*, April–July 1962. Activating the necessary operations inside Cuba for revolution and concurrently

Lansdale critically noted there that the "United States Government was precluded from destroying the current sugar crop." See "Memorandum From the Chief of Operations in the Deputy Directorate for Plans (Helms) to Director of Central Intelligence McCone. Washington, January 19, 1962," *FRUS*, vol. X, p. 720.

applying the vital political, economic, and military-type support from outside Cuba.

"Phase III, *Readiness*, 1 August 1962, check for final policy decision.

"Phase IV, *Resistance*, August–September 1962, move into guerrilla operations.

"Phase V, *Revolt*, first two weeks of October 1962. Open revolt and overthrow of the Communist regime.

"Phase VI, *Final*, during month of October 1962. Establishment of new government."[17]

This Basic Action Plan aimed to organize a counterrevolution inside Cuba and subordinate it to a "responsible opposition" established in exile, which was none other than the so-called Cuban Revolutionary Council (CRC), created days before the Bay of Pigs invasion. The counterrevolution within Cuba was supposed to gain strength until it was capable of launching an open struggle for political power, or at least of controlling a substantial part of Cuban territory, where it could establish a provisional military government. This body would then be quickly recognized and supported by the United States and Latin American governments, which would intervene if necessary with their armed forces under cover of the Rio Treaty.[18]

The plans for support envisaged programs of economic, political, and psychological warfare, military support, intelligence, and sabotage aimed at sowing terror and internal instability to establish suitable conditions for the attack. In short, the goal was within eight months to "overthrow the Communist regime . . . and institute a new government" in accordance with U.S. imperialist interests.[19]

But the key point of Operation Mongoose was the political decision by the United States—at that point still to be taken—to use its own armed forces to support the internal counterrevolution. This was clearly expressed by Lansdale when he sharply posed the question, "Will the U.S. respond promptly with military force to aid the Cuban revolt?"[20]

In mid-March, Lansdale got the "vital decision" he had been

asking for. On March 14, 1962, the Special Group (Augmented) laid out the main guidelines to be followed in planning actions of Operation Mongoose, which were to proceed on the following assumptions:

"a. In undertaking to cause the overthrow of the target government, the U.S. will make maximum use of indigenous resources, internal and external, but recognizes that final success will require decisive U.S. military intervention.

"b. Such indigenous resources as are developed will be used to prepare for and justify this intervention, and thereafter to facilitate and support it."[21]

From the time of this decision, the Joint Chiefs of Staff diligently accelerated their work in relation to Cuba. In April, for example, a study was prepared "on how to impose a 'total blockade' on Cuba," and the CIA analyzed possible repercussions of such an action. In the Pentagon, meanwhile, a working group of the Commander in Chief of the Atlantic Command (CINCLANT) and the Defense Intelligence Agency (DIA) began to coordinate preparing a contingency plan.[22]

The CIA did not lag behind. Between late 1961 and early 1962, William K. Harvey was designated as head of Task Force W, under overall guidance of the Special Group (Augmented). This Operation Mongoose task force set up in Miami the biggest CIA station in the U.S., under the code name JM/WAVE.

Some 400 CIA officials worked in this Miami station and on Cuba assignment in the central office in Langley, not including the approximately 4,000 Cuban agents. JM/WAVE, with an annual budget of about $100 million, lined up a fleet of speedboats and "mother" ships disguised to look like merchant vessels. This fleet was used for infiltrating and evacuating agents, supplying weapons and explosives to armed bands, attacking Cuban merchant ships and fishing boats, and harassing economic targets along the Cuban coasts.

Task Force W also coordinated actions with CIA offices worldwide—with the aim of hampering Cuban commercial and diplomatic relations—by bribing businesses that sold to the island

and by other methods, such as sabotaging cargoes on ships transporting goods to and from Cuba.

Throughout 1962 there was a significant intensification of sabotage, terrorism, burning of canefields, attempts to assassinate leaders of the revolution, acts of piracy, and infiltration of commando groups. Between January and August 1962 there were 5,780 such actions; of these, 716 damaged major economic and social targets.

The planned and attempted assassinations of the head of the Cuban government and other leaders relied on the use of advanced scientific and technological means,[23] including poisoned pills, long-range rifles with silencers, pens and cigars with deadly liquids or powders, and similar monstrous ideas. CIA agents running these operations established ties with elements of the Mafia in the United States.

At the same time, the CIA increased the number of spies infiltrated into Cuba and paid more attention to collecting intelligence on Cuba's defense capabilities, especially the makeup of the new weapons supplies and combat systems arriving from the USSR.

The U.S. Navy and Air Force also undertook intensive airborne and electronic surveillance of the entire Cuban territory, as well as its maritime access routes, including use of u-2 spy planes for aerial photographic reconnaissance. Data collected by these intelligence actions were used to refine the plans to invade Cuba.

General Lansdale reported on the positive and negative results of Phase I of Operation Mongoose in a July 25 memorandum to the Special Group (Augmented). He also proposed taking more aggressive measures for Phase II and presented four options, as follows:

"a. Cancel operational plans; treat Cuba as a Bloc nation; protect Hemisphere from it, or

"b. Exert all possible diplomatic, economic, psychological, and other pressures to overthrow the Castro-Communist regime without overt employment of U.S. military, or

"c. Commit U.S. to help Cubans overthrow the Castro-Communist regime, with a step-by-step phasing to ensure success, including the use of U.S. military force if required at the end, or

"d. Use a provocation to overthrow the Castro-Communist regime by U.S. military force."[24]

In order to discuss the above options, the Special Group (Augmented) had the different bodies represented in the group draw up reports analyzing the feasibility and possible outcomes of those courses of action. To that end, copies of a paper prepared by a representative of the Joint Chiefs of Staff and the Department of Defense, named "Consequences of US Military Intervention in Cuba,"[25] were delivered on August 8 to the Special Group (Augmented).

On August 17 General Taylor informed President Kennedy that the Special Group (Augmented) saw no possibility that the Castro regime would be overthrown by internal subversion without direct military intervention, and that the group favored a more aggressive Mongoose program.[26]

After discussions within this group, Kennedy gave instructions to draw up an expanded version of the second option proposed by Lansdale. On August 23 McGeorge Bundy, Kennedy's special assistant for national security affairs, issued Memorandum No. 181 on "National Security Action" with the president's instructions for implementing as rapidly as possible the course of action laid out in this phase of Operation Mongoose.[27]

Under this directive, the Special Group (Augmented) ordered a list of possible sabotage targets in Cuba, including a large copper mine,[28] presumably the one in Matahambre, Pinar del Río.

Contingency plans for the invasion of Cuba

On April 29, 1961, just days after the defeat at Playa Girón, President Kennedy, Secretary of Defense McNamara, and Chief of Naval Operations Admiral Burke reviewed a contingency plan to deploy U.S. forces in Cuba. According to this plan, the number of ground troops necessary to gain "complete control of the island . . . within 8 days" would reach 60,000, "although it was recognized that guerrilla forces would continue to operate." Two days later, McNamara advised the Joint Chiefs of Staff to be ready to implement the plan, although he clarified that this "should not be interpreted as an indication that U.S. military action against Cuba is probable."[29]

Beginning then, Kennedy told the Joint Chiefs to study and prepare new contingency plans against Cuba. It is believed that these were presented for presidential approval in early April 1962, since on April 10 the president informed Miró Cardona, the counterrevolutionary ringleader, of the U.S. government's readiness to resolve the Cuban problem by force—for which, Kennedy said, six divisions* would be required.[30]

These plans provided for the inclusion of counterrevolutionary Cuban exiles in the invading forces in order to mask direct U.S. intervention and mislead the peoples of Latin America. According to Miró Cardona, Kennedy made an agreement in late October 1961 with representatives of the Cuban Revolutionary Council, under which the U.S. government would be responsible for organizing a new invasion, which could count on direct U.S. military support, while the CRC would recruit personnel of Cuban origin to be part of the expeditionary force.[31]

The problem of using Cuban exiles in future plans was among the issues discussed at the National Security Council meeting on May 5, 1961.[32] Arguments were evaluated for and against organizing a military force made up of these elements, as had been done previously.

Among the reasons given for not doing so was the experience that U.S. involvement in organizing and training such a force—whether on U.S. territory or in any other country of the region—would be very difficult to hide. The U.S. government would then be held accountable at the United Nations and before the court of world public opinion for the implicit intention to invade.

Another problem would be that a special force of this type,

* A division consists of 10,000–15,000 troops.

once organized, would amount to a political commitment that would be difficult to get out of, should it become necessary to deactivate the force. Moreover, experience had shown that such an entity could not succeed without direct U.S. intervention. And in the event of U.S. intervention, a contingent like this would be useful but not essential.

In light of these considerations, the NSC agreed not to organize any separate Cuban military force, while Kennedy instructed the Pentagon to develop plans to enlist Cuban counterrevolutionaries as volunteers in the U.S. armed forces. On June 8, 1961, Defense Secretary McNamara reported to the president on preparations for a program to induct Cuban volunteers.[33]

It was not until 1962 that military contingency plans against Cuba took final form. As these plans were taking shape, the Pentagon was looking at how to justify the use of the armed forces. A secret Joint Chiefs of Staff document, dated March 7, 1962, asserted that the "determination that an internal uprising with any possibility of success is impossible within the next 9 to 10 months demands a decision by the United States to fabricate a 'provocation' to justify a positive U.S. military action."[34]

Two days later, the Joint Chiefs submitted a paper entitled "Pretexts to Justify US Military Intervention in Cuba" for consideration within the Department of Defense. This paper listed a number of harassment measures aimed at establishing conditions to justify direct military intervention. The paper explained:

"1. Since it would seem desirable to use legitimate provocation as the basis for US military intervention in Cuba a cover and deception plan . . . could be executed as an initial effort to provoke Cuban reactions. Harassment plus deceptive actions to convince the Cubans of imminent invasion would be emphasized. Our military posture throughout execution of the plan will allow a rapid change from exercise to intervention if Cuban response justifies.

"2. A series of well-coordinated incidents will be planned to take place in and around Guantanamo to give genuine appearance of being done by hostile Cuban forces."[35]

In accordance with the contingency plans, military training exercises began in April 1962 for combat and operational preparation of the forces that might be involved. It was also necessary to prepare the general staffs and troops to direct and execute large sea and air landings in places similar to the Cuban coasts.

The military exercise designated Landphibex 1/62 (Amphibious Exercise of the Atlantic 1/62) was carried out in late April. It consisted of a powerful military deployment including four aircraft carriers, the *Enterprise* (CVAN-65—nuclear powered), the *Forrestal* (CVS-59), the *Intrepid* (CVS-11), and the *Lake Champlain* (CVS-39), and more than fifty warships, including submarines. Some 40,000 Marines from the 2nd Division landed on the "enemy island" and established a beachhead. The location chosen was the Puerto Rican island of Vieques, eight miles east of the main island.

A few days later, some of these forces carried out a similar exercise at Onslow Beach, North Carolina, called Demolex (Demolition Exercise).

In August 1962, the air force participated in the Swift Strike II exercise in North and South Carolina, training units in air support for troops. Four divisions of the Army, six squadrons of tactical fighter planes, and two squadrons of tactical reconnaissance and transport aircraft—totaling 70,000 soldiers and 500 planes—participated.

In September, another big military exercise, called Jupiter Spring, was carried out. It consisted of air drops of troops of three divisions of the 18th Airborne Corps, the main U.S. elite unit for this kind of operation. During this same period additional air, land, and sea troops reinforced those of the Atlantic Command. For example, in the summer of 1962 ships that had been serving in the Mediterranean and Pacific were assigned to this fleet.

Retired Maj. Gen. Max S. Johnson, a military expert and

former commandant of the Army War College, wrote an article published in *U.S. News & World Report* in September 1962 laying out his view of the Cuban "military problem." He wrote: "Basically, there are two elements involved in a military solution to the problem of Cuba: One element is blockade, by sea and air. . . . The second element is an actual invasion."

The latter, in Johnson's opinion, "one year ago, would have been relatively easy and short. The equivalent of three divisions probably would have been more than enough. . . ." But "today the problem is entirely different," Johnson wrote. A successful invasion now "would require a major effort—one involving perhaps six divisions, or their equivalent. . . .

"Of these divisions, three might comprise the assault echelon, with the rest needed for reinforcement.

"Close air support would be needed for this ground force in sizable amounts. There would be a need for air action, too, to obtain early air superiority over the whole island.

"Naval power would be needed for the amphibious landing operation, and for a supplementary shore bombardment."[36]

The article explains in detail how such an action would unfold. "An initial amphibious landing would be carried out by two divisions, Army or Marine, at several places on the Cuban coast. These forces, with heavy air support, would move quickly inland to neutralize key missile and other military centers, then drive on to Havana to seize the Communists' command echelons there.

"An airborne division, meanwhile, might carry out paratroop drops to knock out new coastal defenses and some airfields, and link up soon thereafter with ground troops as they come ashore.

"For tactical air support of ground forces in this landing phase, probably most of the operation could be covered by Marine and naval air units, flown from aircraft carriers offshore and the U.S. naval base at Guantanamo, Cuba. Other support, if needed, could be flown by jets of the Air Force's Tactical Air Command from bases in nearby Florida. . . .

"After the initial landing, another three divisions could be brought into the secured area, as reinforcements to insure enough effort for quick victory."[37]

The opinions of this retired general were not too far from the Atlantic Command's contingency plan, as the Pentagon's own declassified documents have subsequently confirmed. This confirms the assessment that the air-sea exercises carried out in the Caribbean that year demonstrated a real intention to prepare troops for use.

Today it is known that the Commander in Chief, Atlantic (CINCLANT), drew up three operational contingency plans for military actions against Cuba. According to a September 25, 1962, Pentagon document, these plans were as follows:

"CUBAN CONTINGENCY PLANS

"I. *CINCLANT OPLAN 314-61* is the basic contingency plan for operations in Cuba. It provides for (1) simultaneous airborne and amphibious assault in the vicinity of Havana; (2) reinforcement of Guantanamo; (3) mop-up operations in eastern Cuba. The time schedule for this plan calls for the first U.S. landings on the 18th day after receipt of the order to execute.

"II. *CINCLANT OPLAN 316-61* is the quick reaction plan for operations against Cuba. It uses the same forces as OPLAN 341-61 but commits them in increments. The airborne assault occurs 5 days after receipt of the order to execute; the amphibious assault occurs 3 days thereafter. Reaction time can be reduced to 2 days if advance warning permits pre-positioning of forces.

"III. *CINCLANT OPLAN 312-62* provides for the fast application of U.S. air power to Cuba in time increments of 6, 12, and 24 hours from a no warning condition. Target priorities are: (1) aircraft, anti-aircraft and radar installations, and air fields, (2) selective disruption of communication and transportation facilities; (3) troops and armor concentration, artillery, and naval vessels."[38]

These plans foresaw that the forces involved must be ready to act on October 27. Units chosen to participate would be five divisions of the Army and one of the Marines: two airborne

(82nd and 101st), one infantry (2nd), one armored (1st), and one Marine (2nd); and three permanent divisions of the reserve: one infantry (5th), one armored (2nd), and one Marine (4th).

This stepped-up and dangerous deployment of military forces in the Caribbean, together with the increase of subversive actions against Cuba since early 1962, constituted clear indications of imminent direct military aggression. It was evaluated as such by the Cuban military and political leadership, a judgment shared by the top political and government authorities of the USSR. Such a situation proved that Cuba needed to make enormous efforts to strengthen its defensive capabilities. Before world opinion and in international arenas, Cuba—together with the USSR—denounced Washington's plans, which could seriously threaten world peace.

Chapter 4

Top secret: Operation Anadyr

On Tuesday morning, May 29, 1962, a group of eighteen Soviet hydraulic engineering specialists arrived at the Havana airport.[1]* They were headed by Sharaf Rashidov, alternate member of the Presidium of the Central Committee and general secretary of the Communist Party of the Soviet Union (CPSU) in Uzbekistan. Accompanying the group was Aleksandr Alekseev, who would soon become the Soviet ambassador to Cuba. Among the group were three "technicians" headed by the "engineer" Petrov, whose mission was totally unrelated to that of the rest of the delegation.

Who was that "engineer"? He was Marshal Sergei Biryuzov, vice minister of defense and chief of strategic missile forces in

---

* The main points in this chapter have been reconstructed primarily from oral and written interviews with Soviet and Cuban figures who participated directly in the events, as well as with Soviet combatants who had different responsibilities in the Soviet Troop Force (STF) and with Cuban officials and authorities who were involved in the events. Some of this information has been confirmed by studies in the regions where Soviet troops were stationed.

the USSR. Along with Lt. Gen. Sergei F. Ushakov, deputy chief of the Central General Staff of the air force, and Maj. Gen. Pyotr V. Ageyev, a member of the Central General Staff's directorate of operations, Biryuzov was on a mission from Soviet premier and CPSU general secretary Nikita Khrushchev to personally propose to the top Cuban leadership the installation of nuclear missiles on Cuban territory in order to deter direct U.S. military aggression against the island.

Missiles in Cuba

Khrushchev's idea to deploy medium- and intermediate-range ballistic missiles* outside the territory of the USSR was closely related to the threat posed to Soviet security by the installation of American Jupiter missile bases in Turkey and Italy, as well as to the imminent danger of U.S. aggression that Cuba faced in April 1962.

It is difficult to determine exactly when and where Khrushchev first brought up this idea. There are varying accounts by those who were close to the Soviet leader at the time.

Deputy Premier Anastas Mikoyan's son, Sergo Mikoyan, relates that in late April his father visited Khrushchev at his residence on the outskirts of Moscow. As they walked through the garden, the top Soviet leader confided that he was thinking of proposing to the Cuban government in the next few days the deployment of nuclear missiles on its territory.[2]

Another account is by Fyodor M. Burlatsky,† who mentions that Khrushchev visited the Crimean Peninsula at about that time with Defense Minister Marshal Rodion Ya. Malinovsky. Malinovsky pointed to the horizon and commented that U.S. Jupiter missiles in Turkish territory could strike the USSR ten minutes after being launched, whereas Soviet intercontinental

---

* Medium-range ballistic missiles have a range of 500–1,499 miles (approximately 800–2,399 kilometers). Intermediate-range ballistic missiles have a range of 1,500–3,437 miles (approximately 2,400–5,499 kilometers).

† Fyodor Burlatsky worked at that time in the Central Committee of the CPSU and was part of Khrushchev's personal staff.

missiles would need twenty-five minutes to reach targets in the United States. Khrushchev responded, "We can create a similar situation for the Americans near the border of the United States, if we place missiles in Cuba. After all, the Americans didn't ask our permission to place those weapons next to our borders."[3]

Khrushchev himself gives another version in his memoirs.[4] He says that during a visit to Varna, Bulgaria, on May 14–20, 1962, he had the idea of surreptitiously deploying nuclear missiles in Cuba. This assertion seems doubtful, even though it is recorded in Khrushchev's tape-recorded recollections of those events.

Andrei A. Gromyko, Soviet foreign minister in those years, relates in an article published a few days before his death in 1989 that on a trip back to Moscow, Khrushchev privately expressed to him the considered opinion that in order to preserve Cuba as an independent state it was indispensable to install a certain number of nuclear missiles on the island. "Only that can save Cuba," Khrushchev said, "because Washington won't be deterred by the failure of the invasion at Playa Girón."[5]

In response to Gromyko's objections that such a step could imperil peace, Khrushchev declared: "The Soviet Union does not want nuclear war and does not intend to fight one. In a few days, I will pose the question to the Presidium of the Central Committee."[6]

In the same article, Gromyko says he believed that the subject must have already been taken up with the Soviet military. "I was struck by the fact that Khrushchev would express his ideas to me . . . with no sign of hesitation. I deduced from this that the matter must have been previously agreed upon with at least the military leadership of the country."

The proposal was first analyzed in a very small circle made up of Khrushchev, Anastas Mikoyan, and Frol R. Kozlov, all members of the Presidium. Gromyko and Malinovsky were also present. Biryuzov participated in the discussions too, as did Alekseev later on.

Aleksandr Alekseev's testimony is an important source for understanding the arguments Khrushchev used within the Soviet leadership for his proposal to install missiles in Cuba. Alekseev states: "Around May 1st or 2nd I was called to Moscow—I was working here [Havana] in the embassy—and I spoke to Khrushchev. He said, 'You have been working in Cuba for some time now, for about two years; you have good relations with the Cuban leaders, and we have decided to name you ambassador. . . .' I was also told that I was going to be called again when members of the Political Bureau were there." And that was the end of the conversation.[7]

Four days later Khrushchev again summoned Alekseev to his office in the Kremlin. Kozlov, Mikoyan, Gromyko, Rashidov, and Marshals Malinovsky and Biryuzov were there, in addition to Khrushchev. Alekseev gave the same report about Cuba as in the earlier interview. Khrushchev spoke with great emotion about the Cuban people and in particular about their leaders, their capabilities, and their decisiveness in opposing U.S. pressures. Then he asked, "How would Castro react if the Soviet government proposed to him to install nuclear missiles?"

Alekseev explains that the proposal made him uneasy, and he responded: "It is not likely that he will accept. The Cubans have elaborated a strategy based on the combat readiness of their people and on solidarity from world public opinion, above all from Latin America." Malinovsky then asked for the floor to point out: "The Spanish people agreed to receive Soviet armed assistance in their struggle against fascism."[8]

At that point Khrushchev expressed his ideas on the Cuban situation: "I am absolutely sure that in revenge for the defeat at Playa Girón, the Americans are going to launch an invasion against Cuba, not with mercenaries this time, but with their own armed forces. We have reliable intelligence on that."[9]

The Soviet premier paused as he spoke, thinking out the arguments he was about to make, and exclaimed: "An effective way must be found to deter the Americans from taking that perilous step! It is clear that our statements and interventions at the United Nations in defense of Cuba are no longer enough. Therefore we have to make them understand that if they attack Cuba, they will have to deal not only with that undaunted country, but also with the nuclear might of the Soviet Union.

"We have to make them pay the highest price for a military adventure against Cuba and, somehow, to balance the threat against Cuba with one against the United States itself. Logic dictates this can be accomplished only by deploying missiles with nuclear warheads on Cuban territory."[10]

Khrushchev went on to discuss how the United States was encircling the Soviet Union with its military bases and missile installations—which in his underlying thoughts may have been the determining factor in the proposal to deploy missiles in Cuba. "We have to repay the Americans in kind, to give them a taste of their own medicine, and make them feel what it's like to live with nuclear weapons trained on you." Finally, the premier talked about how he thought it could be done successfully: "The operation must be carried out in strict secrecy, so that the Americans don't find out about the missiles before they are fully ready for action. Above all, there must be no publicity, in view of the strong feelings during the campaign period leading up to the November 6 congressional elections. After that, it can be announced publicly."[11]

At another meeting of the Presidium, after expressing his opinion on how to defend Cuba, Khrushchev asked Malinovsky: "If we had an island like Cuba 140 kilometers from our borders, and we were faced with the need to bring it under control by overcoming desperate resistance, and if you had at your disposal all of our military power except the nuclear weapons, how much time would it take you to accomplish the mission?"[12]

After careful consideration, the marshal gave his opinion: "Three to five days, or maybe a week."

"You see!" Khrushchev commented. "What could we do? Nothing." And hurriedly, before anyone could get in a word, he said, "Even a response in another part of the world would be too late, because every action requires preparation."[13]

The military men did not object to the project—on the contrary, they were interested in it, because it would help redress the USSR's disadvantage compared to the United States in nuclear warheads and delivery systems. Although Khrushchev motivated his idea of deploying missiles as a defense of Cuba, it can therefore be asserted that his real purpose was directly linked to the military relationship of forces in the world at that time.

Militarily the balance of strategic forces favored the United States, both in nuclear warheads and delivery systems. The Kennedy administration's defense secretary, Robert McNamara, later revealed that during the 1962 October Crisis the U.S. had 5,000 nuclear warheads, whereas the USSR had barely 300—a ratio of approximately seventeen to one.[14]

And despite major accomplishments by the USSR in building aircraft and ballistic missiles—intercontinental, intermediate-, and medium-range—the United States was four years ahead, since its strategic forces had more than 1,300 B-47 and B-52 bombers stationed around the world, while the USSR had 155—a ratio of almost ten to one.

In 1962 the Pentagon had 377 strategic missiles, on land and at sea, and another 1,000 advanced Minuteman missiles were under construction.[15] Meanwhile, as of January 1, 1962, the USSR had only 44 intercontinental missiles, 373 medium-range, and 17 intermediate-range.

Ray Cline, former deputy director of the CIA, has revealed that from early 1961 the U.S. intelligence services considered the United States to have a four-to-one strategic advantage over the USSR in intercontinental missiles.*

These figures support the idea that one of the Soviet objectives—albeit implicit—for proposing to shift sixty medium- and

* Ray Cline pointed out that the United States had been "absolutely convinced that the Soviet Union had hundreds of missiles. Well, in August 1961, as I recall, we did fly the first effective reconnaissance satellite mission. . . . This is an extraordinary achievement. The satellite flew ninety miles above the Earth, and . . . circled the Earth every ninety minutes. . . . You could move across the Soviet Union, and cover an enormous area of the country . . . because there were eleven time zones in the Soviet Union, and we were able to cut across them . . . The actual photography from satellites was the key, and what made the United States feel that it had confidence in protecting ourselves. . . . In the fall of 1961, we . . . decided that the

intermediate-range missiles to Cuban territory was to improve the strategic balance vis-à-vis the United States. Based in Soviet territory these missiles could have only a tactical character. But in Cuba, thanks to its geographic location, they would become strategic arms, needing less time to strike their targets, and increasing the Soviet Union's potential to respond until such time as it could achieve nuclear parity.

In this regard, Fidel Castro has stated: "Nikita was very clever in the way he presented the issue to the other leaders of the Soviet party and in his underlying thinking. . . . In light of the facts we know today about the real international relationship of forces, it's clear that a remedy was needed. . . . If what they really had was fifty or sixty missiles, there is no doubt that the presence of those forty-two missiles* significantly improved the situation; it almost doubled the effective delivery systems."[16]

On May 21 the defense council of the USSR made the preliminary decision to deploy missiles in Cuba, and the task was put before the high command of the Soviet armed forces. From that point, discussions began on the military aspects of how the mission could be accomplished.[†]

On May 24 the project was brought up for debate in the Presidium of the CPSU Central Committee, the body empow-

Soviet Union had only twenty-five missiles at that time. . . . By 1962, and the approach of the Cuban missile crisis in October, we thought there were, I believe, perhaps fifty. . . . But the Minuteman in America was being produced very quickly. . . . And in September and October '62, we circled the Earth and found that we had four times as many Minuteman missiles as the Soviet Union had. And in some cases, some of those Soviet missiles were not even very operable. They were still on sites that were not intended for firing, they were intended only for testing. It was only at that time that we learned what was happening." (James G. Blight, Bruce J. Allyn, and David A. Welch, *Cuba on the Brink: Castro, the Missile Crisis, and the Soviet Collapse* (New York: Pantheon Books, 1993), p. 131.)

* The number of medium-range (R-12) missiles stationed in Cuba in October 1962: thirty-six were operational and six were for training.

† The Defense Council was headed by Khrushchev and consisted of Frol Kozlov and Leonid Brezhnev, both secretaries of the Central Committee of the CPSU; Aleksei Kosygin and Anastas Mikoyan, members of the Presidium of the CPSU; Marshal Rodion Ya. Malinovsky, Marshal Andrei Grechko, and General Aleksei

ered to give it final approval. The majority supported the proposal. Mikoyan expressed the opinion that Cuban leaders would not accept such a risk for their country, and pointed out that he did not think the missile operation could be carried out in secret. Khrushchev proposed that Marshal Biryuzov go to Cuba immediately to convey the proposal directly. If the Cubans accepted, Biryuzov—together with two or three specialists—was to study on the spot the possibility of building launch pads without being discovered by U.S. surveillance.[17]

A trip to Cuba had been scheduled around that time for a delegation of civilian technicians, headed by Rashidov, who were going to offer their cooperation in solving water supply problems the country was suffering due to a severe drought. This provided an ideal cover to disguise the trip to Cuba by the chief of strategic missile forces and by the high-ranking military leaders who accompanied him.

To defend the socialist camp

After the Soviet delegation's welcome at José Martí Airport, some of the technicians were taken to the official guest house of the foreign ministry. Alekseev expressed an interest in speaking immediately with Commander Raúl Castro, with whom he had good personal and working relations.

The meeting took place that afternoon. Alekseev informed the minister of the Revolutionary Armed Forces that Marshal Biryuzov and some Soviet generals were traveling incognito among the group of technicians, instructed by Khrushchev to make an important proposal to the Cuban prime minister.[18]

That evening, Fidel met with Biryuzov. Also present were Raúl and, for the Soviets, Rashidov and Alekseev, the latter serving as interpreter. At the beginning of the interview Marshal Biryuzov spoke about the international situation and about Cuba.

Yepishev from the Ministry of Defense; and Col. General Semyon P. Ivanov, head of the Main Operational Directorate of the Central General Staff and Secretary of the Defense Council.

At a certain point he asked Fidel, "What would be necessary to prevent a U.S. invasion?" The Cuban leader answered immediately, "The adoption of measures that tell imperialism unequivocally that any aggression against Cuba would mean a war not only with Cuba."[19]

The Cuban prime minister's reply was consistent with Cuba's position that the socialist camp must be willing to go to war for the sake of any socialist country.

"But, concretely, how?" Biryuzov asked, and immediately stated, "We have to take actions that show this." The marshal wanted to guarantee the success of his mission, and perhaps feared for a second that the Cubans were not going to accept the proposal. He considered his words, and then proceeded to explain Khrushchev's idea to install nuclear missiles.

According to Fidel's recollection, he immediately saw in the proposal something that could consolidate or contribute to the defensive power of the entire socialist camp. From that standpoint he was inclined to accept the proposal, even though he was convinced that missiles were not essential to defend Cuba. The same objective could be accomplished, without the missiles, by a military pact making clear that armed aggression against Cuba would be equivalent to an attack on the USSR. "The United States," he pointed out, "has many of these pacts throughout the world, and they are respected."[20]

Fidel then asked what kind of missiles these were, and how the Soviets thought the operation would be carried out. Biryuzov reviewed the principal characteristics of the missiles, their range, and the explosive force of their nuclear warheads. He explained that deployment would be done quickly, in secret, and under cover. The Cuban prime minister asked for time to discuss the matter in the Secretariat of the National Directorate of the Integrated Revolutionary Organizations (Organizaciones Revolucionarias Integradas—ORI)* before giving a definite an-

---

* At the time, the Secretariat of the ORI was made up of Fidel Castro Ruz (first secretary), Raúl Castro Ruz (deputy secretary), and members Ernesto Guevara

swer. In those days the Cuban leadership had a high degree of confidence in the Soviet Union and its expertise in international and military matters—perhaps "excessive," as Fidel himself later recognized.[21]

The next day the Secretariat met to analyze the Soviet proposal. In presenting the issue to the country's top leadership, Fidel argued that in his judgment, installation of missiles would strengthen the socialist camp. If the party took the stand that the socialist camp should be willing to go to war for the sake of any socialist country, then it should not give the slightest consideration to any dangers for Cuba that this decision might entail. Those present agreed that the proposal would also contribute to Cuba's defense, as a powerful deterrent that the U.S. rulers would have to weigh before undertaking any military action.[22]

It was not lost on the ORI Secretariat that such a decision could have negative political repercussions for the Cuban Revolution in Latin America. Fidel Castro has commented: "We didn't really like the missiles. If it had been a matter only of our own defense, we would not have accepted the deployment of the missiles. But not because we were afraid of the dangers that might follow the deployment of the missiles here; rather, it was because this would damage the image of the revolution, and we were very zealous in protecting the image of the revolution in the rest of Latin America. The presence of the missiles would in fact turn us into a Soviet military base, and that entailed a high political cost for the image of our country, an image we so highly valued."[23]

All members of the ORI Secretariat, however, "without any hesitation, and thinking honestly with a truly internationalist sentiment,"[24] agreed to say yes to the Soviet proposal. The decision was communicated to Biryuzov that same day. "Look, if it serves the interests of the socialist camp," Fidel told him, "we

de la Serna, Osvaldo Dorticós Torrado, Emilio Aragonés Navarro, and Blas Roca Calderío.

here are willing to have a thousand missiles installed."[25] While accepting the Soviet proposal, the Cuban leadership expressed the need to work out a military accord and to announce it publicly at the right moment.

The next day Commander Raúl Castro, along with Marshal Biryuzov and the generals accompanying him, explored places where different Soviet units could be deployed. On that tour, the minister of the FAR got to know in detail the characteristics of the military equipment and the number of personnel to be sent to Cuba. He doubted, as he has since stated, that the Soviets could transport the twenty-meter-long missiles to Cuba without being discovered by the enemy's intelligence services. He reported those concerns to Fidel, but there was confidence in Soviet expertise in such matters.[26]

'I'll send you the Baltic fleet'

The Presidium of the Central Committee of the CPSU made the final decision at the Kremlin on June 10. Work began right away at the Soviet defense ministry on plans to transfer and deploy the military detachment that was to be sent to Cuba. The defense ministry was also asked to prepare a draft of the military assistance pact requested by Cuba.

Commander Raúl Castro, Cuba's minister of the Revolutionary Armed Forces, visited Moscow July 2–16 to discuss the operation and the military accord in detail with Khrushchev and Marshals Malinovsky and Biryuzov. Raúl had instructions from Fidel "to ask Khrushchev a single question: What would happen if the operation were discovered while in progress?" Because Fidel appreciated that "it was not easy to keep the secret, since such a large movement of troops and matériel was difficult to camouflage."[27] All military operations have a critical period. The period between the actual agreement and the final deployment of the weapons was the most dangerous.

Moreover, the Cuban leadership wanted from the outset to make the military accord public, since it did not violate international law or practice. They believed, however, that the final decision was up to the Soviets, who had more expertise in international and military matters and a better understanding of the relationship of forces between the USSR and the United States.

During Raúl's visit, Khrushchev invited him to his country house on the outskirts of Moscow, where they met secretly to discuss the deployment of the missiles. After explaining Cuba's position in accepting the proposal to install the missiles, Raúl asked Khrushchev, "What precautions have you taken in case the operation is discovered by the U.S. before it is made public?" With an attitude intended to show his firmness, Khrushchev replied, "Don't worry, I'll grab Kennedy by the balls and make him negotiate. After all, they have surrounded us with their bases, in Turkey, and other places."

Off the cuff, without pausing to think, he said, "If that problem should arise, I'll send you a warning, an agreed-on phrase in code, and that will mean you should invite the Baltic fleet to visit Cuba, just in case the Americans find out in advance."[28] Khrushchev's response, while showing decisiveness and self-assurance, also revealed that at that point he had made no provisions for such a serious eventuality.

Before concluding his visit, Raúl Castro and his Soviet counterpart, Rodion Malinovsky, both initialed the draft military accord. It was then to be reviewed by both parties, preparatory to signing it and making it public during Khrushchev's visit to Cuba in November. On the basis of the initialed agreement, between August and October the USSR transferred to Cuba most of the agreed-on strategic weapons and the troops and matériel needed to protect them.

On his return to Cuba, Commander Raúl Castro reported to the Cuban central leadership the outcome of his discussions with Khrushchev, as well as Khrushchev's proposed response in case the operation was discovered. Some years later, Fidel Castro talked about how that response was interpreted: "We did not think that it was the Baltic fleet that would solve the problem. What we were thinking about was Soviet will and determination, about Soviet strength. And we got the statement of the top leader of the Soviet Union that there was nothing to worry about. . . . So what was really protecting us was the global strategic might of the USSR."[29]

Preparations for the operation

Once the proposal was approved, the personnel in charge of the operation began making preparations and securing the supplies needed to move and deploy the missile division and other forces that would make up the units assigned to Cuba.

Army Gen. Anatoly I. Gribkov, who was responsible for planning the operation, explained that in giving him the order to work on the project, his superiors said that his mission was to form a powerful military detachment, move it to Cuba, and in a brief period make it completely combat-ready. All this had to be done covertly, quickly, and in total secrecy.[30] General Gribkov pointed out the huge challenge this meant for the Soviet armed forces:

"The task was for us unprecedented: assemble and outfit nearly 51,000 soldiers, airmen and sailors; calculate the weapons, equipment, supplies and support such a contingent would need for a prolonged stay; find 85 freight ships to transport men and gear; put them to sea and ensure them the right reception and working conditions on their arrival in Cuba. Meanwhile, conceal the entire operation and complete it within five months."[31]

After a careful analysis of what the operation required, various plans were devised for selecting and moving the troops, as well as for concealing them and misleading the enemy.

According to their calculations, more than eighty merchant ships of different kinds were required. At that moment those ships were either docked or sailing all over the world. They had to be brought back and made technically ready, and their crews had to be chosen. It took a huge effort on the part of the merchant fleet to accomplish that goal.

One of the first camouflage measures was the story told by

the high command to the military units selected for the mission. They were told to prepare for a secret operation that involved a strategic troop deployment exercise in the north of the USSR. The area where the training was supposed to take place is called Anadyr.* That is how Operation Anadyr came to be the name for the Soviet military mission in Cuba in 1962.

The units chosen for Operation Anadyr had to be extremely well prepared and combat-ready. It was estimated that the Soviet Troop Force (STF) would have as many as 51,000 men. When the crisis broke out, close to 42,000 had already been sent to Cuba.

Along with the process of troop selection, efforts were also made to organize a command structure capable of leading such a diverse military grouping. According to Gribkov, an army command structure was taken as the model. The chief of the STF had to have the highest possible degree of military expertise.

Army Gen. Issa Alexandrovich Pliyev was chosen from among several candidates. General Pliyev was a two-time Hero of the Soviet Union and a Hero of the Republic of Mongolia. He had seen active duty in World War II, distinguishing himself as head of a mechanized troop force and leading raids deep into the enemy's rear guard.

The best-qualified personnel were appointed to the military council of the STF as Pliyev's aides in charge of the different weapons and troops. Col. Gen. Pavel B. Dankevich, who had been a strong candidate for commander of the STF because of his expertise in missile unit command, was assigned as deputy commander to the STF chief. Gen. Pavel M. Petrenko was named deputy commander for political work, and Maj. Gen. Pavel V. Akindinov was named chief of staff.

The other STF deputy commander positions went to Maj. Gen. Leonid S. Garbuz for combat preparation; Maj. Gen. Aleksei A. Dementyev, land troops; Maj. Gen. Stepan M. Grechko,

---

* "'Anadyr': That is the name of a river in the northern region of our country, in a very cold region." General Gribkov, in Blight et al., *Cuba on the Brink*, p. 58.

antiaircraft defense; Col. Gen. Victor Y. Davidkov, air force; Vice Adm. Georgio S. Abashvili, naval force; Maj. Gen. Victor P. Seleznyov, missiles; and Maj. Gen. Nikolai R. Pelipenko, rear guard. Together they made up the military council, chaired by the commander of the Soviet Troop Force. Major Generals Anatoly I. Gribkov and Aleksei S. Butski were appointed as representatives of the Soviet defense minister.

As for the authority the command would have, General Gribkov later pointed to the orders he was given by Malinovsky to convey to General Pliyev, on behalf of Khrushchev and the defense minister: "'The missile forces will fire only if authorized by Nikita Sergeivich Khrushchev'—it was repeated—'only if instructed by the Supreme Commander-in-Chief himself.' Comrade Pliyev was to remember that the missile division had been sent to Cuba to deter aggression. The tactical nuclear forces . . . could be employed with nuclear weapons during a direct invasion by the aggressor. It was said that before arriving at a decision on employing the tactical missiles, the situation had to be very thoroughly and carefully assessed and, in case of extreme need only, then the decision could be made. That was my mission when I was sent to Cuba."[32] Despite the importance of this order, it was never conveyed to the Cuban high command, who learned of it only years later.

The operational group of the Soviet Troop Force

The Soviet military high command decided to send an advance team from the STF leadership to Cuba in early July 1962 to lay the groundwork for receiving and deploying the units that would arrive in early August.

General Pliyev was urgently called to the defense ministry on July 4, while heading up a commanders' and general staff exercise on the outskirts of Rostov. Surprised by this unexpected summons, he left for Moscow right away.

The following morning he was informed by the defense minister of his assignment as chief of the troop detachment that would be sent to Cuba. He was to head up a group of military personnel that would leave for Cuba immediately. That afternoon, Pliyev was introduced to Khrushchev, who personally described to him the objectives and mission of the Soviet troops and his role as commander.[33]

Two days later, on July 7, Khrushchev and Marshal Malinovsky met in the Kremlin with the six generals[*] who made up the operational command group of the STF. One of the participants, retired Maj. Gen. Leonid S. Garbuz, later wrote an account of the meeting. According to Garbuz, there are no minutes or tape recordings of the event. The Soviet head of state opened the meeting by stating, "In the Central Committee we have decided to sow a field of thorns for the United States: to supply Cuba with missiles and to protect Cuba. The missiles are the main thing. We have Cuba's consent."

That statement could lead to the conclusion that the purpose of the operation was to do everything possible, in one single blow, to improve the relationship of strategic forces with the United States. Garbuz, however, does not believe this was the Soviet leader's goal. Khrushchev stated more than once, "The objective of the missile installation is to protect the Cuban Revolution from an attack by the United States." Lest there be any doubt, at one point during the meeting Khrushchev made the remark he was fond of, that somewhere in the south the USSR "was producing missiles like sausages."[†]

[*] The generals who participated in that meeting were P.B. Dankevich, P.V. Akindinov, S.N. Grechko, L.S. Garbuz, A. Dementyev, and N.R. Pelipenko.

[†] Concerning this, Sergei Khrushchev—the Soviet premier's son—explained that "as of the beginning of the Cold War, the Soviet Union lived under the threat of a U.S. nuclear strike, and the Soviet Union was always looking for a chance to respond to this strike. And this led to the development of missiles in our country, although, in view of the events of the October crisis, we overestimated our potential.

"The United States learned that we did not have as many missiles as they thought. At one point, Khrushchev said that we built missiles like sausages. I said then, 'How can you say that, since we only have two or three?' He said, 'The important thing is to make the Americans believe that. And that way we prevent an attack.'. . . We threatened with missiles we didn't have. This happened in the case of the Suez crisis." (Blight et al., *Cuba on the Brink*, p. 130.)

Khrushchev also underlined the military requirements and conditions for a successful mission. He stressed that the entire force had to be deployed in total secrecy, especially the missile division. He also emphasized the need to obtain a high degree of combat readiness as soon as possible.

At one point, Khrushchev directly asked Maj. Gen. Aleksei A. Dementyev, head of Soviet military specialists in Cuba at the time, "Is it possible to deploy the troops in secrecy in a short time?" Dementyev replied, "No, Nikita Sergeievich, that is impossible."

Surprised by this unexpected reply, Khrushchev asked the general, "Why?" Dementyev argued his position so convincingly that a significant change was then made to the operational plan for deploying the force. It was decided that the missile division would be moved only after the general assignment units.[34]

The decision turned out to be justified in the long run, according to General Garbuz. The United States became used to the idea that a reinforcement of the Cuban armed forces with conventional weapons was taking place, thus diminishing the effectiveness of U.S. surveillance. This allowed the camouflage of the first missiles arriving in Cuba for a whole month.

One of Khrushchev's concerns in laying out the mission, however, was to safeguard peace and avoid the unleashing of nuclear war. He stated that "the Soviet government has the means and capability to prevent in a timely fashion any unfavorable turn of events that could lead to the outbreak of war."[35]

According to Garbuz, the assignment of General Pliyev as commander came as a surprise to everyone at the meeting. They all expected Colonel General Dankevich to be chosen, because of his experience in command of missile units.

General Pliyev was introduced to his future deputies and members of the operational group at the defense ministry two days later. They were informed that as part of the camouflage plans, all the principal leaders of the force would have pseudonyms. Pliyev would now be called Ivan Alexandrovich Pavlov.

At this meeting they were also given details about their trip to Cuba. The flight was to stop for one day in the Republic of Guinea, and Soviet Civil Aviation Minister Evgenii Loginov would be on the plane. Loginov was to attend the inauguration of the new airport in Conakry, built with the help of Soviet specialists. In Cuba, Loginov was to sign an air travel agreement for flights between Moscow and Havana with a stopover in Guinea. The flight was to be made in a TU-114, at that time the biggest commercial aircraft in the world, which was making its first flight to Cuba.

The Soviet military leaders would therefore fly to Guinea under the guise of Aeroflot specialists and later as agricultural technicians. They were to depart in the dawn hours of July 10 from the Vnukovo airport.

The operational group arrived in Havana two days later, on July 12. Prime Minister Fidel Castro met with them the following morning to extend his welcome and offer whatever help they needed to accomplish their mission.[36]

Reconnaissance work for the location and deployment of the Soviet units began immediately. Cuban officials participated as guides and helped to resolve any problems encountered.[37] With help from a group of Cuban speleologists, caves were chosen that met the requirements for storing arms and ammunition and protecting troops.

Peasant families living in some of the places selected had to be moved and given new land and housing. Although this was inconvenient for the families involved, they were cooperative, due to the careful political work done by the ORI, together with the National Institute of Agrarian Reform (INRA) and the National Association of Small Farmers (ANAP).

Transferring the Soviet troops

The troops and military matériel were shipped from seven seaports located on the Barents, Baltic, North, Black, and White Seas. The Soviet civil fleet carried out 185 crossings moving the military force. According to Khrushchev, the USSR had to contract with outside companies, at a cost of 16 million rubles,* to provide freighters to carry out Soviet foreign trade during that period.[38]

To maintain the secrecy of Operation Anadyr and to prevent intelligence leaks, the troops that were chosen did not know their destination. The units were put into full combat readiness, assigned to move with all their matériel and weapons, including winter equipment—skis, snow sweepers, etc.—to areas close to the naval ports, where engineering forces camouflaged all military equipment as commercial export merchandise, agricultural implements in particular.

The troops arrived at the merchant ships at night in small groups. During the ships' voyage, the troops were forbidden to be on deck. According to the testimony of three officers of the missile units—retired Cols. Victor Semykin, Ivan Shishenko, and Aleksandr Kovalenko—the conditions on board the ships were very difficult.

"The men could not go on deck during the day," Semykin said, "only at night and in small groups to get fresh air. And the voyage lasted many days."[39]

"Throughout the trip, the men had to be kept hidden," Shishenko said. "The heat was intolerable. It was humid and we were exhausted and covered in sweat."[40]

Colonel Kovalenko explained: "To make the troops look as much as possible like the crew of the ship, twenty-five to thirty men were kept on deck. They were rotated regularly, as there were 1,200 men on board. All of them were traveling in the hold of the ship and, due to the heat there, it was necessary to use hoses to spray them down with water. The troops were instructed that if anyone were to fall overboard and then be rescued by ships of other countries, we were to say that we were working for Autoexport and were taking automobiles to Ghana."[41]

At a preestablished point along the route, the military chief

---

* At the official exchange rate, 1 ruble was equal to $1.11.

of each voyage had orders to open a sealed envelope, containing the orders for traveling to Cuba and the security measures to be adopted. When they arrived near the island, the troops were to be given civilian clothes. Kovalenko recounted: "We weighed anchor with the order to go to Gibraltar and there to open a box containing the relevant instructions, which told us to set course for the Azores. When we got near these islands we were to open an envelope with a certain name. There we read, 'Go to Mariel seaport, Cuba.'"[42]

The captains of the ships and the military chiefs of the crossing had explicit orders not to allow the cargo to be inspected for any reason and, in the worst case, to blow up the ships to prevent detection.

"We received the order to prevent and repulse any pirate attack or attempt to board," Kovalenko said. "For this purpose, we had a battery of 37-mm. guns and twelve heavy machine guns, hidden in boxes marked as automobiles, in addition to the individual weapons of the troops. From that moment, we began the training necessary to carry out the mission."[43]

From the very beginning, the unusual increase of Soviet ships heading for Cuba attracted the attention of British and West German intelligence, which stepped up surveillance, provoking several incidents. The intelligence agencies of both countries maintained close links with the United States.

Aleksei F. Maslov and Victor Potelin, then sergeants who belonged to the antiaircraft missile troops, recounted their experiences during the voyage. "Several things happened during our trip on the ship *Bavier*," Maslov commented. "West German intelligence, for instance, was interested in the cargo that we were carrying while sailing through the Dardanelles Strait. Also, British intelligence tried to inspect our ship's cargo when we passed Gibraltar, but the energetic response of our crew stopped them."[44]

Potelin commented on the aerial reconnaissance that the Soviet ships were subjected to. "The Americans acted as if they were the masters of the Mediterranean," he said. "They were very arrogant, flying between the masts of the ships, grazing them over and over again. The situation made us very tense."[45]

"In the Atlantic Ocean, five days out from Cuba," Maslov said, "there were more and more U.S. warships and reconnaissance aircraft, carrying out dangerous and provocative maneuvers against our ship. We knew that a U.S. plane crashed into the sea while carrying out a maneuver over the ship *Leninski Komsomol* near the Bermuda Islands."[46]

Colonels Kovalenko and Semykin also commented on this. "From the time we reached the Azores, enemy aerial reconnaissance was constant, and we observed many submarine periscopes," Kovalenko said, "although I cannot be certain whether they were Soviet or U.S."[47]

"When U.S. planes were flying over the ships, as they did several times," Semykin pointed out, "people who had guitars or cameras would go out and act as if they were a group of tourists on their way to Cuba."[48]

Soviet units started to arrive in early August through the seaports of Santiago de Cuba, Nuevitas, Casilda, Havana, Bahía Honda, Cabañas, and Mariel. The troops landed, regrouped, and left at night in caravans of thirty to forty vehicles. To make sure that they could travel, Soviet and Cuban engineering units had to repair roads or build new ones, and prepare fords in order to detour around bridges unable to withstand such heavy loads.[49]

The Cuban command selected dockworkers to help these units unload and assigned troop detachments to protect the seaports and escort caravans. Officers were also designated to serve as guides and to coordinate the necessary tasks.[50]

Once the Soviet units arrived at the areas where they were to be permanently stationed, living arrangements for the troops were made, such as constructing rural barracks. Military instruction also had to be undertaken, so they could attain a high degree of combat readiness.

Retired Lieutenant General Beloborodov, who was head of the special unit in charge of the nuclear warheads, and retired Colonel Shishenko, chief of the unit where they were stored, recalled the shipment of the warheads.

"This sensitive cargo," Shishenko said, "was all brought to Cuba on board two ships, the icebreaker *Indigirka*, which arrived on October 4, and the *Aleksandrovsk*, on October 23. The former moved the bulk of the warheads, while the latter transported supplemental munitions, which were not unloaded. Both ships weighed anchor from Murmansk and arrived in Cuba at the port of Mariel."

Beloborodov explained: "One of the big problems that had to be resolved in connection with the nuclear warheads was the climate in Cuba. The warheads required humidity below 50 percent and a temperature not higher than 20 degrees [Celsius], so air-conditioned vehicles had to be built for their transportation and maintenance."[51]

Warheads were kept in a depot in Bejucal, Havana province, where a special unit guarded them until the missile regiments could prepare the conditions for their staging and authorize their positioning. On October 26 all the warheads were moved to missile regiments near the launch sites.[52]

General assignment troops

These units—including infantry, antiaircraft, naval, and air forces—were the first ones to be transferred to and stationed in Cuba. Like the missile units, they were directly under the orders of the commander of the Soviet Troop Force. Once deployed in the different regions, they set up communications with their high command and, together with the Cuban military, drew up plans for cooperating with the FAR units in the event of enemy aggression.

Infantry, consisting primarily of four motorized regiments, were deployed in areas of Holguín, Remedios, Managua, and Artemisa. With the exception of the Holguín regiment, they each received a battery of short-range (twenty to twenty-five miles) surface-to-surface Luna missiles.

This missile system was mobile, installed on PT-76 armored transports. Each of the batteries had four launchers with twelve missiles. According to Soviet veterans who were involved in Operation Anadyr, the three batteries each had twenty-four missiles equipped with conventional warheads and twelve missiles with two-kiloton nuclear warheads.*[53]

Every motorized regiment was made up of some 3,000 troops with three infantry battalions in BTR-60 armored transports and one T-55 tank battalion. They also had batteries of 120-mm. mortar, antitank guns, and antiaircraft artillery.

This gave the regiments great firepower and the ability to carry out rapid maneuvers. The mission assigned to these units was to protect the missile troops deployed in their territory against airborne landings by the enemy and to cooperate with the FAR in the defense of Cuba. Two T-55 tank battalions stationed in the western region were part of the reserve forces of the STF command. The communications units, as well as the engineering troops, made great efforts to ensure the lines of command and administration of all Soviet units deployed over the length and breadth of the country, as well as keeping the Soviet command in Cuba in direct contact with the defense ministry of the USSR.

The antiaircraft defense forces consisted of two SA-75 surface-to-air missile divisions. One division provided cover for the eastern region, the other for the west. Each division was made up of three regiments, each with one technical and four combat groups. Each missile group had six launchers for a total of twenty-four groups and 144 launchers in the country. This ensured an effective antiaircraft defensive cover, because their missiles had the power to shoot down targets under any weather conditions, day or night, at an altitude of one to twenty-seven kilometers, with a maximum range of thirty-five kilometers. However, they were not effective against aircraft flying low, for example, under 1,000 meters. A battery of 100-mm. antiaircraft guns was also under the command of the STF leadership.

---

* One kiloton is equivalent approximately to the explosive force of 1,000 tons of TNT.

Two radar battalions were also deployed, increasing the capacity for fast and timely detection of the enemy. These were able to cover Cuba's air space from altitudes below 150 meters up to stratospheric levels.

The air force included a regiment, stationed in Santa Clara, of MIG-21 (F-13) fighters, with forty of these planes; six MIG-15s (UTI); and one MIG-17 (AS). The supersonic MIG-21 fighters were excellent aircraft for air, land, and sea combat. They could also intercept U.S. F-101, F-105, A-4, and F-4 planes, used at the time for aerial photographic reconnaissance. They also had an independent squadron of six IL-28 bombers carrying six-kiloton nuclear bombs.[54] The Soviet command also had a regiment of MI-4 helicopters, stationed in Baracoa, Havana province, and a squadron of transport planes.

The air force had two FKR cruise missile regiments: one deployed in Nicaro, Upper Mayarí (formerly Oriente province), and the other in Quiebra Hacha, Pinar del Río. These missiles could hit the enemy up to a range of ninety miles. According to statements from Soviet officers, the Soviet command sent eighty tactical nuclear warheads for these missiles with payloads of 5.6 and 12 kilotons.[55]

The naval forces were originally supposed to include one squadron of surface ships—consisting of two cruisers and four destroyers, two with missiles and two with artillery—and one squadron of eleven submarines—seven diesel- and four nuclear-powered. Those units, however, were not sent.

The actual naval forces included a brigade of Komar-class missile boats (design 183R), each carrying two R-15 missiles with a twenty-five-mile range. This unit was made up of three squadrons of four boats each; two of them were stationed in the naval air base at Mariel and the other one at Banes. At the right distance, these ships could inflict massive missile strikes against enemy naval detachments in remote approaches off the Cuban coasts, either during the crossing or at probable landing sites.

A surface-to-sea Sopka missile regiment, consisting of four groups each with two launch sites, was stationed on the Isle of

Pines (now the Isle of Youth), Santa Cruz del Norte, Cienfuegos, and Banes. Thirty-four missiles of this kind, with a range of thirty to fifty miles, arrived in Cuba and were set up. They were expected to be used against invading enemy ships, either independently or in cooperation with the missile boats, reaching distances beyond what the latter could with their guns.

This force also included an IL-28 tactical bomber regiment in San Julián, Pinar del Río, with thirty-six aircraft, only six of which were assembled. These planes made their test flights to the air base in Holguín. They were intended mainly for mining sea access and torpedoing enemy naval concentrations.

According to statements by Soviet officials, seven attack submarines would protect sea transport of forces and matériel to Cuba. According to these same sources, each sub was armed with three R-13 missiles, with a 340-mile range, and four torpedoes. Construction was started on a new station for recharging submarine batteries at the Mariel naval base, in preparation for the submarine squadron foreseen as part of the Soviet Troop Force.

Such submarines were to function independently, with their combat capabilities determined by their nuclear-armed missiles. According to witnesses, the missiles' warheads were 1.5 megatons, and the torpedoes between eight and ten kilotons. This would permit them to defend naval communications by attacking groups of surface ships and annihilating enemy submarines, as well as inflicting nuclear strikes at an operational depth into enemy territory.[56]

The force also had several independent units for combat supply; among them, one communications regiment; six independent battalions—two of them tank, one sapper, one reconnaissance, one radio, and one microwave; an independent 100-mm. antiaircraft artillery battery; and other units for technical and material support.

Strategic forces

The large missile unit chosen for Operation Anadyr was the 43rd Division of the Smolensk Guard, which had been decorated with the "Suvorov" and "Kutuzov" orders. This unit belonged to the Strategic Missile Forces of the Soviet Union.* In Cuba it came to be known as the "Statsenko Division," since it was commanded by Maj. Gen. Igor D. Statsenko. Its regiments were headed by Lt. Cols. Y.A. Solovev, A.Z. Bandilovsky, I.S. Sidorov, I.I. Cherkesov, and A.A. Kovalenko.†

The division took up positions in several locations across Cuba. One of the two regiments with R-14 intermediate-range ballistic missiles was stationed in the El Esperón hills—between Caimito and Guanajay in Havana province—and the other at a place called Bartolomé, in Remedios, Las Villas province (now Villa Clara). The three R-12 medium-range ballistic missile regiments were located in the San Cristóbal hills, Santa Cruz de los Pinos, and Candelaria, in Pinar del Río; and at Cifuentes and Encrucijada, in Las Villas.

The regiments of this division consisted of two combat groups each. Each group had four launchers, with one-and-a-half missiles per launcher. So there were to be in Cuba twenty-four launchers for R-12 missiles, sixteen for R-14s, and a total of sixty missiles. Each R-12 group had an instructional missile for personnel training, so there were six of those missiles. Since the R-14 missiles had a range of 2,800 miles, and the R-12s a range of 1,400 miles, these missile systems made it possible to effectively strike targets throughout the strategic depth of the continental United States.

The R-14 missiles did not make it to Cuba. The Soviet freighters transporting them were just passing the Azores on October 24, when the United States imposed a naval blockade. On October 25 the Soviet government ordered the ships to return to their ports of departure, even though many of the missile crews

---

* This unit was on a combat footing from January 1, 1962. All of its crews were well trained and had experience in firing training missiles, including one combat missile with a nuclear payload.

† Lieutenant Colonel Bandilovsky headed the R-12 regiment until October 20. Lieutenant Colonel Kovalenko was in command of an R-14 regiment until October 20, when he replaced Bandilovsky.

were already in Cuba doing engineering work to prepare for installation of the R-14s. This reduced the striking power of the missile division, in both range and nuclear payload, but its power was still significant.

The engineering support units of the missile division were the first to arrive, and they quickly started work preparing positions in the areas assigned to each group. The R-14s required more construction work.

The R-12 missiles reached Cuba in late September through three ports: Bahía Honda, Mariel, and Casilda. Liquid fuel was unloaded at Bahía Honda in the western region, while other equipment and components were unloaded at Mariel. The delivery systems were transferred at night, staying clear of cities and towns as much as possible, to the regions where they were to be deployed. However, it was impossible to avoid some urban areas, where obstacles such as electricity and telephone poles had to be removed so the cargo could pass through. The caravans were organized in vehicle columns that transported five or six missiles each, along with an escort detachment.[57]

When the missiles reached the assigned regions, engineering troops and missile group personnel stepped up their work to prepare the launchers and lay the groundwork for technical support. Major General Garbuz recalled the troops' efforts to get their units ready for combat: "Soviet forces worked twenty-hour days, working right through the night and stopping only at midday for the sake of concealment. As a result, the installations were ready in less time."[58]

Each installation required a great deal of work. It was necessary to prepare four launchers, build a silo twenty to twenty-five meters long and eleven meters wide with a system of three-part reinforced concrete arches, prepare floors for six tents to store the missiles, build barracks for the troops, and set up headquarters for the group and regimental commanders. The equipment was stored all together at first, until the launching positions were finished, when it could be dispersed.[59]

A regiment had two missile groups, each of which was spread

over an area of 1.5 to 3 square kilometers with specific topography: wooded flatland next to mountains. The launchers were placed in a zigzag pattern, about 200 meters apart. The network of roads built on each site was separated from the main road by what was apparently a buffer zone of 800 to 1,000 meters, in which no engineering works were undertaken.

The site of each missile group was ringed by barbed wire with sentry posts. Soviet troops took charge of protection and security. They built surveillance posts, as well as checkpoints at the entrances. The perimeter fences were far enough away from the launching positions so that infantry weapons fire could not damage the missiles.[60] The outer perimeter of each installation was guarded by Cuban troops.

It was scheduled to take two hours and thirty minutes to get an R-12 missile system ready for combat. According to Major General Garbuz, that time was broken down as follows: two hours and ten minutes for mounting the nuclear warhead onto the missile and raising it up on its launcher, then sixteen to thirty minutes for loading fuel and oxidizer, checking the various systems, and entering data for firing.[61]

The three regiments that arrived in Cuba with missiles of this kind were made operational.[62] The first R-12 launcher was ready on October 4, 1962, and four others on October 10. Ten days later, twenty launchers were ready, and by October 25, all launchers in the three R-12 regiments were operational. So when President Kennedy announced measures against Cuba on October 22, construction had already been completed on the launch sites of two regiments, and those of the third regiment were within three days of completion. At no time, however, were nuclear warheads mounted on the missiles, nor were they ever loaded with fuel and oxidizer, since that was to be done only when they were about to be launched.[63]

According to data provided by Major General Garbuz, the total nuclear capability of the division was to be 75.6 megatons: twenty warheads of 1.65 megatons each for the R-14 missiles, and thirty-six warheads of 1 megaton each for the R-12 missiles. Since the R-14 missiles never reached Cuba, that figure was reduced by a little more than 52 percent. The actual capability totaled 36 megatons.[64]

Errors in concealment

Although the maritime transport of troops and matériel and their deployment in Cuba in just seventy-six days could be considered perfect from a logistical standpoint, mistakes were made that allowed the missiles to be detected by U.S. surveillance sooner than anticipated.

According to Major General Garbuz, the missile regiments carried out the general plan for concealment; nevertheless, they failed to avoid detection. One factor may have been the pressure to complete engineering work on the launch sites, which required the crews to work long hours, neglecting to apply the camouflage measures most suitable in Cuba. The installations being built were identical to others with the same purpose that the United States had photographed from the air over Soviet territory.

Reflecting on this issue, General Gribkov pointed out: "We foresaw, naturally, the possibility that U.S. intelligence might discover us. As it turned out, on October 14 they photographed areas that we had not been able to camouflage . . . there were white slabs of concrete. Naturally, they could be seen quite well from the air and were very difficult to disguise. . . . Some of our comrades . . . thought that the missiles could be placed in such a way that they could not be distinguished from palm trees, but that was a stupid conclusion, because all the missile sites had to be prepared, cables hung, launching pads built—in other words, everything was complicated. Naturally, their intelligence discovered us, for all those reasons. That's what intelligence is for. But the fact is, they discovered us late."[65]

Nevertheless, Cuban leaders believe there might have been a chance to camouflage things adequately, had they been consulted about it. "If we had known what those missiles were like," Fidel Castro has stated, "and if the question of camouflage had been posed to us, it would have been easy to decide what to do." He went on to say, "In a country where there are so many construction projects, so many big chicken barns and all sorts of things, it would have been the easiest thing in the world to build all those installations under roofs or something else, and they never would have been discovered."[66]

Nor were measures taken to prevent U.S. aircraft from exploring the island with impunity. Again and again Cuban authorities denounced before world opinion the increasingly frequent violations of Cuba's air space. At the time, however, the Cuban armed forces did not have antiaircraft weapons capable of deterring or shooting down the enemy's modern planes, which flew at high altitude over the country's territory. These facts were known to the Soviet government and high command.

In the midst of a military operation such as Anadyr, which the Soviets wanted to keep secret at all costs, stopping these flights was a strategic necessity. Why then didn't the Soviet military prevent U-2 aircraft from flying overhead and photographing its installations? Fidel Castro has stated that those illegal flights could have been prevented. "The question arises: What were the surface-to-air missiles there for? What were they doing there? Why put in surface-to-air missiles, and allow U-2s to fly over? To permit this was, I believe, unquestionably a political mistake. I don't blame the military men for that. . . . Undoubtedly, they had strict orders. . . . I am sure that they had orders not to fire on the U-2s. . . . But it is incredible to me that . . . those planes were allowed to fly over. . . . What were those surface-to-air missiles doing there?"[67]

On the basis of these considerations, Fidel Castro concluded that there were, "from that standpoint, mistaken political conceptions, excessive caution. On the one hand there was . . . great audacity on Khrushchev's part, which I don't deny. . . . But unquestionably, along with the great audacity involved in sending troops, there were vacillations. . . . For I could also ask, what would have happened if the U-2s had not gotten through? What would have happened if the U-2s had been brought down and had not taken photographs? If we had had those missiles and had been in that operation, you can be sure that u-2s would not have gotten through, that's for sure. To do otherwise would be inconceivable."[68]

Despite these mistakes, which facilitated discovery of the missiles, the full extent of the Soviet Troop Force in Cuba was not detected by U.S. or other Western intelligence. This is confirmed by statements made September 11, 1963, to a subcommittee of the U.S. Senate Armed Services Committee that was investigating the record of its intelligence services in relation to Cuba's military buildup. These statements seriously underestimated the number of Soviet troops during the days of the crisis. On October 22, 1962, U.S. intelligence officials calculated that 8,000 to 10,000 Soviet personnel were on the island.

The reality on that date was quite different: some 42,000 Soviet soldiers had already arrived with their weapons and combat equipment. Even after examining Cuban territory from every angle, the U.S. did not obtain accurate evidence of the deployment of medium-range missiles until mid-October, when a good number of them were already operational.

Likewise, Washington did not know the status of the nuclear warheads. U.S. officials never did manage to find out how they arrived in the country, where they were located, or how many there were. In fact, one of the main military objectives of the U.S. naval blockade was supposedly to prevent the entry of nuclear warheads into Cuba.

What was the nuclear capability of Soviet troops in Cuba?

An assessment of the strategic nuclear capability of the Soviet Troop Force in Cuba indicates that in October 1962 there were thirty-six nuclear-armed r-12 missiles, and seven submarines with twenty-one r-13 missiles, able to launch a total payload of 67.5 megatons to strategic depths inside the United States.

The STF also had tactical nuclear warheads for Luna and FKR missile systems. In terms of conventional forces as well, these military units had excellent weapons with great firepower, and modern combat techniques. Even without counting the strategic troops, they increased the number of active-duty military personnel in Cuba by a third, with a high degree of combat preparation and military expertise.[*]

These facts show the danger that humanity faced during the days of greatest tension in the October Crisis. A miscalculation by U.S. intelligence services of the real strength of Soviet troops in Cuba—and we now know that they did miscalculate—could have led them to undertake military actions against the missile sites, as some high-ranking military and political figures were urging President Kennedy to do. That could have unleashed not only a confrontation with conventional arms but also the use of nuclear weapons, provoking a world holocaust.

The Soviet internationalist troops in Cuba during the October Crisis were willing to fight alongside the Cuban people to defend their national independence against imperialist aggression. As General Gribkov put it, "We were all ready and willing to fight to the very last man. . . . We even decided that if it proved necessary . . . we would form guerrilla units. . . . We did not have anywhere to withdraw to. No retreat was possible. Our Soviet fighters were willing to give their all to defend Cuba."[69]

---

[*] According to FAR rosters, permanent personnel in Cuba numbered around 100,000 troops (CID-FAR archives), and the STF had around 32,000—according to interviews—not counting the 10,000 troops of the missile division.

Chapter 5

The secret and the deception

Due to the nature of Operation Anadyr, Soviet intelligence agencies devised measures of concealment and disinformation to keep secret the deployment of troops, weapons, and other combat and logistical supplies in Cuba. Official documents, public statements, and interviews with Soviet functionaries suggest that the political leadership of the Soviet Union was confident in the effectiveness of its disinformation measures, and did not prepare an adequate response in case the United States discovered the operation—as in fact happened.

Despite repeated warnings from Cuba, Nikita Khrushchev stubbornly insisted the operation should not be announced until it was an accomplished fact, which the U.S. would then have to accept. This determined two different stances—Cuban and Soviet—toward the news media campaigns and pressure from the United States.

If Khrushchev had proceeded as the Cuban leadership—with a clear view of the problem—repeatedly suggested, the crisis might have been avoided, or at least might have followed a course less dangerous for humanity.

'Why not make public the military agreement?'

The Cubans' opinion on the difficulty of concealing Operation Anadyr began to be confirmed in early August. Reports of the arrival of Soviet troops in Cuba circulated in the U.S. press beginning August 8. U.S. authorities discounted those reports as exaggerated, even though they admitted that more Soviet ships were traveling toward Cuba.

The first reports that came to light in the U.S. press were based on correspondence between Cuban émigrés in the United States and their relatives in Cuba, as well as from Western diplomatic personnel and journalists stationed in Havana. They referred to caravans of military vehicles moving in the middle of the night, with large trucks transporting what appeared to be missiles covered with tarps. There were also reports of construction and repair of roads along various routes where the convoys moved, and reports confirming transfer of the civilian population from some of those rural areas.

As already noted, the intelligence services of Great Britain and the Federal Republic of Germany, which maintained constant surveillance of maritime traffic through the Straits of Gibraltar and the Dardanelles, warned the U.S. government of unusual movements of Soviet ships headed for the Atlantic. So Washington stepped up its surveillance of sea lanes leading toward Cuba, with continuous reconnaissance flights from the Azores.[*]

In his book *Presidents' Secret Wars*, John Prados recounts that CIA Director John McCone asked Philippe Thyraud de Vosjoli—the chief of French intelligence in Washington and an expert on this kind of weaponry—to travel to Cuba to verify on-the-ground reports of the presence of Soviet missiles. In August the expert carried out that mission. He found evidence of antiaircraft missile emplacements, but not of other types of missiles.[1]

---

[*] In August, U.S. air and naval reconnaissance registered the arrival of fifty-five Soviet ships in Cuba, compared to twelve in the same period a year earlier.

Nevertheless, U.S. intelligence services subjected Cuban territory to intensive scrutiny. Kennedy adviser Theodore Sorensen wrote that beginning in August movements of Russian personnel and equipment in or toward Cuba were the subject of secret meetings and reports in the White House. Naval forces and aircraft photographed every Soviet ship headed toward Cuba. Reconnaissance flights covered all of Cuban territory twice a month. According to Sorensen, beginning August 27 the intelligence services prepared special daily reports devoted exclusively to Cuba.[2]

On August 29 aerial photography by u-2s detected antiaircraft missile sites in western Cuba, which led the intelligence services to pay special attention to that area.

Days before, on August 11, Aleksandr Alekseev had arrived in Havana as the new ambassador, bringing with him the draft of the military agreement. When Fidel Castro examined the draft he found major political lapses in it. Since in Castro's view the problem was fundamentally political, the agreement needed to be, in his words, "clear, precise and concrete."[3] From that standpoint, the top Cuban leader made the corrections he considered necessary.

The first thing he modified was the title of the accord. He proposed three alternatives. The one that in his opinion best fit the essence of the accord was: "Agreement between the Government of the Republic of Cuba and the Government of the Union of Soviet Socialist Republics on military cooperation and mutual defense." Since the goal was not only "the defense of Cuban territory," as stated in the initial draft, but also "military cooperation and mutual defense" between the two countries, this would express the spirit of solidarity in the agreement.*

According to the text of the document, the Soviet military

---

* See pages 207–12 for the full text of the draft agreement. The original handwritten document is in the archives of the Havana Office of Historical Affairs of the Council of State.

contingent was to be directly subordinated to the Soviet government, and was to cooperate with the Cuban armed forces in the event of external aggression. The USSR was to cover the expenses of its forces and all the supplies its troops required. For its part, the Cuban state would assist the Soviet forces and provide the necessary facilities for their deployment.

The agreement also established that the Soviet armed forces had to respect Cuban sovereignty and Cuban law. They thus had no rights to occupy territory or do anything aside from their assigned functions. The agreement was to be valid for five years, although either side could terminate it giving one year's notice. The agreement also stipulated that the installations built would be turned over to the Cuban government when the troops withdrew.

Meanwhile, in the United States, rumors of the presence of Soviet missiles touched off a fierce media campaign against Cuba and the Soviet Union, which was manipulated by the inner circles of power in that country for their own political interests. There were more and more public statements about the military buildup in Cuba by high officials of the government, Congress, and political parties, as well as by leaders of the counterrevolutionary groups based in the United States.

The top Cuban leadership considered this political atmosphere to be quite dangerous, and thought it necessary to make an immediate, strong response. In late August, the Secretariat of the ORI National Directorate analyzed the situation and concluded that the propaganda campaign unleashed in the United States was an unmistakable sign of a new crisis brewing. Faced with that reality, the Secretariat thought it best to take the initiative by making public the military accord.

The Secretariat decided to send two of its members—Commander Ernesto Che Guevara and Captain Emilio Aragonés Navarro—to Moscow with the corrected draft of the military agreement, in order to propose personally to Khrushchev that it be made public. The final decision, however, was to be up to the Soviet side.

Aragonés and Guevara were in the Soviet Union from August 26 to September 1. According to Aragonés, during their exchange of ideas Khrushchev agreed with the corrections Fidel had made to the military agreement, but he did not think it was yet time to make it public. "Be calm," he recommended. "For the Americans a rumor is not the same as real proof of the missiles' existence."[4]

Che repeated their concern that the missiles might be discovered before they were operational, and that the United States might take advantage of the situation to attack. Khrushchev asserted with great assurance, "Relax, I don't think they will find out. When they do find out, they will have no choice but to accept the situation."[5]

Besides, the Soviet leader thought an announcement of the agreement right then would interfere with Kennedy's political activity in the midst of the off-year election campaign. Khrushchev may also have been influenced by the fact that the missile divisions' main weapons had not yet arrived in Cuba. Perhaps he considered it better to publicize the agreement after the missiles had been installed, and in that way present it as a fait accompli. He concluded by repeating to Che and Aragonés what he had said previously to Raúl Castro: "You can relax. If any problem should occur, if we have to send the Baltic fleet over there, we'll send it."[6]

Those talks resulted only in getting a paragraph included in a joint communiqué on the visit publicly expressing Soviet willingness to contribute to the reinforcement of Cuba's defense against the threats of external aggression. It stated: "As long as threats against Cuba by the above-mentioned circles persist, the Republic of Cuba will be fully entitled to adopt measures to guarantee its security and the defense of its sovereignty and independence, and all sincere friends of Cuba will have the full right to respond to those legitimate requests."[7]

Meanwhile, in the United States, the campaign around Soviet weapons in Cuba was becoming more bellicose. The most reactionary politicians demanded immediate action against

Cuba. A group of congressional Republicans headed by Senators Homer E. Capehart, Kenneth Keating, and Barry Goldwater was publicly pressing the Kennedy administration to do something. Those statements were directly linked to the November 1962 off-year elections, which drew numerous congressmen into the debate.

Some Latin American governments joined the campaign. The Venezuelan foreign minister, for example, predicted that if Cuba carried out aggression, his country would be the first target. Argentina and Peru also expressed alarm over what was happening on the island. In Central America other governments supported the idea of an invasion, as well.

On September 4 President Kennedy revealed that a reconnaissance flight over Cuba on August 29 had detected surface-to-air missiles and an increased number of Soviet military personnel. He warned Moscow that he would not tolerate the installation of offensive weapons on the island. On September 7 he requested congressional approval to call up 150,000 reservists to active duty if necessary to be able to respond quickly and effectively "to challenges in any part of the Free World."[8]

A week later, on September 13, with his government under political pressure, the U.S. president stated in a press conference that if the growth of communism in Cuba should at some point endanger or interfere in any way with the security of the United States and other nations of the Western Hemisphere by turning the island into an important offensive base for the Soviet Union, he would do everything possible to protect their security. He also warned that if he were to take military action against Cuba, all the weaponry and military advisers provided by the communists would not be able to change the outcome.

On September 26 the U.S. Congress adopted Joint Resolution 230, presented by the Senate Foreign Relations and Armed Services Committees. This resolution authorized the president to take armed action against Cuba over its supposed aggressive and subversive activities in the hemisphere, and also authorized the use of force to prevent the establishment or use of military power on the island that might endanger the security of the United States.*

A meeting of Latin American foreign ministers on October 3 adopted a communiqué, at the request of the U.S. State Department, condemning the secret military buildup in Cuba and calling on OAS member countries to take individual or collective action to prevent the spread of communism in the hemisphere.

Two different positions

In face of the U.S. campaigns, Cuba's stance was to defend the country's sovereign right to take the measures necessary for its defense, while the Soviet Union's position was to turn to deception to keep the operation secret. Compare, for example, statements made by both countries at the time.

Cuban president Osvaldo Dorticós Torrado, in a meeting with workers leaders on September 7, said this about the U.S. campaign against Cuba: "What they are trying to do is deny us the right to defend ourselves. . . . Cuba has the legitimate right to use all means necessary for its defense, and Cuba's friends have the right to respond to our requests as needed for defense."[9]

That same day in Washington, Soviet ambassador Anatoly Dobrynin, speaking on behalf of his government, assured the U.S. representative to the United Nations, Adlai Stevenson, that the Soviets were giving only defensive weapons to Cuba.

Three days later, speaking to the Third National Congress of Municipal Education Councils, Fidel Castro sounded the alarm about pressures on the U.S. administration to attack the island, and pointed out: "An invasion of Cuba by U.S. military forces would place imperialism outside international law, as vulgar violators of the rights of the peoples, as perpetrators of genocide." He also warned the U.S. rulers: "We have said on other occasions that we do not want imperialism to commit suicide

* On September 25, the Congress also approved President Kennedy's request to call up 150,000 reservists to active military service.

on our account. We proclaim our desire to live in peace. We proclaim our desire that good judgment and the most elementary common sense should govern the destiny of that country."[10]

On September 11, 1962, the Soviet news agency TASS broadcast a statement by the government of the USSR reaffirming its intention to provide needed military assistance to Cuba in the event of aggression. But paradoxically, the statement denied the existence of strategic weapons on the island: "The Soviet Union does not need to transfer to any other country—Cuba, for example—the means it possesses to repel aggression, to strike back. Our nuclear resources are so powerful in their explosive force and . . . we have such powerful missiles for delivering nuclear warheads that we have no need to look for a place to deploy them anywhere outside the boundaries of the USSR."[11]

In response to the joint congressional resolution authorizing President Kennedy to use armed force against Cuba if it threatened U.S. security, the Council of Ministers of the Cuban revolutionary government released a statement September 29 reaffirming Cuba's principled policy:

"Do we not have the rights that international norms, laws, and principles recognize for every sovereign state in any part of the world?

"We have not surrendered nor do we intend to surrender any of our sovereign prerogatives to the Congress of the United States.

"If the U.S. government harbored no aggressive intentions toward our country, it would not care about the quantity, quality, or type of our weapons.

"If the United States could give Cuba effective and satisfactory guarantees with respect to our territorial integrity and would cease its subversive and counterrevolutionary activities against our people, Cuba would not need to strengthen its defenses. Cuba would not even need an army, and we would be happy to invest all the resources this implies to the nation's economic and cultural development.

"Cuba has always been ready to hold discussions with the

U.S. government and to do everything possible on our part, if only we were to find a reciprocal stance by the U.S. government of reducing tensions and improving relations."*

This is how the revolutionary government expressed itself in response to the slanderous campaigns being whipped up in the United States. Cuba steadfastly maintained this principled stance and never vacillated in the slightest in the face of all types of pressures. Nor did Cuba negate its sovereign right to possess whatever weapons might be necessary to confront military aggression, and it warned of the consequences such aggression could bring.

In assessing the information supplied and the position taken by Soviet officials, the testimony of Georgi Bolshakov is very interesting. Bolshakov was a press officer in the Soviet embassy in Washington, and at that time acted as a secret "channel" of communication between Kennedy and Khrushchev. "The U.S. had already installed their missiles right under our noses, in Turkey, some time ago," he commented. "That was not secret. The whole world knew it, including the Soviet Union. However, our own deliberate secrecy was hindering Soviet diplomacy, because whenever the topic of Cuba came up, the question arose: 'Are there Soviet missiles in Cuba?' The fact that we denied it was used in the only possible way: 'They lie.' That idea took hold easily in the minds of the American people, sowing mistrust of our intentions. Perhaps this is why President Kennedy managed to secure support in advance for a planned invasion of Cuba from the Organization of American States and from several European countries, such as Great Britain, the Federal Republic of Germany, and France."[12]

Years later, Fidel Castro explained the major mistakes made by the Soviet government, not only keeping the operation secret—which certainly didn't help—but also their repeated denial of the presence of missiles in Cuba. He analyzed how

* See pages 213–23 for the full text of the statement. Published in *Noticias de Hoy*, September 30, 1962, p. 1.

Khrushchev, in his eagerness to cover up the strategic character of those weapons, used the categories Washington had contrived of "offensive" or "defensive" weapons. Khrushchev always made assurances that the weapons sent to Cuba were defensive in character. For the U.S., the distinction depended on whether the weapons could reach the continental United States, not on the purpose for which they were intended. Consequently, to define the weapons in this way was a highly dangerous political error by Khrushchev. It made things easy for Kennedy, because when nuclear missiles were discovered, Kennedy presented himself as a man who had been lied to, which gave him the moral high ground in public opinion.[13]

Unlike the Soviet government, the Cuban government maintained a principled stance on the matter. "We refused to play that game," Fidel said, "and in the public statements of the government, and then at the United Nations, we always said that Cuba considered that it had the sovereign right to have the kind of weapons it considered convenient, and that no one had any right to establish what kind of weapons our country could or could not have. We never denied the strategic character of the weapons. We did not want to play that game."[14]

Chapter 6

The crisis begins

In the early morning hours of Sunday, October 14, an American u-2 plane on a south-to-north flight path over Cuba took photographs of the western part of the island. The pictures were carefully analyzed the following day, and the presence of an r-12 missile launch site was detected in the San Cristóbal region of Pinar del Río province.

Ray Cline, the CIA deputy director for research and analysis who headed up the National Photographic Interpretation Center, has pointed out that as of October 14 he already had indications that there were missiles in San Cristóbal. To check them out, "we finally decided that we had to make a u-2 overflight in order to discover whether these missiles were actually there. Fortunately, we did find them."[1]

Kennedy received the pictures on the morning of October 16. He immediately ordered the intelligence services to assess the operational readiness of the missiles, and he insisted that the information be kept secret.[2] He also established a special group of senior government officials, later known as the Executive

Committee of the National Security Council (ExComm), for the purpose of analyzing the situation and determining what actions to take.*

The ExComm and the decision

This committee worked between October 16 and 22 in absolute secrecy. Its main mission was to find the best way to get rid of the Soviet missiles before they became operational. Those were extremely dangerous days for Cuba, because the United States held the military initiative. With the secret in hand, it was free to consider, without any pressure at all, what political or military measures it might take to eliminate the missiles.

On October 16, the ExComm began its working sessions with a detailed analysis of the aerial photographs, counting sixteen to twenty-four missile launchers that, according to experts, would be ready in two weeks. There were no signs that nuclear warheads were being stored, but this could not be ruled out. The president ordered an increase in reconnaissance flights, because more photographs were needed right away as clear and solid evidence. Kennedy also told everyone at the meeting to set aside all other tasks and concentrate their efforts on a thorough study of this problem and future actions. He demanded that the strictest secrecy be observed until an appropriate response had been prepared.

---

* The ExComm included—in addition to President Kennedy—Vice President Lyndon Johnson; Secretary of State Dean Rusk; Defense Secretary Robert McNamara; Treasury Secretary Douglas Dillon; Attorney General Robert Kennedy; Gen. Maxwell Taylor, chairman of the Joint Chiefs of Staff; CIA Director John McCone; Deputy Defense Secretary Roswell Gilpatric; George Ball, undersecretary of state; national security adviser McGeorge Bundy; Special Counsel to the President Theodore C. Sorensen; and Llewellyn Thompson, former U.S. ambassador to the Soviet Union. In addition, regularly participating in ExComm meetings were U. Alexis Johnson, deputy undersecretary of state for political affairs; Edwin Martin, assistant secretary of state for inter-American affairs; and Paul Nitze, assistant secretary of defense. Adlai Stevenson, U.S. representative to the United Nations, took part in some ExComm sessions as well, as did others. This committee remained in permanent session throughout the crisis as Kennedy's advisory council.

In that first working session, the members of the ExComm did not reach any agreement, but they did lay out some of the main options that would be discussed that week. These ranged from applying diplomatic pressure on the Soviet Union through the United Nations, to negotiations at a summit meeting between the two powers, to various types of military attacks on Cuba.

According to Theodore Sorensen, an adviser to Kennedy and a member of the ExComm, one participant said the way to accomplish their goal was either through an air strike or pressuring the Soviets to withdraw all the missiles from Cuba. Someone else offered the opinion that the proposed air strike could not be limited to missile sites, but would also have to include storage depots, Cuban air bases, and other military targets, and might lead to an invasion of the island. A third person spoke of organizing a naval blockade, combined with warnings to all parties involved, as well as stepped-up surveillance.[3]

Following up on these proposals, the ExComm devised various options, such as a naval blockade that would lead step by step to an invasion, following either massive or limited air strikes. Some of these ideas are stated in a highly revealing document that was discussed on Wednesday, October 17:

"The following possible tracks or courses of action have each been considered. Each has obvious diplomatic and military disadvantages, but none others as yet occur.

"*Track A*—Political action, pressure and warning, followed by a military strike if satisfaction is not received.

"*Track B*—A military strike without prior warning, pressure or action, accompanied by messages making clear the limited nature of this action.

"*Track C*—Political actions, pressure and warning, followed by a total naval blockade, under the authority of the Rio Pact and either a Congressional Declaration of War on Cuba or the Cuban Resolution of the 87th Congress.

"*Track D*—Full-scale invasion, to 'take Cuba away from Castro'.

"Obviously any one of these could lead to one of the others—but each represents a distinguishable approach to the problem."[4]

All of these proposed actions show beyond any doubt that military options were studied in detail and were at the center of the discussions, while diplomatic initiatives were relegated to the background. The transcripts from the committee meetings held that week prove that the option considered most attractive was a surprise air attack to destroy Cuba's missile installations.

On October 18, as discussions continued within the ExComm, the U.S. president met at the White House with Andrei Gromyko, the Soviet minister of foreign affairs. Among the issues they discussed was the Cuban situation. Kennedy blamed the actions of the Soviet Union and Cuba for tensions in the Caribbean, but he did not show Gromyko the photographs of missile installations that were in his possession. Gromyko, for his part, repeated the argument that his country's aid to Cuba was designed only to strengthen Cuba's defensive capability, and he made no reference to nuclear missiles.

One may ask: How could the Soviet foreign minister have failed to realize that the U.S. president was alluding to the missiles in Cuba, and let pass the opportunity to take the initiative?

We can find the answer to this question in the volume of memoirs of the Soviet premier, titled *Khrushchev Remembers: The Glasnost Tapes.* "Andrei Andreyevich Gromyko was in New York at a United Nations session," Khrushchev says. "It was a difficult moment; storm clouds were gathering. Gromyko was invited by [Secretary of State Dean] Rusk to Washington. Our position was neither to confirm nor to deny presence of missiles. In answer to a direct question, we would deny."[5]

Participants at the January 1989 Moscow conference on the October crisis asked Gromyko about his October 18 meeting with Kennedy: "Why didn't you bring up the issue of the missiles in Cuba during your meeting with Kennedy?"

"Kennedy didn't ask me," he replied laconically.

"And if Kennedy had asked you," persisted one of the delegates, "how would you have responded?"

"I would have given an appropriate response," Gromyko replied.[6]

Discussions within the ExComm continued October 18. Most members were initially in favor of a limited air strike, which they called "surgical," aimed at destroying the missile sites.

Defense Secretary Robert McNamara reported during the night that "the necessary planes, men, and ammunition were being deployed and that we could be ready to move with the necessary air bombardments on Tuesday, October 23, if that was to be the decision."[7]

However, when Kennedy asked about the effectiveness of this military action, Gen. Maxwell Taylor could give assurance of destroying only 90 percent of the known missile sites. As a result, beginning that night the option of a blockade gained favor in the debates, with the president himself leaning that way, in spite of the disadvantages it entailed.

Within the ExComm, "at first there had been very little support of a blockade," one of the members wrote. "It appeared almost irrelevant to the problem of the missiles." Among the drawbacks attributed to blockade was, "If Soviet ships ignored it, U.S. forces would have to fire the first shot, provoking Soviet action elsewhere. We could not even be certain that the blockade route was open to us."[8] This action could be considered a violation of the UN Charter and international law.

The naval blockade was seen as a less provocative action than an air strike, one that would initially avoid a direct military clash that would force the Soviets to respond immediately. According to Sorensen, the president "liked the idea of leaving Khrushchev a way out, of beginning at a low level that could then be stepped up; and the other choices had too many insuperable difficulties."[9]

Another issue discussed in the ExComm was the weakness of the U.S. military position in West Berlin. Edwin Martin, at that time assistant secretary of state for inter-American affairs, later stated: "West Berlin was not just ninety miles away from the U.S., as Cuba was, but was surrounded directly by Soviet, or Soviet allied, forces. We were very vulnerable there, if there was a desire to retaliate or to make threats that would persuade us not to take action against Cuba. I think that needs to be kept in mind, because it did come up rather often in our considerations of what action to take against Cuba, and was certainly a deterrent to the military option at the time we were making our choices in that first week of ExComm."[10]

On the other hand, a confrontation in the Caribbean resulting from the blockade would be more advantageous to the United States, since its naval forces were stronger than those of the Soviets, should the Soviets decide to retaliate with submarines. By this line of reasoning, Khrushchev, in order to avoid a military defeat, would have to order his ships back to their home ports.

Another argument in favor of the blockade was that it was a limited action that could be escalated step by step as the situation called for. The blockade would also prove somewhat more acceptable to other countries than an air attack, thus making it easier to obtain allied support when the time came to carry out more drastic action. Nevertheless, some members of the ExComm felt that the biggest drawback of the blockade in comparison to an air attack lay in the greater amount of time it would take.

On October 19, after the different options had been studied, President Kennedy instructed the State Department to come up with a way to present the naval blockade to the world as a legal act. The specialists assigned to this task explained that a blockade could be one of two types: pacific or belligerent. A pacific blockade is imposed in peacetime to retaliate for a specific act. In the past this type of action had been limited to ships from the affected nation—therefore, Cuban ships could be stopped, but not those of the USSR or any other nation, making such a blockade totally ineffective. A belligerent blockade takes place in wartime, and means that all ships, including those from neutral countries, are prevented from entering blockaded ports. Any ships that try to break the blockade can be captured, and their cargo confiscated as spoils of war.

Neither of these two types of blockades was well suited to the situation at hand, the State Department pointed out. It felt it would be best to establish a new type of blockade specifically concerning armaments, and to base it on the precepts of the Monroe Doctrine.

It was recommended that the blockade begin at the lowest level—that is, it was to be directed only at "offensive" weapons—and then, ten days after being put into effect, it could be expanded to include a ban on transport of petroleum products, gasoline, and lubricants to Cuba. This was expected to contribute indirectly to the collapse of the Cuban economy, thus bringing about political results favorable to Washington's anti-Cuba plans.

On Saturday, October 20, at 2:30 P.M., the ExComm met to make its final decision. Kennedy asked CIA Director John McCone to open the session with a report on the latest intelligence data. Then the two main alternatives were discussed, along with their advantages and disadvantages. The options were to start with a blockade and later take more drastic actions, or to start with an air strike that, as far as could be seen, would culminate in an invasion of Cuba.[11]

After the decision was made in favor of the blockade, discussion began on the legality of the action. On this point, McGeorge Bundy explained much later in a television interview, Dean Acheson—an unofficial foreign policy adviser to President Kennedy—had suggested that "if some people objected to the term 'blockade,' why was that word being used? Why not 'quarantine'?" Kennedy thought it was beneficial to use this term for the naval blockade, to camouflage from the public the illegality of the action. "This was a huge accomplishment," Bundy stated, "because under international law a blockade is an act of war—or it can be interpreted as such—while a quarantine is simply to prevent an infection from spreading over the area."[12]

Finally, the draft of the president's speech was reviewed, as well as the timing of its delivery. Kennedy urged Sorensen, his speechwriter, to emphasize the sudden, secretive, and deceptive nature of the deployment of offensive weapons in Cuba. Kennedy was concerned that the Soviets would appeal to public opinion and invoke international law, since they had every legal right to install those weapons so long as the Cuban government had authorized it.[13]

From that moment, experts from the State, Defense, and Justice Departments worked on drafting the official proclamation of the blockade. The Pentagon was asked for a list of the "offensive" weapons that were to be prohibited from reaching Cuba, for a study on the possibility of blockading aircraft, as well as for what military forces were available from Latin American countries that might join the blockade.

The Defense Department developed a list of military supplies to be covered by the blockade, including surface-to-surface missiles, air-to-surface missiles, warheads for these missiles, bomber aircraft, bombs, and mechanical and electronic equipment for operating the missiles. It was also ordered that cargo ships needing to cross the area of the blockade would have to declare their cargo and request a departure certificate from the U.S. consulate at the last port they called on before reaching the blockade line.

The ExComm also analyzed the possible reaction to the naval blockade among the peoples of Latin America. It was presumed that there could be demonstrations, rallies, and actions outside U.S. embassies and other locations. It was therefore agreed to send riot control equipment to Latin American governments. The State Department instructed all its Latin American ambassadors who were in Washington for consultations or on vacation abroad to return immediately to their posts.

The president's speech was set for Monday, October 22, at 7:00 P.M. It was decided to notify cabinet members and Republican and Democratic Party congressional leaders of the decision ahead of time. Kennedy also instructed the State Department to obtain OAS support for the blockade.

The president wanted to hear in person the opinion of Gen. Walter Sweeney, commander of the Tactical Air Command (TAC), about the effectiveness of a massive air strike, in case that were resorted to. This meeting was held on October 21 at 11:30 A.M., with the participation of Defense Secretary McNamara; Gen. Maxwell Taylor, who was now chairman of the Joint Chiefs of Staff; CIA Director John McCone; and Attorney General Robert Kennedy.

An account of that meeting has survived in notes taken by McNamara on what the TAC commander told Kennedy about plans for an air attack to destroy the missile capability detected in Cuba.

"a. The 5 surface-to-air missile installations, in the vicinity of the known missile sites, would each be attacked by approximately 8 aircraft; the 3 MIG airfields defending the missile sites would be covered by 12 U.S. aircraft per field. In total, the defense suppression operations, including the necessary replacement aircraft, would require approximately 100 sorties.

"b. Each of the launchers at the 8 or 9 known sites (a total of approximately 32 to 36 launchers) would be attacked by 6 aircraft. For the purpose, a total of approximately 250 sorties would be flown.

"c. The U.S. aircraft covering the 3 MIG airfields would attack the MIG's if they became airborne. . . .

". . . General Sweeney stated that he was certain the air strike would be 'successful'; however, even under optimum conditions, it was not likely that all of the known missiles would be destroyed. . . . General Taylor stated, 'The best we can offer you is to destroy 90% of the known missiles.' General Taylor, General Sweeney and the Secretary of Defense all strongly emphasized that in their opinion the initial air strike must be followed by strikes on subsequent days and that these in turn would lead inevitably to an invasion."[14]

This last factor influenced Kennedy's decision not to begin with air strikes, since his military advisers could not be certain that all the missiles would be destroyed—a response capability that could reach U.S. territory would remain. This option was preserved, however, and on more than one occasion the ExComm analyzed the possibility of carrying it out. McNamara's notes record that Kennedy "directed that we be prepared to carry out the air strike Monday morning or any time thereafter."[15]

Kennedy met again with the ExComm at 2:30 P.M. that day to review State Department instructions to U.S. embassies and presidential letters to be sent to U.S. allies. He also finalized everything that was to take place within the Organization of American States and statements to be made before the United Nations Security Council.

The White House chief ordered air surveillance over Cuba stepped up and requested of Adm. George W. Anderson, chief of naval operations, a briefing on plans and procedures for the blockade. According to Sorensen: "First, said the Admiral, each approaching ship would be signaled to stop for boarding and inspection. Then, if no satisfactory response was forthcoming, a shot would be fired across her bow. Finally, if there was still no satisfactory response, a shot would be fired into her rudder to cripple but not to sink."[16]

On the morning of Monday, October 22, in accordance with the plan, President Kennedy telephoned his predecessors—Herbert Hoover, Harry Truman, and Dwight Eisenhower—to inform them of the situation. At 3:00 P.M. he met with the National Security Council and the Joint Chiefs of Staff to specify actions to be taken. An hour later he held a meeting with the cabinet, at which he reported briefly on the latest events and, finally, he did the same with leaders of Congress.

According to Robert Kennedy, the meeting with members of Congress was very tense, because some strongly criticized the president. "They felt that the President should take more forceful action, a military attack or invasion, and that the blockade was far too weak a response."[17]

Dean Rusk summoned Soviet ambassador Anatoly F. Dobrynin to the State Department at 6:00 P.M. to give him a message;

RAÚL CORRALES

" **The imperialists began preparing their war on us five months after the triumph of the revolution, simply because the revolution decreed an agrarian reform law.** "

FIDEL CASTRO, OCTOBER 23, 1962

In response to the aspirations and initiatives of sharecroppers, tenant farmers, and squatters, the revolution on May 17, 1959, decreed an agrarian reform law granting deeds to more than 100,000 families. The vast sugar plantations and cattle ranches, the majority of them U.S.-owned, were expropriated. **Top,** Cuban farmers receive their deeds. **Inset,** *New York Times* article reporting the measure.

> " The U.S. government carried out sabotage and terrorist acts in Cuba; assassination attempts; support to counterrevolutionary bands; efforts to isolate Cuba diplomatically; and an economic blockade. "

GRANMA

VERDE OLIVO

GRANMA

Facing page: El Encanto department store after April 13, 1961, counter-revolutionary arson attack in Havana. That night, working people in the city marched to condemn perpetrators of the attack.

In addition to sponsoring counterrevolutionary terror, Washington in 1960 organized U.S.-owned refineries to stop processing oil purchased from the Soviet Union and slashed imports of Cuban sugar by 95 percent. In response to these escalating attacks, the revolutionary government in the summer of 1960 led the nationalization of major U.S. holdings and contracted with the Soviet Union to buy Cuban sugar. **This page, top,** workers and militia members take down plaques of Bank of Boston, September 1960. **Bottom right,** Cuban prime minister Fidel Castro and Soviet premier Nikita Khrushchev at United Nations General Assembly, September 1960.

The U.S. rulers pressured Latin American regimes to join in efforts to overturn the Cuban Revolution. **Bottom left,** Ernesto Che Guevara answers Washington's attacks at conference of Latin American governments in Punta del Este, Uruguay, August 1961.

" The immediate causes of the October Crisis are found in the U.S. government's defeat at the Bay of Pigs. It was clear that after this failure, the White House would consider direct intervention by its own armed forces. "

GRANMA

BOHEMIA

On April 17, 1961, a U.S.-organized, -trained, and -financed force of 1,500 men invaded Cuba at the Bay of Pigs. In less than 72 hours, Cuba's militia and Rebel Army defeated the mercenaries, the last of whom surrendered at Playa Girón (Girón Beach). **Top left,** Fidel Castro with members of tank crew during battle. **Bottom left,** Cuban militia members at antiaircraft gun. **Top,** militiamen celebrate victory, April 19, 1961. **Bottom,** captured mercenaries.

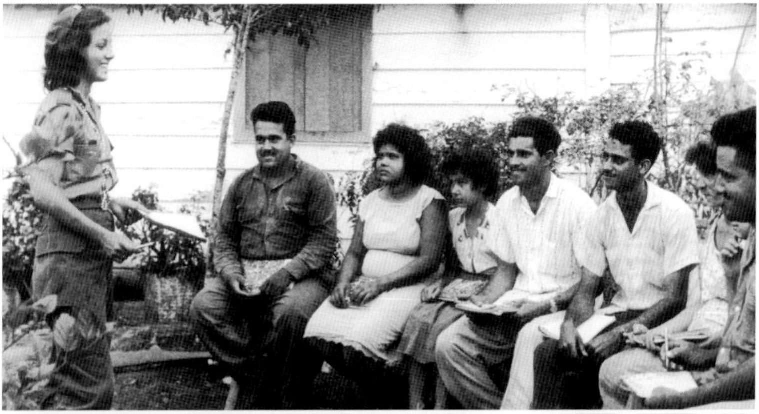

BOHEMIA

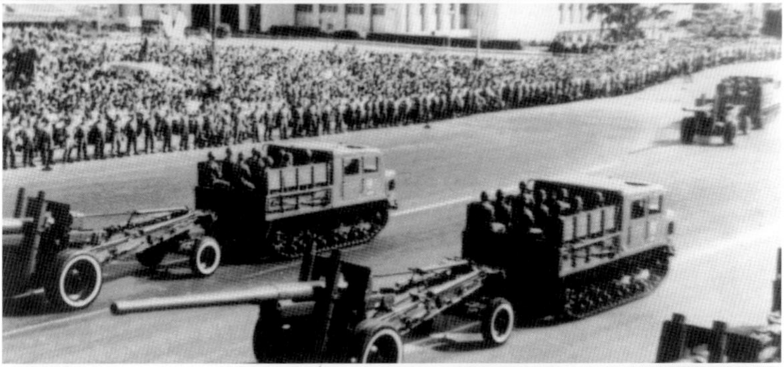

GRANMA

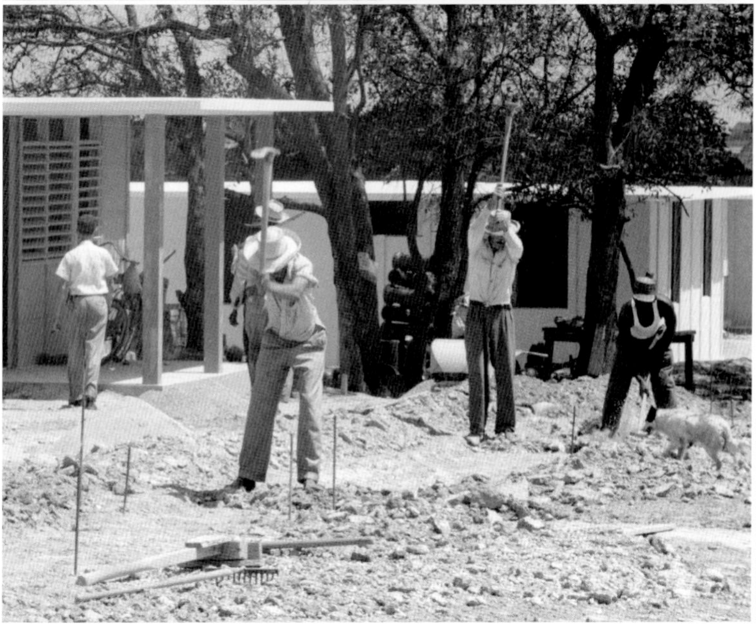

JOSEPH HANSEN / MILITANT

" It was necessary to develop education and health care; keep up production; prepare the country for defense; and fight the bandits. All these efforts drew on the same forces: the working people and, in the first place, the youth. "

BOHEMIA

Top left, in the 1961 National Literacy Campaign more than 100,000 young brigadistas taught a million Cuban peasants and workers to read and write. **Center left,** January 2, 1962: Cuba displays artillery just obtained from Soviet Union. **Bottom left,** the revolution embarked on a crash program to build housing, roads, schools, and factories. In early 1960, members of a new farming cooperative, most of whom lived in thatch-roof, dirt-floor huts, build housing with materials provided by the government. **Above,** U.S.-organized counterrevolutionary bands in the Escambray mountains and elsewhere were defeated by the Lucha Contra Bandidos (LCB) units of the armed forces and militias.

" **Fidel saw in Khrushchev's proposal something that could contribute to defense of the entire socialist camp. From that standpoint he was inclined to accept it, even though he was convinced missiles were not essential to defend Cuba.** "

Top left, following the Soviet proposal to install missiles in Cuba, Raúl Castro (on right) visits Soviet Union in July 1962 with instructions to ask Khrushchev (on left) what would happen if the missiles were discovered before the agreement was published. **Bottom left,** Havana harbor, 1962. Following the visit, tens of thousands of fully equipped Soviet troops began arriving in Cuba. **Center left,** in late August Che Guevara (right) headed a delegation to the USSR to take Khrushchev a copy of rewritten mutual defense pact drafted by Fidel Castro and to urge Soviet government to make the agreement public. **Above,** Fidel Castro (left) with members of a Soviet military unit participating in Operation Anadyr. At his side is the interpreter (center) and a member of the Soviet unit.

> " Cuba's stance was to defend the country's sovereign right to take the measures necessary for its defense, while the Soviet Union's position was to turn to deception to keep the operation secret. "

Facing page, photographs taken by U.S. U-2 spy planes of Soviet missile emplacements.

Top, Kennedy (center) meets in October 1962 with National Security Council's special Executive Committee (ExComm). **Bottom,** Soviet foreign minister Andrei Gromyko visited the White House on October 18. In his talks with Kennedy—who did not reveal that Washington knew of the missiles—Gromyko denied the Soviet Union had strategic weapons in Cuba.

> " The Kennedy administration devised various options, such as a naval blockade that would lead step by step to an invasion, following either massive or limited air strikes. "

Right, Kennedy delivering televised address October 22, 1962, announcing naval blockade of Cuba. The broadcast publicly initiated the "Missile" Crisis that brought humanity to the brink of nuclear war. **Top,** earlier that same day, U.S. Marine reinforcements had arrived at the U.S. naval base on occupied Cuban soil at Guantánamo.

a few minutes later, the U.S. representative in Moscow, Foy D. Kohler, delivered an identical document to Vasily V. Kuznetzov, vice minister of foreign relations of the USSR.

Dean Acheson had left the previous day as a high-level White House emissary to meet personally with top leaders of the NATO allies in Western Europe and with authorities in West Berlin.

That night, in a televised address from the White House, President Kennedy read a speech meticulously prepared to influence public opinion in the United States and worldwide in favor of the military actions he proposed to implement. In a tone of recrimination, he announced that the Soviets—suddenly and secretly—were installing offensive missile bases in Cuba, whose purpose "can be none other than to provide a nuclear strike capability against the Western Hemisphere." This "constitutes an explicit threat to the peace and security of all the Americas." He went on to assert: "This action also contradicts the repeated assurances of Soviet spokesmen, both publicly and privately delivered, that the arms build-up in Cuba would retain its original defensive character, and that the Soviet Union had no need or desire to station strategic missiles on the territory of any other nation."[18]

To support that claim, he cited fragments of Soviet declarations on September 11 as well as his meeting with Gromyko on October 18. In this way, Kennedy presented the arguments to justify politically the military actions he was about to undertake against Cuba.

"Neither the United States of America nor the world community of nations," Kennedy said, "can tolerate deliberate deception and offensive threats on the part of any nation, large or small."[19]

In order to reassert the claim that he had been deceived, justify military measures against Cuba, and ascribe hegemonistic intentions to the Soviets, Kennedy compared their action to U.S. conduct elsewhere in the world. He said, "Our own strategic missiles have never been transferred to the territory of any other nation under a cloak of secrecy and deception; and our history, unlike that of the Soviets since the end of World War II, demonstrates that we have no desire to dominate or conquer any other nation or impose our system upon its people."[20]

In threatening language, the U.S. president stated: "This sudden, clandestine decision to station strategic weapons for the first time outside of Soviet soil—is a deliberately provocative and unjustified change in the status quo which cannot be accepted by this country."[21]

Kennedy then listed the actions that he had ordered. The first stipulated a strict quarantine, under which all ships bound for Cuba—of any kind, coming from any seaport or nation—would be obliged to turn back if they transported offensive weapons. He threatened that the blockade would be expanded, if necessary, to other types of cargo and carriers.

The second measure was increased surveillance over Cuba. Kennedy maintained that if military reinforcement of the island continued, additional actions could be taken. He had ordered the armed forces to be ready for any eventuality.

Third, Kennedy proclaimed the United States to be the guardian of the continent, declaring that any attack launched from Cuba against any other country in the hemisphere would be treated as Soviet aggression against the United States, and would be met with full retaliation. Fourth, the U.S. president reported on the reinforcement of the U.S. naval base at Guantánamo and the evacuation of civilians from there. The fifth and sixth measures were the diplomatic actions with which the United States would try to legalize the naval blockade, by immediately convening the OAS consultative body and the United Nations Security Council.[22]

Kennedy's address announced to the world the beginning of the gravest crisis of the Cold War era, which threatened the end of humanity.

Deployment of U.S. military forces

After October 16, the U.S. armed forces went to higher levels of combat readiness. Troops, weapons, and supplies were moved to their designated combat areas.

Also starting October 16, the White House began to organize a unified Atlantic Command, the main command body for military actions, to which were subordinated all land, sea, and air forces involved—including the units intended for the air strikes against Cuba and the invasion of the island. This huge array of forces was commanded by Adm. Robert L. Dennison.

The Joint Chiefs of Staff assigned responsibility for the blockade to Adm. George W. Anderson, chief of naval operations. Decisions were to be made by the U.S. president, as commander in chief of the armed forces, and transmitted through the secretary of defense.

Naval forces

On October 21 the United States put the various Navy commands on alert and established Defense Condition 3 (DEFCON-3) for the five naval districts located on the Atlantic coast.[*] In this situation, units prepared to undertake long-term combat actions, and ships were sent out from their permanent bases onto the high seas.

A considerable number of those forces were already operating in the conflict region at the time of the crisis because they were participating in various military exercises, such as Unitas III and Sweep Clear II.[†] But the training that involved the most troops, ships, and aircraft was Phibriglex 62, an amphibious assault exercise scheduled to take place October 15–30 in the Caribbean.

For this exercise, four task forces were organized, totaling

---

[*] The five naval districts were 3rd Naval District, headquarters in New York; 4th, Philadelphia, Pennsylvania; 5th, Norfolk, Virginia; 6th, Charleston, South Carolina; and 8th, New Orleans, Louisiana.

[†] Unitas III was a joint submarine exercise involving naval units from the U.S. and several South American countries. Sweep Clear II was a minesweeping exercise that started in mid-October involving naval units from the United States and Canada in the vicinity of Nova Scotia..

20,000 men and forty ships: two aircraft carriers (one attack and one antisubmarine), two assault helicopter carriers, fourteen amphibious ships, fifteen destroyers, three submarines, and four auxiliary ships. The landing exercise included 6,000 marines from a reinforced regiment of the 2nd Marine Corps Division and a battalion of the 1st Marine Corps Division, which was to carry out an airborne mobility test.[*]

Deployment of these forces in the vicinity of Cuba, prior to announcing the blockade, made it easier for the United States to carry out large movements of troops and warships there after October 16 without attracting as much attention.

The Guantánamo naval base was reinforced in the early hours of October 21 with the arrival of the 2nd Battalion of the 1st Regiment of the 1st Marine Corps Division. The base commander later deployed this unit on the defense perimeter of the installation, where various engineering projects were being carried out. On October 22, two Marine Corps battalions landed; one with the 8th Amphibious Squadron and the other sent from Cherry Point, North Carolina. That day, 2,890 civilians were evacuated, 390 in aircraft and 2,500 in various ships.

The total number of Marine Corps troops at Guantánamo increased from 8,000 to 16,000 men, equivalent to a reinforced regiment. In addition to the units mentioned above, the 4th and 7th mobile construction battalions, which carried out engineering projects, were also there.

The aircraft concentrated there remained on a state of alert, making daily flights and carrying out bombing exercises, while helicopters patrolled the border perimeter. Aircraft and ships patrolled access north of the former Oriente province, the Windward Passage, and south of Jamaica, using P-2 "Neptune" and S-2 "Tracker" patrol planes, destroyers, and submarines, in co-

---

[*] The Phibriglex 62 exercise was preannounced—an unusual step—and was to be carried in the Caribbean during the second fortnight of October 1962. It envisioned a naval landing on the island of Vieques, supposedly to overthrow an imaginary tyrant named Ortsac—Castro spelled backwards.

ordination with other units based in Puerto Rico.

In order to carry out the blockade and the air attack or invasion of Cuba, the Atlantic Command established different task forces that day:

• Task Force 136, under the command of Vice Adm. Alfred G. Ward, with the mission of imposing the blockade between the Bahamas and Puerto Rico. Naval units in this task force had supplies of all types for sixty days from the beginning of the blockade.

• Task Force 135 was assigned to act as a strike and protection force for the Guantánamo naval base, under the command of Rear Adm. John T. Hayward. Its main units were deployed in the Caribbean near the southeastern coast of Cuba. This naval force included two attack carriers, the *Enterprise* (CVAN-65) and the *Independence* (CVA-62), and nine destroyers.

• Task Force 137, activated on November 12, 1962, was called the Combined Inter-American Blockade Force, under the command of Rear Adm. John A. Tyree. Its primary mission was to assist Task Force 136 in the area southwest of Cuba. This task force included naval units from the United States, Argentina, Venezuela (countries involved in the Unitas III military exercise), and the Dominican Republic.

• Task Force 129, under the command of Rear Adm. Horacio Rivero, had as its main mission the transport of troops and matériel in case of an invasion of Cuba. This task force comprised sixty-five amphibious ships, concentrated around Mayport and Jacksonville, Florida.*

• Task Force 83 participated in the antisubmarine defense of the Atlantic and was under the command of Vice Adm. Edmund Battelle Taylor. Its units were deployed mainly in naval bases in Puerto Rico, Guantánamo, and Key West.†

---

* The U.S. Navy believed there was a shortage of amphibious ships that could land directly on the coast and that Cuban seaport capacities were limited. In case of an invasion, this might have delayed the introduction of troops, equipment, and supplies in the landing zone.

† Task Force 83 carried out the inspection on the high seas of Soviet ships that

The units of the 2nd Marine Corps Division, equivalent to two expeditionary brigades, were on board the ships of the 6th, 8th, 10th, and 12th amphibious squadrons by October 28 and ready for combat. In early November they were joined by the 50th Expeditionary Brigade, deployed in Mayport and Jacksonville, Florida, consisting of one Marine Corps regiment reinforced with a small squadron of helicopters and other forces.

Naval units also executed exploratory missions, and radio surveillance ships, known as DERs, DDRs, and AGTRs, kept up intensive surveillance around Cuba.

In short, during the crisis 85,000 men and 183 warships of the U.S. Navy, including eight aircraft carriers, were involved. Of that total, 40,000 were Marine Corps combat troops, ready for the invasion.

Air Force

The air force of the unified Atlantic Command, under Gen. Walter C. Sweeny, Jr., consisted of the 19th Air Army, to which units of the 9th and 12th armies were operationally added. This force was charged with the task of preparing tactical actions by air to act independently or in support of ground troops. A forward headquarters was established at Homestead Air Force Base, Florida, to direct air operations, using Atlantic Fleet and Marine Corps aircraft.

During the crisis, the United States used and drew upon 2,142 aircraft in support of operations, including those on aircraft carriers.* The plan for a surprise air strike against Cuba anticipated

---

were withdrawing R-12 missiles from Cuba, as a result of the agreements between the governments of the United States and the USSR. After the blockade was lifted, this task force's mission was to find and photograph ships leaving Cuba with IL-28 bombers.

* The force of aircraft comprised 75 heavy and medium fighter bombers, 790 Air Force fighter bombers, Navy attack fighters and bombers, 367 fighter interceptors, 145 surveillance aircraft, 600 transport aircraft, and 165 patrol aircraft and submarine chasers. (Information Directive of the EMG of the FAR, pp. 39–40)

1,190 sorties on day one for which 579 warplanes were ready.[23] The Air Force mobilized around 148,000 troops. Of these, approximately 15,000 men and 1,000 aircraft, with supplies for two weeks, were sent to Florida.

In order to concentrate tactical aircraft in preparation for operations, the U.S. administration started October 19 to move such forces to bases in Florida. All civil aviation flights over the peninsula and nearby areas were prohibited as a security measure. Rapid construction of a control tower at the naval air station in Key West began October 22; the tower has operated provisionally ever since.

That day, radio surveillance and antiaircraft defense units were sent to those areas. A radar network able to detect targets at a distance of 370 kilometers was installed. According to the U.S. command, this system ensured, in case of attack, the ability to give five minutes advance notice for the middle part of the U.S. East Coast and fifteen minutes notice for most Strategic Air Command (SAC) bases in the rest of the country.

The U.S. command intensified photographic surveillance of Cuban territory after October 23, following in detail construction of Soviet missile sites and other important military installations. In addition to U-2s, the RF-8A "Crusader," RF-101 "Voodoo," and RF-100 "Super Sabre" aircraft were used. On October 24, President Kennedy authorized low-altitude flights in groups of four to eight planes. In all, from October 22 to December 1, 1962, there were 386 flights over Cuba.

At noon on October 22, SAC bombers with their nuclear payloads started to spread out to thirty-three civilian airports in the United States, and on October 24 they went to highest alert (DEFCON-2). These forces* were ready to act against the socialist countries and against the USSR in particular. A quarter of the B-52 bombers were kept in the air at all times with their nuclear weaponry, a situation that was maintained for two

---

* At the time, the SAC comprised 600 B-52 and 800 B-47 bombers and 100 Atlas, 54 Titan, and 12 Minuteman missiles.

weeks. The rest of the aircraft had similar weaponry and were ready to take off in fifteen minutes.

The U-2 spy planes employed ten pilots. They belonged to the 4080th Strategic Reconnaissance Wing of the SAC, headquartered at Laughlin Air Force Base, Texas.

During the crisis, B-52 and B-47 bombers; F-4 and F-104 fighters; P-2, P-5, and S-2 aircraft and helicopters daily patrolled one million square miles over sea. Around ninety B-52 and B-47 heavy and medium bombers crossed the Atlantic, ready to carry out Kennedy's orders. In addition, F-4 and F-104 fighters from the 41st Fighter Squadron in Key West were on duty twenty-four hours a day over the Straits of Florida.

In all, U.S. aircraft logged 115,000 hours of flight time in direct support of the operations—30,000 hours by Navy aircraft and 85,000 by the Air Force. They are known to have suffered sixteen casualties for various reasons.[*]

Army forces

The army component of the unified Atlantic Command was made up primarily of troops and resources of the 18th Army Corps and the 1st Armored Division of the 3rd Army Corps, under the command of Gen. Herbert B. Powell. For the command and administration of these land forces a general staff was established at Fort Monroe, Virginia. A forward command post at Homestead Air Force Base, under the command of Gen. George T. Duncan, was responsible for activities of those forces in the southeastern United States.

The main units intended for use against Cuba were as follows: two airborne divisions (101st and 82nd); two infantry divisions (1st and 2nd); and one armored division (1st), which was

---

[*] Casualties were due to accidents during landing of two RB-47 aircraft, one in MacDill and the other in Bermuda; an accident in landing a C-135 aircraft in Guantánamo; a fourth accident when an F-104 fighter crashed during a military exercise carried out by a brigade of the 1st Armored Division on Hutchinson Island; and finally the death of Maj. Rudolf Anderson Jr. when his U-2 aircraft was shot down over Cuba.

transferred to the U.S. East Coast, unlike the others, which remained on alert in their respective bases.* Including 14,500 paratroopers, the army forces totalled 100,000 men, larger than the force that landed in Normandy. These divisions would make up a joint strike task force.

When the state of military alert was decreed, all units carried out intensive training to maintain and increase their combat readiness. They executed paratroop drops, airborne transports, and an amphibious landing exercise by a brigade of the 1st Armored Division, supported by tactical aircraft. Simultaneously, plans were readied for mobilizing reserve units to active duty.

The Second Logistic Command (SLC) was responsible for administrative matters and for material and combat supplies for the army. The SLC was transferred to Opa-Locka Air Base, Florida. Its troops comprised approximately 10,000 men, and its main units included engineering, communications, weapons technicians, transportation, medical supplies, and others.

The 3rd Army Corps was entrusted with defense of the continental United States. Antiaircraft units such as the 2nd Battalion of Nike-Hercules missiles of the 52nd Artillery Regiment and the 6th Battalion of Hawk missiles of the 65th Artillery Regiment were transferred by rail and air from Texas and from the Northeast to mainland Florida and the most important Florida keys for this purpose.

After October 16, in accord with the contingency plans under way, the armed forces of the United States were moving from one level of combat readiness to another. When President Kennedy announced the naval blockade, however, all U.S. troops worldwide went from peacetime status (DEFCON-5) to high-alert status (DEFCON-3). And when the "quarantine" was put into effect on October 24, the highest state of combat readiness

---

* The 82nd Airborne Division was based in Fort Bragg, North Carolina; the 101st Airborne Division in Fort Campbell, Kentucky; the 1st Infantry Division in Fort Riley, Kansas; and the 2nd Infantry Division in Fort Benning, Georgia.

short of actual war—DEFCON-2—was adopted.

The U.S. military preparations and mobilization continued even after the agreements on withdrawing Soviet missiles from Cuba. Some of the deployed units returned to normal readiness status starting on November 15, but the majority did so only in late November. The actions taken by the United States gives evidence of its preparedness not only for aggression against Cuba but also for a world war.

Chapter 7

The brilliant yet sad
days of the crisis

On October 22 the crisis erupted. From then on, not only the countries directly involved but the entire world was shaken by these momentous events, which posed a real and imminent danger of nuclear war.

The military measures taken by the United States were directed not only against Cuba but also against the USSR. These steps included putting the Strategic Air Command (SAC) on maximum alert, ordering nuclear submarines armed with Polaris missiles to leave their bases and take up attack positions, and placing in a state of combat readiness the ring of U.S. bases, with all their troops and equipment, that encircled the Soviet Union from Turkey to Japan. For its part, the Soviet Union made its strategic missile forces combat-ready and put its entire armed forces on maximum alert. In Europe the North Atlantic Treaty Organization (NATO) and the Warsaw Pact armies took similar measures.

The stance taken by the superpowers created worldwide turmoil. Starting on October 23 there were demonstrations in many countries against these actions, which threatened peace and endangered all humanity. Public opinion on the gravity of the events was expressed in various ways around the world. However, political conditions were not favorable for the protests to directly condemn the actions of the U.S. rulers, given the way in which the Soviet Union had deployed the missiles in Cuba and Kennedy's adroit manipulation of public opinion.*

Seven days on the brink of nuclear war

Cuba was not caught off guard. Noting the increase in U.S. military actions in the Caribbean,† the Cuban government had already begun taking action to meet the threat. Cuban intelligence units were kept on alert. Increasingly alarming reports poured in to the General Staff of the armed forces.

On October 21 it was learned that the U.S. naval base at Guantánamo had been reinforced with additional troops and matériel. Information was also obtained—through a secret channel—that in the early morning hours of October 22 the base commander had ordered the evacuation of civilian families of troops stationed at Guantánamo.[1] In accordance with Operational Directive no. 1,‡ and in light of the political-military situ-

---

* Voices were raised around the world, however, calling on the parties involved to act cautiously in order to avoid the outbreak of war. The telegrams sent by the well-known British philosopher and writer Bertrand Russell to both Kennedy and Khrushchev were one example. Russell criticized the U.S. president for taking a rash and unjustifiable step, and asked him to put an end to such foolishness. Russell also urged the Soviet leader to avoid hasty actions that might lead to the destruction of humanity. Another important protest was the message sent to the UN Security Council by Professor John D. Bernal, president of the World Peace Council, in which he condemned the blockade against Cuba as a serious threat to world peace.

† See chapter 6 for the October 15–30 air-and-sea military exercise called Phibriglex-62.

‡ On October 10, 1962, the General Staff had begun distributing Operational Directive no. 1 to the various armed forces commands, in order to ensure the strategic deployment of the FAR in the event of foreign aggression. See General Staff, Operational Directive no. 1, CID-FAR Archives, Military Unit 1081 Collection, Inventory 1, Record 2, File 1.

ation, orders began going out to Cuban combat units.

At noon on October 22, news arrived that the White House press secretary, Pierre Salinger, had reserved time that evening on all U.S. radio stations and TV channels for President Kennedy's address to the nation. From then on, the news media started to report on all meetings held in the presidential office.

Cuban authorities concluded that the flurry of activity in the U.S. capital had to do with discovery of the Soviet missile sites. Although they could not predict exactly what military action the U.S. would launch or where it would strike, they were certain that an attack was imminent. At 3:50 P.M. that day Prime Minister Fidel Castro, in his capacity as commander in chief, placed the armed forces on combat alert. Shortly afterward, at 5:35 P.M.—nearly an hour and a half before Kennedy spoke—a state of combat alarm was decreed for the entire country.[*]

That evening, Foreign Minister Raúl Roa instructed the Cuban ambassador to the United Nations, Mario García Incháustegui, to request an emergency session of the Security Council because—as Roa stated in his instructions—the naval blockade against Cuba announced by the U.S. president constituted "an act of war carried out behind the backs of international organizations, with absolute disdain for the Security Council, creating an imminent danger of war."[2]

Cuba's plans for wartime defense of the island involved organizing the military and political command structure into three operational regions based on the mountain ranges—eastern,

---

[*] During the night of October 22 and early morning of October 23, hundreds of thousands of Cubans were mobilized, with their weapons, and moved to their battle posts. A total of fifty-four infantry divisions, four brigades (one of tanks, and three of artillery), seventeen independent battalions, six artillery groups (multiple rocket launchers), three independent 120-mm. mortar groups, twenty units of the Revolutionary Navy, one hundred and eighteen antiaircraft batteries, and forty-seven warplanes were mobilized. A total of 269,203 people were mobilized, including 169,561 reservists and 99,612 on the active-duty rosters of the FAR. See "Draft Report Analyzing Experiences of the Recently Concluded Mobilization." Operations Directorate, Havana, December 19, 1962. CID-FAR Archives, Military Unit 1081 Collection, Inventory 1, Record 28, File 4.

central, and western. Each was headed by an authoritative commander who could lead the struggle and armed resistance independently. Commander Raúl Castro, minister of the Revolutionary Armed Forces, assumed command of Oriente province and its army. Commander Juan Almeida headed up the central provinces, with his headquarters in Santa Clara. Commander Ernesto Guevara, based in Pinar del Río, led the western region. Fidel Castro remained in Havana, at the head of the nation.

Meanwhile, the news reached Moscow that the Cuban high command had decided to put the armed forces first on alert and later on a full combat footing.* One hour before Kennedy's televised address,† moreover, U.S. ambassador Foy Kohler delivered to the Kremlin a personal message from the U.S. president to Soviet Premier Nikita Khrushchev, along with the public statement on the discovery of the missiles and the imposition of the naval blockade of Cuba. In the message, Kennedy warned Khrushchev that "the United States is determined that this threat . . . be removed." At the same time, he underlined that "the action we are taking is the minimum necessary." He stated that he hoped "that your Government will refrain from any action which would widen or deepen this already grave crisis and that we can agree to resume the path of peaceful negotiation."[3]

Khrushchev immediately convened a meeting of the Presidium of the CPSU Central Committee and the Soviet Defense Council to take whatever actions were necessary given the serious situation. General Gribkov later wrote that the Soviet command in Havana received a message from Defense Minister Malinovsky thirty minutes before the U.S. president began his October 22 address. Malinovsky ordered General Pliyev to "take immediate steps to raise combat readiness and to repulse the

---

* Both the Soviet embassy in Cuba and the Soviet troop command promptly reported the situation to Moscow.

† October 22, 6:00 P.M., in Washington—1:00 A.M. the following day in Moscow. There is a seven-hour time difference between the capital of the USSR and Cuba and the eastern United States in the Western Hemisphere.

enemy together with the Cuban army and with all the power of the Soviet forces, except Statsenko's means and Beloborodov's cargoes."*

Early on the morning of October 23, Marshal Malinovsky reported on the military actions by the United States, and proposed to put the Soviet armed forces on full combat alert. Khrushchev, on the other hand, called for caution, for projecting an image of calm, and for not rushing to make decisions that might touch off a war.† At the same time, Kruschchev gave instructions that the submarine fleet, antiaircraft defense, and strategic missile units cancel all leaves and put on hold retirements based on age until further notice.

Faced with the threat of war, Warsaw Pact countries ordered similar military measures. The TASS news agency ran a statement by the Soviet government denouncing the naval blockade as a serious threat to peace and a step toward unleashing thermonuclear war. It also warned the United States not to implement the measures Kennedy had announced against Soviet ships headed toward Cuba, and requested that the UN Security Council be convened promptly.

At the same time, the Soviet Foreign Ministry gave U.S. ambassador Kohler a copy of the official statement and a message from Khrushchev to Kennedy, which repeated that the weapons in Cuba were defensive and called the actions announced the previous day outrageous interference in the affairs of the Republic of Cuba as well as a provocative act against the

---

* "Statsenko's means" refers to the R-12 missiles. "Beloborodov's cargoes" were the Soviet nuclear warheads. Gribkov and Smith, *Operation Anadyr*, pp. 62, 181.

† The Soviet premier's daughter, Rada Khrushcheva, explained: "He [Khrushchev] decided that we should show that everything was all right and calm. He was therefore going to attend a performance at the Bolshoi Theater that night along with other top government and Party officials. The chief of his personal guard called and told me, 'I will send a car to take you to the Bolshoi Theater.' My father enjoyed the Bolshoi in particular, and theater performances in general, so I happily got dressed and we went to the Bolshoi Theater." Television program on the Cuban Missile Crisis broadcast October 17, 1992, by the ABC network in the United States.

Soviet Union. The Soviet premier also sent a letter to Fidel Castro, calling the U.S. actions piratical, perfidious, and aggressive. Khrushchev told Castro that he had given instructions to the Soviet military representatives in Cuba to take all necessary measures to be completely combat-ready.[4]

This message was interpreted by the Cuban leadership as a clear sign of Soviet determination not to give in to U.S. demands. Years later, Fidel exclaimed: "The idea of retreating never entered my mind."[5]

Coincidentally, on the morning of October 23 the Soviet ship *Aleksandrovsk* docked at the Cuban port of Isabela de Sagua, carrying on board the remaining nuclear missile warheads, without being detected by U.S. intelligence. This was very significant militarily, since it meant that the so-called quarantine announced by Kennedy had no strategic value. Politically, it was a powerful deterrent for the Soviets to use in negotiations to end the conflict. But this advantage was never utilized or even mentioned.[*]

In the morning, after giving the necessary instructions, Fidel Castro went to the central command post to get the latest reports on the state of mobilization. There he learned that U.S. warplanes were making low-altitude flights over Cuba—a dangerous military escalation.

That night the Cuban prime minister appeared on radio and television to refute charges made by the U.S. president the day before.[†] Fidel made it clear that he had no obligation to explain anything to the U. S. government, and he rejected the idea that the United States had the right to decide what kind of weapons

---

[*] As a result, for several years after the crisis it was believed that the Soviet forces in Cuba never had nuclear payloads. The facts were referred to for the first time at the tripartite conference in Moscow in January 1989, when General Dimitri Volkogonov gave the erroneous figure that there had been twenty nuclear warheads in Cuba. (For the actual number of warheads, see pages 123–24.) This issue was widely debated later at the Havana conference in 1992.

[†] For the October 23, 1962, address by Fidel Castro to the Cuban people, see pages 224–55.

or how many weapons Cuba should or should not have. He warned categorically that "appropriate measures to resist and . . . repel any direct aggression" had been taken. The Cuban leader also opposed the U.S. demand to inspect the island, because "we will never renounce our sovereign prerogatives. Within our borders we are the ones who rule, and we are the ones who will do the inspecting—nobody else."

One by one, Fidel refuted Kennedy's arguments for imposing the blockade. He denounced U.S. violations of the standards of conduct among nations, such as its repeated trespassing into Cuban air space and territorial waters. In another part of his speech, he stated that the government of Cuba was always willing to resolve its differences with the United States—under conditions of equality.

At the same time, the prime minister asserted that Cuba was in favor of dismantling all military bases and not stationing any foreign troops in the territory of another country. "If the United States desires disarmament, magnificent!" he said. "Let us all support a policy for the dismantling of bases, of troops throughout the world. . . . But we are not in agreement with a policy that calls for disarming ourselves in the face of the aggressors."

Meanwhile, in the United States the press and other media were spreading alarming news that frightened the population. People stocked up on food and all kinds of supplies. Some well-to-do families in the South began moving north for fear of a nuclear strike in their region.

In Washington, as part of U.S. maneuvers to obtain international backing for its actions and demands, Secretary of State Rusk was assigned to pressure OAS members to approve a resolution of support.

The OAS Council met in special session the morning of October 23. Despite U.S. pressure, it was not until the afternoon—an hour before the start of the UN Security Council meeting—that the proposal was approved, with nineteen votes in favor, none against, and one abstention, by Uruguay. The representatives of Mexico, Brazil, Chile, and Bolivia declared that their votes were subject to the constitutional limitations on their governments.[6] This OAS resolution called for the withdrawal of weapons classified as offensive, and for taking collective and individual action, including the use of force if necessary.*

Meanwhile, in the White House Oval Office, the ExComm met at 10:00 A.M. to track in detail the progress of events and military preparations. The State Department contacted the governments of Guinea, Senegal, Jamaica, and Trinidad and Tobago to pressure them to prohibit landings of Soviet aircraft. CIA Director McCone reported an increase in transmissions between the Soviet ships and Moscow. He also reported that submarines had been detected heading toward the Caribbean. The ExComm approved a new message from Kennedy to Khrushchev warning him to abide by the "quarantine."

At 7:00 P.M. Kennedy signed Proclamation 3504, ordering a naval blockade to start at 10:00 A.M. the following day, under the unified Atlantic Command. That night, Pentagon chief McNamara announced that twenty-five ships were approaching the interception line. Tension mounted. Admiral Anderson, chief of naval operations, warned that boarding the first two ships could result in a confrontation with Soviet submarines.

President Kennedy assigned his brother Robert to meet with Soviet Ambassador Dobrynin that night. In their conversation, Robert Kennedy insisted that Khrushchev had deceived the United States. The ambassador—still unaware of the existence of missiles in Cuba—denied that they were present on the island.

At UN headquarters in New York, the Security Council was

---

* In accord with this resolution some Latin American countries—Argentina, Venezuela, and the Dominican Republic—participated in the blockade of Cuba alongside U.S. forces. The governments of Ecuador, Colombia, Costa Rica, Honduras, Haiti, Guatemala, and Peru made offers of support to the United States of lesser magnitude. Some expressed willingness to send troops and weapons if necessary. Others offered their territory and authorized use of their harbors and airports by military units involved in the actions.

convened the afternoon of October 23 to hear representatives of the United States, Cuba, and the Soviet Union. The first to speak was Adlai Stevenson. He delivered a long speech seeking to present the blockade as an act of self-defense. He accused Cuba of receiving strategic weapons, and denounced the USSR for not making public the decision to provide them. He insisted that those weapons systems had altered the "precarious balance of forces" in the world. He also asserted that the Cuban government had allowed the Soviet Union to establish a beachhead and base of operations in the Western Hemisphere, inviting a foreign power to infiltrate the American family.

Cuban representative García Incháustegui spoke next, refuting Stevenson's assertions. He stated that Cuba had been compelled to arm itself due to repeated acts of aggression by the United States in flagrant violation of the UN Charter and inter-American agreements. He criticized the U.S. stance of adopting military actions first and later calling on the council, since the UN Charter obligates its members to settle differences through peaceful negotiations before resorting to such extreme measures. He commented on the striking contradiction that the United States was the only country that maintained a military base in Cuba—against Cuba's will—while at the same time it denounced Cuba for allowing the deployment of friendly troops from the Soviet Union. In conclusion, he presented the principled position of not allowing any kind of inspection of Cuban territory, because "the first thing that ought to be inspected are the U.S. bases from which invasions are launched. We do not accept observers of any kind in matters that fall under our internal jurisdiction."[7]

Soviet representative Valerian Zorin analyzed the pretexts and sophisms used by the U.S. government to justify its aggression, and denounced its actions as having no legal basis. He pointed out that the United States "has endangered maritime shipping of several countries—including its own allies—which do not accept such a foolish policy toward Cuba." He also denounced the diplomatic maneuver by the United States in the

OAS, which "openly violates the prerogatives of the Security Council—the only body that can authorize any acts of force."[8] After his statement the session was recessed.

While these debates were taking place in the Security Council, representatives of forty-five nations, mostly members of the Nonaligned Movement from Asia and Africa, met at the United Nations to discuss ways of resolving the crisis.* They agreed to ask the UN acting secretary-general, U Thant, to act as mediator and to convene a meeting of the General Assembly if the Security Council was not able to agree on a solution.

On the morning of October 24, Fidel—in his capacity as commander in chief of the armed forces—met with a group of commanders and officers at the General Staff headquarters to analyze the implementation of military measures to defend the country. The chief of intelligence, Captain Manuel de Jesús Quiñones *(Pedro Luis)*, estimated that in case of an invasion of Cuba, the United States would use five or six divisions, and that transporting them would require 120 or 130 ships and take at least six days. He pointed out there was no evidence that such an invasion was imminent. He said, however, that if the 82nd Airborne Division were activated, the first stage of the invasion could be carried out in five or six hours, although the increase in communications traffic and the number of aircraft involved would mean the operation could be quickly detected and pinpointed. He thought the most likely action was an air strike.[9]

Fidel Castro put special emphasis on antiaircraft defense, and he insisted the reserve batteries based in Havana had to be in a position to move quickly if necessary. Therefore, he ordered at least twenty-four of these batteries to be deployed at three points on the outskirts of the city, clustered in such a way that they could rapidly be moved to any location.

During the meeting it was reported that the previous day ten

* Five Latin American countries—Brazil, Mexico, Chile, Bolivia, and Venezuela—and four European countries—Finland, Sweden, the United Kingdom, and Austria—were also present.

enemy aircraft had violated Cuban air space, flying over Cuba at an altitude of 100 meters and then climbing sharply once they crossed the coastline. These aircraft could not be allowed to fly with impunity, Castro said. He proposed an investigation of the places where antiaircraft defense needed to be strengthened, so that such flights into Cuban airspace could be shot down. "There is no political reason whatsoever why we shouldn't shoot down an aircraft flying 300 feet over our heads," Fidel said.[10]

In closing the meeting, Fidel explained the military and political considerations that led to ordering the mobilization of October 22. He said that the Cuban leadership had indications an attack was being organized and therefore decided to put troops on alert and order a full mobilization, because "the harm done by taking precautions that later turned out to be unnecessary was preferable to the consequences of being caught by a surprise enemy attack."[11] The subsequent course of events fully justified such a decision.

That afternoon Castro visited a unit of Soviet surface-to-air missiles northeast of the capital. There he became aware how vulnerable they were to attack by low-flying aircraft,* since they had only one 14.5-mm. ZPU-2 double-barrelled antiaircraft machine gun. He ordered that fifty antiaircraft batteries from the reserves be immediately deployed to protect those positions and the mid-range missile sites.

As expected, the U.S. naval blockade was put into effect in the waters surrounding the Cuban archipelago at 10:00 A.M. that same morning, October 24, and aircraft raids—above all low-altitude flights—increased. Meanwhile, at the Pentagon, the Joint Chiefs of Staff ordered Gen. Thomas Powers, commander in chief of the Strategic Air Command (SAC), to put all his units on full-alert status, DEFCON-2, for the first and only time in the SAC's history. Then Powers, on his own initiative, decided to broadcast the orders to SAC commanders through uncoded

---

* As noted in Chapter 4, these antiaircraft missiles were not effective against targets flying below 1,000 meters.

messages, stressing that the operation was fully prepared and the alert process was proceeding smoothly. As General Powers himself commented, he felt it "important that [the Soviets] knew the state of combat readiness of SAC."[12] The military situation was becoming more and more dangerous to world peace.

The situation grew even more tense when Kennedy signed National Security Memorandum 199, authorizing the deployment of multiple nuclear weapons by the Supreme Allied Command in Europe. At the same time, France put its armed forces on Alert Status 2, one step below a general mobilization, further heating up the atmosphere in the European theater of operations.

At the United Nations on October 24, the Security Council began its 9:00 A.M. session with speeches by the representatives of Venezuela and the United Kingdom declaring their support for the U.S. action, while the Romanian delegate condemned it. Secretary-General U Thant explained that, at the request of a group of governments, he would mediate the conflict, and that he had already sent messages to Khrushchev and Kennedy, appealing to them not to take any action that might aggravate the situation and increase the risk of war. He also requested time for the parties involved to meet, with a view toward resolving the crisis peacefully and normalizing the situation in the Caribbean. To achieve this, he proposed a voluntary two-to-three-week suspension of both weapons shipments to Cuba and measures to "quarantine" the island.

U Thant made a similar appeal to the government of Cuba, urging it to look for some area of common interest to serve as a basis for discussions seeking a negotiated way out of the situation. He suggested that a halt in the construction of Soviet military installations during negotiations would contribute significantly to their success.

On the morning of October 25, Khrushchev responded to U Thant's appeal: "I understand your concern. . . . The Soviet Government also considers this situation as highly dangerous and requiring an immediate intervention by the United Nations. I am informing you that I agree with your proposal, which meets the interest of peace." For his part, Kennedy avoided giving U Thant a direct response that would commit the United States to anything. He said, "Ambassador Stevenson is ready to discuss these arrangements with you. I can assure you of our desire to reach a satisfactory and peaceful solution of the matter."[13]

The government of Cuba, through Ambassador Mario García Incháustegui, reaffirmed to U Thant Cuba's peaceful intentions, but reiterated that the United States had not provided any evidence that Cuba posed a threat to the security of the Western Hemisphere. The ambassador also stressed Cuba's right and obligation to defend itself in the face of the aggressive and interventionist U.S. stance.

Later on October 25, upon receiving information that a group of Soviet ships was approaching the blockade zone, U Thant made a second appeal to both governments to draw back from a confrontation. Once again he asked for time to continue efforts to mediate the issues.

The government of the USSR was the first to respond. It instructed the captains of its ships to stay outside the blockade zone. Those ships were carrying R-14 missiles and had submarine escorts, so any attempt to carry out an inspection could have provoked a serious incident.

By October 25, more and more Cubans, men and women of all ages and professions, were asking to take their place in defending the country. In face of the sharpening crisis and imminent danger of direct attack, a decision was made to organize People's Defense (Defensa Popular—DP) combat battalions and also to set up special civil defense units, including health and sanitation brigades, firefighters, and repair brigades.*

Another session of the Security Council took place on the

---

* By November 4 the Western and Central regions reported establishing 260 People's Defense battalions of 432 militia members each, totaling 112,320 troops. In the special units, Pinar del Río, Havana, and Matanzas provinces reported 3,038 health and sanitation brigades, with a total of 78,988 members. The Eastern region organized People's Defense battalions in the main cities and in Gibara, Moa, and Nicaro, as well as infantry companies in important towns and sugar mills, for

afternoon of October 25. According to various observers, these were the most heated discussions that had ever taken place in the Security Council. The U.S. representative opened the debate, acknowledging the steps taken by the Soviet government to preserve peace but then justifying once again the U.S. decision to take military action before turning to the United Nations. He claimed that military measures were necessary to defend the republics of the Americas. As evidence, he displayed the OAS resolution, in an effort to legalize his country's actions in the eyes of the international community. Stevenson also referred to Kennedy's letter to U Thant, accepting the secretary-general's offer to mediate the conflict. Stevenson said nothing, however, about lifting the blockade.

Valerian Zorin spoke next, explaining that the United States was trying to find a legal basis for its illegitimate conduct. The U.S. delegate interrupted Zorin's speech, trying to interrogate him—in a hectoring tone—and demanded he confirm the presence of offensive weapons in Cuba. Immediately afterwards, the U.S. delegate displayed aerial photos on an easel in the hall as proof of missile deployment in Cuba.

Faced with this clear evidence, the Soviet representative responded by asking why, if President Kennedy had this proof as early as October 16 (as he stated in his October 22 speech), he had said nothing about it during his long meeting with Soviet foreign minister Gromyko on October 18. If the U.S. president had no aggressive intentions and wanted to maintain normal, peaceful, and tranquil relations, why did he keep silent on October 18 and then four days later put the world at the brink of thermonuclear war by announcing a blockade? Zorin then mentioned the letter of Premier Khrushchev, clearly stating the

a total strength of around 25,000 combatants. Taking into account People's Defense militia members and troops belonging to regular units of the FAR, the number of armed men mobilized during the crisis was 400,000. "Documentos de la Defensa Popular relativos a la movilización durante la Crisis de Octubre" [Documents of the People's Defense concerning mobilization during the October Crisis], CID Archives, Military Unit 1081 Collection, Inventory 1, Record 8, Box 2.

intentions of the Soviet Union to seek a negotiated solution to the crisis and refuting Stevenson's interpretation of the Soviet Union's stance.

U Thant announced in this Security Council session that discussions would begin the following morning among representatives of Cuba, the United States, and the USSR to seek a solution to the crisis, and that the Security Council would postpone further deliberations until after those discussions.

Meanwhile Kennedy's third letter to the Soviet premier arrived in Moscow, in response to Khrushchev's letter the day before stating that the USSR would not accept the naval blockade. In this new message, the U.S. president strongly reproached Khrushchev for having deceived him and urged Khrushchev to permit a restoration of the earlier situation.

For the Soviet leadership, Kennedy's request for "restoration of the earlier situation" was the same as saying there should be no missiles in Cuba. This, together with the increasing danger of the situation, led Khrushchev on the evening of October 25 to instruct his aides to prepare a draft response to Kennedy. The missiles would be withdrawn under two conditions: first, a commitment by the United States not to invade Cuba, and second, U.S. withdrawal of its Jupiter missiles from Turkey and Italy.[14]

On the morning of Friday, October 26, the U.S. government continued its dangerous but calculated game—courting war, but not completely closing the door to the Soviet Union or forcing it to take drastic military action. The ExComm discussed whether the "quarantine" could accomplish the desired result of getting the missiles out of Cuba. Kennedy himself doubted that the blockade alone would result in withdrawal, which is why he proposed discussing other options, such as an invasion or possibly a trade-off—a tacit allusion to the Jupiter missiles stationed in Turkey. One of his decisions was to increase the frequency of low-altitude spy planes, from two flights a day to one flight every two hours.

On a parallel track, the White House tried using diplomatic

channels. The U.S. ambassador in Brazil, Lincoln Gordon, was instructed to give the Brazilian government a note on October 26 to be transmitted to Cuba. In peremptory terms, the note warned that, if the emplacement of so-called offensive weapons were not halted, then "further steps will have to be taken against Cuba and very soon."[15] The Brazilian representative in Havana, Luis Baian Pinto, gave Fidel Castro a message from President João Goulart outlining the U.S. plans. This information was interpreted in Cuba as a warning that Soviet missile installations would be attacked within twenty-four to seventy-two hours.

The possibility of a surprise air strike grew. One indication was the growing number of low-altitude flights; there had been eleven flights from October 22 through October 24, but on October 25 alone there were fifteen flights.

On the morning of October 26, the Cuban prime minister decided to stop such flights and gave the order that, as of the morning of October 27, Cuban forces were to open fire on any enemy aircraft flying at low altitude. He immediately called a meeting with General Pliyev, commander of the Soviet Troop Force in Cuba, to inform him of the decision.*

The meeting started the afternoon of October 26 and lasted into the night. All the main Soviet military leaders were present. Fidel, after outlining the reasons for the Cuban decision, used the occasion to try to persuade Pliyev of the need to turn on the radar detectors so that the antiaircraft missile installations would have sufficient advance warning of enemy incursions. He also strongly urged Pliyev: "Please don't keep all these missiles in the same sites. Deploy them in relatively distant sites, and preserve them from surprise air attacks, so that in the event of a

---

* Fidel also drafted a public communiqué to U Thant, which said: "Cuba does not accept the vandalistic and piratical privilege of any warplane to violate its airspace, as this threatens Cuba's security and prepares the way for an attack on its territory. Such a legitimate right of self-defense cannot be renounced; therefore, any warplane that invades Cuban air space does so at the risk of meeting our defensive fire." *Noticias de Hoy*, Havana, October 27, 1962, p. 1.

surprise air attack not all the missiles will be destroyed. . . . A surprise attack is not successful if at least one-third of the missiles survive."[16]

In that meeting, Fidel recounted later, General Pliyev "spoke to the commanders of the various units. They presented a report, and he said, 'Motorized mechanized units in combat readiness, the air force regiment in combat readiness, antiaircraft units ready, naval units ready, missile units ready.' That is exactly what he said: 'Missile units ready for combat.'"[17]

As October 26 ended, after verifying the country's preparations for defense down to the smallest detail, Castro sent a message to Khrushchev that was intended to give heart to the Russian leader, strengthen his moral resolve, and encourage him to stand firm, without errors or indecisiveness that could prove irreparable. In the letter Fidel told Khrushchev that, in light of the information and analysis he had received, "the aggression is almost imminent within the next 24 or 72 hours." In his judgment, Castro continued, "There are two possible variants: the first and likeliest one is an air attack against certain targets with the limited objective of destroying them; the second, less probable although possible, is invasion. I understand that this variant would call for a large number of forces and it is, in addition, the most repulsive form of aggression, which might inhibit them."

Fidel also reiterated his confidence that Cuba would "firmly and resolutely resist attack, whatever it may be," because "the morale of the Cuban people is extremely high and the aggressor will be confronted heroically."[18] Castro thought it necessary, however, to communicate to Khrushchev his opinion that an invasion of Cuba would in fact mean war against the Soviet Union, a war whose dynamic would lead—either simultaneously with the attack on Cuba or soon afterwards—to a U.S. nuclear strike against Soviet territory. Castro warned that the United States would not hold back and wait for the Soviet reaction, but would instead take the initiative, and he urged Khrushchev not to be caught by surprise and not to permit a repetition of Soviet mistakes in the Second World War.*

This message, drafted by Fidel at the Soviet embassy in Havana late on the night of October 26 and in the early morning hours of October 27, has sometimes been used to justify why the Soviets gave a rapid response to the United States without consulting Cuba. It has even been used to advance the tendentious theory that the leader of the Cuban Revolution was urging Khrushchev to carry out a preemptive nuclear strike against the United States. Both theories lack any objective basis. It is a proven fact that a U.S.-Soviet solution was already in the works before Fidel's message was decoded and read by the Soviet leadership at 1:15 A.M. October 28 (Moscow time). The content of the note itself shows it is completely false that Castro was suggesting a Soviet first strike. He warned that if an invasion occurred—which he said was the less likely variant—this would inevitably turn into total war. This danger was confirmed by history, when it was revealed that Soviet commanders in Cuba had tactical nuclear weapons and the authority to use them.

In addition to the discussions in international organizations like the United Nations, there was increasing private contact between the top leaders of the USSR and the United States, as well as the establishment of various secret channels for communication between Kennedy and Khrushchev.[19]

On October 26, despite attempts at negotiations in the UN, the Soviet leadership considered the situation to be deteriorating dangerously. At that point Khrushchev sent a coded message to Kennedy through the Soviet embassy in Washington, proposing to withdraw the missiles in exchange for an end to the naval blockade and assurances that the United States would not invade Cuba. "The question of armaments would disappear," the message said, "since, if there is no threat, then armaments

---

* The surprise attack by the Nazis on the USSR began June 22, 1941. The Soviet government had received intelligence that such an attack was coming and dismissed the reports as a provocation. It therefore failed to take the necessary defensive measures, which allowed the enemy to deal a powerful blow and to maintain the strategic initiative through the first months of the war.

are a burden for every people. Then, too, the question of the destruction not only of the armaments that you call offensive, but of all other armaments as well, would look different."[20]

That evening a secret meeting took place between Soviet ambassador Anatoly Dobrynin and Robert Kennedy. In the course of their conversation, Dobrynin took up the arguments thrown out by the United States in unleashing the conflict. He recalled that a U.S. missile base had been installed in Turkey, on the border of the USSR, without provoking a crisis. Robert Kennedy responded that if the USSR was interested in the withdrawal of missiles from Turkey, he would immediately consult his brother. He left the room and returned shortly to tell Dobrynin that the president had said the matter of missiles in Turkey could be examined. The substance of this meeting was immediately reported to the Kremlin.*

At 9:00 A.M. on October 27, Khrushchev sent a second message to Kennedy over Radio Moscow. It included the proposal for withdrawal of missiles from Turkey in exchange for the ones installed in Cuba, and for commitments by the Soviet government not to threaten the territorial integrity of Turkey, and by the U.S. government not to invade Cuba.[21] When the ExComm analyzed the two letters sent by the Soviet Premier, it concluded that the second message reflected a harder line on the part of the Moscow leadership. So Kennedy decided to respond not to that one but to the first. He wrote that day:

---

* Georgi Kornienko has revealed that when Khrushchev found out through various channels that the danger of confrontation between the two powers was escalating, the demand for withdrawal of U.S. missiles from Turkey and Italy was dropped. This explains why Khrushchev's first letter to Kennedy on October 26, transmitted through coded channels, did not include that demand. After the talks between Robert Kennedy and Dobrynin, when Moscow realized that other demands could be satisfied, a second message was drafted that same day that included the call for withdrawal of missiles from Turkey. It was sent through open channels so that it would reach Kennedy faster. Kornienko stated that it has never been explained why withdrawal of the missiles in Italy was omitted from the second message, and speculation was that this might have been a typographical error. (Tripartite conference on the Cuban Missile Crisis in Antigua, January 1991.)

"As I read your letter, the key elements of your proposals—which seem generally acceptable to me as I understand them—are as follows:

"1) You would agree to remove these weapons systems from Cuba under appropriate United Nations observation and supervision; and undertake, with suitable safeguards, to halt the further introduction of such weapons systems into Cuba.

"2) We, on our part, would agree—upon the establishment of adequate arrangements through the United Nations to ensure the carrying out and continuation of these commitments—(a) to remove promptly the quarantine measures now in effect and (b) to give assurances against an invasion of Cuba. I am confident that other nations of the Western Hemisphere would be prepared to do likewise.

"If you will give your representative similar instructions, there is no reason why we should not be able to complete these arrangements and announce them to the world within a couple of days. . . .

"But the first ingredient, let me emphasize, is the cessation of work on missile sites in Cuba and measures to render such weapons inoperable, under effective international guarantees."[22]

At the same time that Kennedy sent this message to Khrushchev, the White House released a public statement on the proposals made by the Soviet Union. It read: "It is therefore the position of the United States that as an urgent preliminary to consideration of any proposals, work on the Cuban bases must stop; offensive weapons must be rendered inoperable; and further shipment of offensive weapons to Cuba must cease—all under effective international verification."[23]

On Saturday, October 27, the situation was extremely tense and complex. When U.S. aircraft flew into Cuban air space, all the antiaircraft batteries opened fire, as ordered. Fidel later explained, "We could say that the war started in Cuba on October the 27th in the morning. Of course, those fast-flying jet planes, as soon as they heard the first shots, went higher to evade our artillery. . . . We couldn't shoot down any of the low-flying planes.

But we demonstrated our resistance."[24]

That same day, a u-2 flew over Cuba, as had become common. Soviet troops in Cuba also decided to fight back, out of an elementary spirit of solidarity at a time when Cubans had begun firing on enemy aircraft. The u-2 was shot down over Banes, in eastern Cuba, at 10:17 a.m., killing the pilot, Maj. Rudolf Anderson.

This event has been used to try to show that by giving the order to fire on U.S. aircraft, it was the Cuban leaders who put the world on the brink of nuclear war, at a time when the crisis had practically been resolved. But that assertion is utterly false. First of all, nobody in Cuba knew about the secret negotiations between Khrushchev and Kennedy. Moreover, the U.S. side—including the U.S. military—did know of the negotiations, and yet took no steps whatsoever to reduce tensions.

That same day, October 27, Fidel Castro wrote to the UN secretary-general assuring him that "Cuba is willing to discuss its differences with the United States as much as necessary, and to do everything it can to cooperate with the United Nations to resolve the present crisis; but Cuba flatly rejects any act violating the sovereignty of our country."[25] This letter was proof of Cuba's willingness to seek a peaceful solution to the crisis, while not backing off from its principles or yielding its sovereignty under pressure from the United States. The letter also reaffirmed that negotiations were possible only under conditions of equality.

The Soviet command in Cuba immediately reported the downing of the u-2 to the Soviet defense minister, who did not express disapproval. Marshal Malinovsky only sent a coded message saying that the troops had acted hastily, since the crisis had entered a phase of negotiations. That same day, Pliyev received another coded message from the defense minister that issued an order categorically prohibiting Soviet forces "to use nuclear armaments for missiles, the FKRs, the 'Lunas' and the aircraft without authorization from Moscow."[26]

Another dangerous incident occurred that day, when a U.S. spy plane of the same kind violated Soviet air space over the

Chukotsk Peninsula at the far eastern end of Siberia.

Meanwhile, a second nighttime meeting took place in Washington between the Soviet ambassador and Robert Kennedy. At that meeting Kennedy threatened Dobrynin that he must give an immediate answer, because events were accelerating and could get out of the president's control at any time. He indicated that the problem of missiles in Turkey would be resolved, but that this should not be made public, because the matter would first be taken up within NATO.

On Sunday, October 28, the White House received the Kremlin's response, broadcast over Radio Moscow with evident urgency. It confirmed the terms of Khrushchev's letter of the 26th, accepted by Kennedy, "in your message of 27 October 1962 that there would be no attack, no invasion of Cuba, and not only on the part of the United States, but also on the part of other nations of the Western Hemisphere, as you said in your same message. Then the motives which induced us to render assistance of such a kind to Cuba disappear.

"It is for this reason that we instructed our officers . . . to take appropriate measures to discontinue construction of the aforementioned facilities, to dismantle them, and to return them to the Soviet Union. . . . We are prepared to reach agreement to enable U.N. representatives to verify the dismantling of these means."[27]

In the White House, Kennedy also hastened to respond to Khrushchev: "I consider my letter to you of October twenty-seventh and your reply of today as firm undertakings on the part of both governments which should be promptly carried out. I hope that the necessary measures can at once be taken through the United Nations, as your message says, so that the United States in turn will be able to remove the quarantine measures now in effect. I have already made arrangements to report all these matters to the Organization of American States, whose members share a deep interest in a genuine peace in the Caribbean area."[28]

Along with the letter to the head of the Soviet government,

Kennedy released a public statement that same Sunday, expressing satisfaction with Khrushchev's decision to discontinue the construction of bases in Cuba, to dismantle "offensive" weapons, and to return them to the Soviet Union under UN verification.[29]

All humanity breathed a sigh of relief. The threat of confrontation between the two nuclear superpowers had passed. For Cuba, however, the danger was not over. U.S. armed forces maintained the naval blockade and were poised for an air strike or invasion. Not all members of the ExComm received Khrushchev's message with relief. Some military and civilian members voiced dissatisfaction with the solution agreed to, arguing that Washington had failed to take advantage of the situation to overthrow the Cuban regime. Adm. George Anderson, chief of naval operations, complained loudly—to the surprise of some—that "We have been had." Gen. Curtis LeMay, air force chief of staff, backed him up and expressed the idea, "Why don't we go in and make a strike on Monday anyway."[30] But the idea went nowhere. At that point the United States had no pretext to justify an attack.

Chapter 8

In defense of principles

The Cuban leadership learned from a Radio Moscow broadcast of Khrushchev's October 28 letter to Kennedy ordering the removal of missiles from Cuba. Hours later, Fidel received a brief message from the Soviet leader, who recommended that the Cubans not let themselves be carried away by emotion.[1] In the same vein, he requested that they suspend the order to fire on low-flying aircraft, in order to avoid a new incident that might scuttle the agreement with Kennedy at the last minute and allow the foolhardiness of the militarists in the United States to prevail.

Fidel later described the repercussions in Cuba of those agreements: "When this news reached us . . . it produced great indignation, because we had felt that we had become some kind of bargaining chip. Not only was this a decision taken without *consulting* us, several steps were taken without *informing* us. They could have informed us of the messages of the 26th and the 27th. . . . We heard over the radio on the 28th that there had been an agreement. . . . The reaction of our nation was of profound indignation, not relief."[2]

Khrushchev argued that given the seriousness of the situation, there had not been time for consultation, but the Cubans were not convinced. The problem went deeper than merely bad procedure. Even allowing a supposed "lack of time," it was unacceptable that Khrushchev, in drafting the message to Kennedy, failed to consider Cuba's participation in the negotiations. As Fidel said, "The simple solution of withdrawing the missiles because the United States gave its word it wasn't going to attack us was inconsistent with everything that had been done, and inconsistent with the circumstances in our country that had to be overcome. It would have been enough for Nikita to say, 'We agree to withdraw the missiles if you give satisfactory guarantees for Cuba.'"[3]

Besides, Khrushchev's response could open the door for the U.S. government to make new demands, as in fact Washington did by demanding on-site verification of the withdrawal of missiles and other weapons. Thus Washington, in flagrant violation of Cuba's sovereignty, tried to claim rights that belonged exclusively to Cuba.

On the afternoon of October 28, Fidel Castro reported Cuba's position in a public statement. "The guarantees mentioned by President Kennedy that there will be no aggression against Cuba," it said, "will be ineffective unless, in addition to the removal of the naval blockade that he promises, the following measures, among others, are adopted:

"1. Cessation of the economic blockade and all measures of commercial and economic pressure being carried out by the United States against our country throughout the world.

"2. Cessation of all subversive activities, of the dropping by air and landing by sea of weapons and explosives, of the organization of mercenary invasions, and of the infiltration of spies and saboteurs—all of which are being carried out from the territory of the United States and certain accomplice countries.

"3. Cessation of the acts of piracy being carried out from bases in the United States and Puerto Rico.

"4. Cessation of all violations of our air space and territorial waters by United States aircraft and warships.

"5. Withdrawal of the Guantánamo naval base and return of the Cuban territory occupied by the United States."[4]

Cuba's position was sharp and clear: if a true solution were to be found to the tension and problems, these guarantees had to be conceded. They were five concrete points, soundly based. Yet the U.S. rulers did not want to consider them. They declared the five-point program to be unfeasible at that time, while they also demanded inspection of Cuban territory as a way of verifying the Soviet commitment.

Why were the five points considered unfeasible? Weren't Cuba's demands absolutely just and based on the country's indisputable rights? An end to the economic blockade and trade pressures, as stipulated by Cuba, were a necessity, because those were elements aggravating the situation that produced the crisis. Moreover, what was impossible about demands to end U.S. subversive and covert actions, acts of piracy, and violations of Cuba's territorial waters and airspace? The Cuban government was simply asking that those crimes and other illegal acts not be committed against its country.

And as for the last demand—withdrawal from the U.S. naval base in Guantánamo and the return of occupied Cuban territory—was this not a logical, reasonable request under the circumstances? It was simply absurd to ask for the withdrawal of the weapons provided to Cuba by a friendly power while leaving an enemy military enclave on Cuban territory. No one with a modicum of dignity anywhere in the world would question the inalienable right of the Cuban people on this issue.

The five-point program received great popular support, because the Cuban people had long and bitter experience with the U.S. government's lack of sincerity. The repeated violations of international law by U.S. administrations, economic aggression, the infiltration of teams of saboteurs, weapons, munitions, and other supplies into different points of the country to promote counterrevolutionary groups, as well as the latest pirate attacks along the Cuban coast, all made it imperative to demand something more than words from the White House.

On October 28 Fidel Castro drafted a reply to Khrushchev to convey the position of the Cuban government and to clarify why it had given the order to fire on low-flying aircraft, noting that the Soviet command in Cuba could furnish additional reports on the downing of the U-2. Castro also indicated that he agreed on the need to avoid an incident at that moment, when it might cause major harm to the negotiations. He said that he would therefore instruct Cuban antiaircraft batteries to hold their fire, but only for as long as negotiations continued, and without revoking the previous day's declaration on defending Cuba's airspace. This message showed Fidel's willingness to avoid obstructing the steps being taken by the Soviets, in spite of his disagreement with the basis on which they were taken. Finally, he reaffirmed that Cuba was as a matter of principle opposed to allowing inspection of its territory.[5]

Events proved him right. On the afternoon of October 28, four State Department officials went to New York to try to persuade U Thant to order an immediate inspection of the missile bases in Cuba, since on-site verification had been approved by the Soviets. The UN secretary-general did not accept such a request, because it went beyond his authority.

Two days later, on October 30, the Cubans received Khrushchev's reply to Fidel, seeking to explain the events leading up to the October 28 commitments. In an obvious attempt to justify his conduct, the Soviet leader argued that any other stance would have meant a global holocaust and the destruction of the Cuban Revolution. As an argument for his decision to withdraw the missiles, Khrushchev recalled that prior to that he had received various messages from Cuba, "each one more alarming." He craftily claimed that Fidel's cable of October 27 represented a sort of exchange of ideas between the two governments. "Wasn't this consultation on your part with us?" Khrushchev asked. As if that were not enough, he criticized the Cuban leader for— according to Khrushchev—proposing that the Soviet Union launch a nuclear first strike against the enemy. Finally, he maintained the negotiations had won the objective for which the missiles had been sent to Cuba, since a promise had been extracted from the United States not to invade Cuba nor to allow its Latin American allies to do so.[6]

Fidel lost no time in replying. On October 31 he sent a message reaffirming the point of view of the Cuban leadership. "We knew," Fidel wrote, "that we would have been annihilated, as you insinuate in your letter, in the event of nuclear war. However, that didn't prompt us to ask you to withdraw the missiles, that didn't prompt us to ask you to yield. Do you believe that we wanted that war? But how could we prevent it if the invasion finally took place? The fact is that this event was possible, that imperialism was obstructing every solution and that its demands were, from our point of view, impossible for the USSR and Cuba to accept."

Regarding Khrushchev's serious allegation that he had proposed launching a nuclear first strike, Fidel replied that he never said any such thing "because that would be more than incorrect, it would be immoral and contemptible on my part." He explained that "once aggression is unleashed, one shouldn't concede to the aggressor the privilege of deciding." Likewise, he reaffirmed, "Everyone has his own opinions and I maintain mine about the dangerousness of the aggressive circles in the Pentagon and their preference for a preemptive strike." Fidel ended his message saying, "I do not see how you can state that we were consulted in the decision you took. . . . There are not just a few . . . but in fact many Cubans who are experiencing at this moment unspeakable bitterness and sadness."[7]

The Cuban leadership took up these disagreements directly with their Soviet counterparts, seeking not to harm friendly relations between the peoples of the two countries. That is why, after everything that had happened, when Fidel addressed the Cuban people on November 1, 1962, he explained that—in those moments when misunderstandings and disagreements had provoked hard feelings—it was good to remember that "in every one of the difficult moments we have had, every time the Yankees lashed out at us—with economic aggression, with the revocation of our sugar quota, with the cutoff of oil deliveries to our country . . . we have had the friendly hand of the Soviet Union at our side. We are grateful."[8]

Negotiations to end the crisis

On Monday, October 29, at the United Nations, the Soviet delegation announced the appointment of Vice Minister of Foreign Affairs Vasily V. Kuznetzov to lead its negotiations with the United States. It was also announced that Secretary-General U Thant would leave for Havana the next day, at the invitation of the revolutionary government, for direct discussions. U Thant arrived along with undersecretaries Omar Loufti and Hernane Tavares de Sa, and military adviser Gen. Indar Jit Rikhye.

Talks began immediately and lasted into the following day.[*] The Cuban participants were Prime Minister Fidel Castro, President Osvaldo Dorticós, Foreign Minister Raúl Roa, and Carlos Lechuga, newly appointed Cuban representative to the UN.

U Thant explained the efforts he had made and the proposals by the U.S. and Soviets to verify removal of the missiles. He explained that the United States wanted to devise a UN mechanism that could provide assurance that missile sites were dismantled and withdrawn, and that such weapons did not enter Cuba thereafter. To do that, he proposed that an aircraft with Cuban, U.S., and Soviet crew members verify the process for several weeks. Concerning the Soviet proposal, he said that they would allow a commission of the International Red Cross to monitor the movement of their ships. U Thant stated that he had no authority to associate himself with those initiatives unless the Cuban government agreed to them. He also reported that the Movement of Nonaligned Countries was willing to assist.

Fidel asked him what right the United States had to demand

---

[*] See pages 256–84. The minutes of the October 30–31 talks between the government of Cuba and the secretary-general of the United Nations are in the archives of the Institute of Cuban History.

those conditions of verification. None, replied U Thant, since something like that could be done only if it were accepted by Cuba's government. The Cuban leader then argued for the guarantees that Cuba was demanding, based on its five points. If these were taken into account, then the negotiating process could lead to real peace in the region. Fidel also put forward the reasons of principle underlying Cuba's rejection of the proposed verification. "If what the United States is actually seeking is to humiliate our country," he stated, "it will not succeed!"[9]

The reasons for not permitting inspection were based, in the first place, on the country's unwillingness to sacrifice its sovereignty, especially when the power that demanded those conditions wanted to interfere in Cuba's internal affairs—in this case, trying to dictate what kind of weapons Cuba could possess. Secondly, this was a demand under threat of force, to which Cuba would never give in. Finally, there was the logical question: if the Soviets and the United Nations both trusted Washington's public promise not to invade Cuba, why then did the U.S. government doubt that the USSR would remove the missiles? Why impose the additional guarantee of inspecting Cuba?

Throughout the second day of talks, Cuba maintained its point of view and warned of the danger of violations of its airspace, stressing that these must cease.

U Thant expressed his view of what was happening: "My colleagues and I believe—and I have let the United States know this—that the blockade is illegal, that no state can tolerate a blockade, whether military or economic. . . . I also told them that the reconnaissance flights being made over Cuba were illegal and unacceptable. These three things—economic blockade, military blockade, and aerial reconnaissance—are illegal." Likewise, the secretary-general told the Cuban leaders that in his talks with U.S. representatives he had told them that "if they were to take some drastic action, I would not only report it to the Security Council, but I would also accuse the United States in the Security Council; and that even though the United States might have the votes and the veto, there could still be a moral sanction."

U Thant requested the return, on humanitarian grounds, of the body of the U.S. pilot who had been shot down, to which the Cuban government immediately agreed.

When he returned to New York, U Thant indicated that his talks with Cuban authorities had been fruitful, and he reported having reliable evidence that the missile sites were being dismantled and the necessary measures were being taken for their return to the USSR. This last statement was based on meetings held at the Soviet embassy in Havana, where Soviet officers assured him that the missiles would be dismantled by November 1 and sent to the ports from which they would be shipped.

The withdrawal of medium-range missiles had begun October 31, as promised by the USSR. Cuba did not put up any obstacle to the withdrawal. The Soviet and Cuban attitude stood in contrast to that of the U.S. administration, which maintained the naval blockade and stepped up its low-level flights over Cuba.

Soviet Vice Premier Anastas I. Mikoyan was sent to Cuba to discuss the differences that had arisen between Moscow and Havana. Prior to his arrival he made a brief stop in New York, where he talked with Vasily V. Kuznetzov, head of the Soviet delegation at the United Nations, and with U Thant. In addition, he exchanged opinions with Adlai Stevenson and John J. McCloy, the U.S. representatives appointed by Kennedy to negotiate with the Soviet delegates. Stevenson and McCloy insisted on inspection of the dismantling of the missile sites in Cuba, and hinted at new demands.

U Thant assured the press in New York that the Cuban perspectives for peace in the region seemed good for all involved, and said that he would not convene the Security Council until an agreement was reached among the parties. Meanwhile, in Washington, President Kennedy continued to insist on international inspection of the missile sites before he would agree in the United Nations that Moscow had fulfilled its commitments. The U.S. administration tried to ignore Cuba, and would not make contact with Cuba to discuss matters that directly concerned it. This attitude hampered the process of negotiations.

Mikoyan arrived in Havana on Friday afternoon, November 2. His stay in Cuba would stretch out to three weeks.* The talks, which began the morning of November 4, were by no means easy for the Soviet leader. No matter how strongly he argued for the necessity of precipitously withdrawing the missiles, it was no simple matter to defend the unilateral decision to withdraw them without consulting Cuba—the main interested party and participant in the events. The first point discussed was the proposed verification of the missile withdrawal by an international commission. The Soviet leader proposed various alternatives, none of them essentially different. Fidel argued Cuba's position of rejecting inspection, on the grounds that the U.S. goal was to violate Cuba's sovereignty.

Mikoyan then proposed allowing inspection of the ships. Fidel responded that this was up to the Soviet Union, as long as it was not done in Cuban territorial waters. The Cuban attitude was not capricious, he pointed out, because if Cuba gave in to the asserted U.S. right to inspect, Washington would then demand new concessions. Mikoyan promised he would not allow the imposition of new conditions, such as withdrawal of the IL-28 bombers. Later he had to explain that the Soviets had given in to that demand, which was undoubtedly very embarrassing. Nevertheless, both parties made efforts to overcome stumbling blocks, so as not to make their relations more tense than they already were.

On Tuesday, November 6, the U.S. government—now convinced that the missiles had been dismantled, and accepting the Soviet proposal to inspect its ships on the high seas—officially added a new demand: withdrawal of the IL-28s, which were suddenly declared to be "offensive" weapons. In an attempt to step up tension and exert more pressure on Cuba, the U.S. Defense Department reported that it was closing the Panama Canal to other traffic to allow passage of seventeen warships—includ-

---

* Upon his arrival, Mikoyan received news of his wife's death. He decided to send his son Sergo, his secretary on this trip, back to the USSR, and to continue his talks with the Cuban leadership.

ing aircraft carriers, destroyers, and submarines—to join the forces already deployed in the Caribbean.

On November 7, the U.S. delegation at the United Nations announced agreement with the USSR on visual verification of the missile withdrawal and inspection by the International Red Cross of Soviet merchant ships bound for Cuba. This still wasn't enough for Washington, however, which maintained that adequate verification had to be performed on site and demanded withdrawal of the IL-28s. This stance was maintained as a lever of political pressure, in order at the right moment to justify its failure to fulfill its own commitments.

Negotiations continued at the United Nations. On Thursday, November 8, U Thant met separately with Lechuga and Kuznetzov to discuss the new U.S. demand to withdraw the bombers. Later, U.S. and Soviet delegates met about the same issue, but after four hours of talks were unable to reach any agreement. The United States insisted that the IL-28s were "offensive weapons" and therefore had to be removed in line with the Khrushchev-Kennedy agreement. The Soviets replied that they were outmoded aircraft and represented no threat to the United States.

On Monday, November 12, the head of a CIA special operations group, Miguel A. Orozco Crespo, was shown on Cuban television. He had been captured on the Malas Aguas farm in Viñales, Pinar del Río province, while preparing a bloody sabotage of the Matahambre copper mine and the Sulfo-metals plant in Santa Lucía. Had this sabotage been carried out, hundreds of workers would have lost their lives.*

Meanwhile, an official statement by the U.S. administration reported that the withdrawal onboard Soviet ships of forty-two missiles installed in Cuba had now been verified. With the hysteria around the missiles dissipated, the United States tried to step up pressure to obtain a second demand. The White House press secretary announced November 12 that the U.S. govern-

---

* The terrorist commando squad had been infiltrated into Cuba on the northern coast of Pinar del Río in the early morning hours of October 20.

ment had not changed its position that the IL-28s were offensive weapons and therefore must be removed before the naval blockade would be lifted.

New declarations were issued for the purpose of maintaining tensions in the Caribbean. On Wednesday, November 14, State Department spokesman Lincoln White declared that the United States would not tolerate the building of "military installations" in Cuban ports. He was referring to the construction of a fishing port near Banes, in Oriente province.

Washington compounded all these threats with constant violations of Cuban airspace by low-flying reconnaissance aircraft. A policy of force and pressure was being given top priority in order to block resolution of the crisis. Under those circumstances Fidel sent a letter to U Thant on Thursday, November 15, protesting the incursions by U.S. aircraft, which were photographing not only the dismantled sites but the entire territory of Cuba. The prime minister explained in his letter that such actions not only infringed upon the vital security of the country, but also insulted the dignity of the Cuban people. It was not possible to ask Cuba to tolerate such an outrage in the name of negotiations, Fidel said. He warned: "To the extent of the firepower of our antiaircraft weapons, any warplane that violates the sovereignty of Cuba by invading our airspace will do so at the risk of being destroyed."*

A U.S. State Department spokesman replied to the Cuban protest the next day, insisting that such flights over Cuba would continue and that they were being carried out in accordance with OAS agreements of October 23. In fact, however, the low-level flights ceased, while high-altitude U-2 flights continued. During a television interview on November 17, Roswell Gilpatric, deputy secretary of defense, went to the extreme of declaring

---

* Fidel Castro, "Carta al Secretario General de las Naciones Unidas U Thant, 15 de noviembre de 1962" [Letter to UN Secretary-General U Thant, November 15, 1962]. *Política Internacional*, no. 1, 1963, p. 237. After withdrawal of the R-12 missiles, low-level flights increased considerably. Between November 4 and 8, 124 overflights were carried out, with 36 on one single day, November 8.

that such flights "were a right" of the United States.

Negotiations continued at the UN on Sunday, November 18, with none of the parties yielding. The White House had officially said it would lift the blockade as soon as the Soviet Union agreed to remove the IL-28s, but the Soviets refused to do so without Cuba's consent.

A press campaign was now unleashed in the United States accusing Cuban leaders of obstructing resolution of the crisis because they refused to accept on-site inspection, would not tolerate reconnaissance flights over Cuba, and opposed withdrawal of the IL-28s. With the deterrent threat of the missiles removed, and with the Soviet Union showing signs of vacillation on the U.S. demands, conditions were being created in the eyes of U.S. and world opinion to justify a military attack on Cuba.

Kennedy rejected various offers by Khrushchev, maintained the "quarantine," and then announced that he would report to the press on November 20 what further steps the U.S. government might take. On November 19 he prepared letters for British Prime Minister Harold MacMillan, German Chancellor Konrad Adenauer, and French President Charles DeGaulle informing them that the crisis was about to heat up again and that he was considering extending the naval blockade and carrying out a massive air strike against Cuba.[10]

On Monday, November 19, the Cuban prime minister made public a new message to the UN secretary-general, in which he warned about the dishonesty of the anti-Cuba campaign by the U.S. administration and press. "The Government of Cuba," Fidel stated, "has not created the slightest obstacle to the negotiations that are taking place. This has been and it is our position. Our attitude to the threats and insults of the Government of the United States is something very different." He also explained how Washington had made withdrawal of the IL-28s the crux of the problem, and how this showed its arrogant attitude aimed at maintaining tension, prolonging the conflict, and continuing the U.S. policy of force. Fidel pointed out that those aircraft were the property of the Soviet Union, and that if the USSR considered their withdrawal beneficial to the negotiations and the solution of the crisis, Cuba would not object to such a decision.[11]

On Tuesday, November 20, fifteen hours after Fidel's communiqué to U Thant, a message from Khrushchev arrived at the White House, in which he announced that the IL-28s would be withdrawn within thirty days.

In a news conference that day, Kennedy stated that dangers had been reduced due to the Soviet decision to withdraw "offensive weapons." He added, "If all offensive weapons systems are removed from Cuba and kept out of the hemisphere in the future, under adequate verification and safeguards, and if Cuba is not used for the export of aggressive Communist purposes, there will be peace in the Caribbean." He immediately added the threat: "We will not, of course, abandon the political, economic, and other efforts of this hemisphere to halt subversion from Cuba nor our purpose and hope that the Cuban people shall some day be truly free. But these policies are very different from any intent to launch a military invasion of the island."[12]

Kennedy also let it be known that he would continue air incursions over Cuba, under the pretext that the Cubans had not permitted international observers into the country. These words expressed the determination to maintain a provocative and aggressive policy against the Cuban Revolution.

Moments after the news conference ended, Defense Secretary McNamara announced that he had ordered the Navy to end the blockade that had begun on October 24. Also on November 20, the USSR and other members of the Warsaw Pact declared that their armed forces had returned to normal status. Similar measures were taken in Cuba two days later.

Conclusion of the negotiating process

The National Directorate of the Integrated Revolutionary Organizations and the Council of Ministers of the Republic of Cuba met in joint session on the afternoon of Sunday, November 25, to take up issues involved in resolving the crisis and to discuss their reply to President Kennedy's statement of November 20, when he announced the lifting of the naval blockade. The meeting resolved to make a public declaration so that the people of Cuba and the world would know the position of the party and the government of Cuba.

This document rejected the U.S. demand for on-site verification to fulfill the agreement with the USSR and stated, "Cuba has a sovereign right, based on the United Nations Charter, to agree or not to agree to inspection of its territory. Cuba has never offered or agreed to such verification. . . . President Kennedy's claim is groundless. It is merely a pretext for not carrying out his part of the agreement and for persisting in his policy of aggression against Cuba."*

It also stated that inspection would be undertaken only on a reciprocal basis and argued that if "the U.S. government demands that the United Nations should verify, in our territory, the withdrawal of strategic weapons, then "Cuba demands that the United Nations should verify in the territory of the United States, Puerto Rico, and other places where attacks on Cuba are prepared . . . the dismantling of the training camps for mercenaries, spies, saboteurs, and terrorists; of the centers where subversion is prepared; and of the bases from which pirate vessels set out to attack our coasts. . . . Only through reciprocal concessions and guarantees will it be possible to reach a broad and honorable agreement acceptable to all."

Faced with repeated efforts by the U.S. government to intervene in Cuba's internal affairs, and decide what kind of weapons it could possess, the statement proclaimed that Cuba "reserves the right to acquire weapons, of whatever type. for its defense and will take such steps as it deems appropriate to strengthen its security."

The party and the Cuban government reaffirmed their conclusion that the results obtained so far in the U.S.-Soviet negotiations had prevented an armed conflict, but they had not

* See pages 285–91 for the full text of the statement. Published as "Posición de Cuba ante la Crisis del Caribe" [Cuba's position on the Caribbean Crisis"], *Ediciones COR*, no. 9, December 1962, p. 90.

achieved peace in the Caribbean. To that end, the document concluded, "We do not believe in mere promises of nonaggression; we need deeds. Those deeds are set forth in our five points."

At 10:00 A.M. on Monday, November 26, Mikoyan left for the United States, where he talked with the Soviet and U.S. representatives at the United Nations and met with President Kennedy. The Soviet vice premier met that day with U Thant to exchange opinions on the progress of the negotiations and to inform him that both the Soviet and Cuban governments supported his plan for establishing UN control posts in Caribbean countries, including on United States territory, where international observers would oversee compliance with the commitments agreed to by the three countries.[13]

Furthermore, the USSR and Cuba had drafted a tripartite protocol presented for approval by the three countries. The intransigent position of the U.S. government, however, blocked any negotiations in which Cuba was represented, thus dooming both U Thant's initiative and the draft protocol. Cuba's UN representative, Carlos Lechuga, had instructions from his government that if the protocol were not accepted, the Cuban points were to be firmly maintained in a separate statement.

From then on, the three countries drew up separate draft statements to be discussed in the Security Council. The U.S. delegation presented its draft on November 27, introducing new demands. It called for withdrawing all weapon systems that have "offensive" goals, for example, a vague formulation that could imply any kind of weapon that the United States asserted to be for that purpose. Thus the U.S. continued trying to legitimize its interest in controlling what weapons Cuba could have for defense. Washington also tried to assert the right to continue reconnaissance flights through Cuban airspace, which it justified as a means of supervising the Soviet government's obligation not to send "offensive" weapons to the island.[14]

The document also made the U.S. commitment not to invade conditional on Cuba not taking actions that endangered the peace and security of the Western Hemisphere. By accepting such a demand, Cuba would hand over to the U.S. rulers the ability to fabricate any kind of pretext or incident to breach the agreement. Thus if social or revolutionary conflicts broke out in Latin America, these could be considered "subversive actions" by Cuba, providing the pretext for the U.S. to intervene militarily.

The draft statement presented by the USSR clearly laid out the commitments made by the USSR and the United States during the negotiating process. This document supported the proposal of creating UN control posts in the Caribbean as a way to verify fulfillment of the commitments by all countries and to ensure that no party could take unexpected steps detrimental to the others.[15]

The Cuban government made its comments on both drafts and stood by its position of rejecting the validity of any agreement that failed to include the five points formulated by the Cuban prime minister on October 28. Cuba denounced the U.S. attempt to bring up new demands and refused as ineffectual any conditional offer of military nonaggression. To mount an invasion is not a right of the United States, but an international crime, Cuba said. Cuba's remarks clarified, once more, that it would not accept any kind of inspection. It would allow only multilateral verification, which must include U.S. territory, in the context of an agreement for a permanent and general solution of the crisis. Likewise, Cuba opposed the U.S. claim to arrogate to itself the right to use other means of inspection and control, since they undermined national sovereignty. Furthermore, Cuba considered unacceptable the U.S. reference to the Rio Treaty, because all agreements reached on the conflict should be in the framework of the United Nations.[16] On November 29 the Cuban draft statement laying out its point of view was presented to the Security Council.[17]

On November 28, Mikoyan met with Stevenson and McCloy. In their discussion the Soviet vice premier expressed his opinion that the U.S. draft submitted to the Security Council left out some of the conditions included in Khrushchev's and Kennedy's messages, and also added new demands. He also said that the

Soviet government supported the Cuban position set forth in the five points, because it considered them essential for a true and definitive solution to the crisis.[18]

Stevenson and McCloy assured Mikoyan that the United States would meet its commitments and said they would prefer international monitoring by the United Nations to ensure that no more nuclear weapons entered Cuba. But since Havana's refusal made this impossible, they would continue using their own means to carry out whatever observations they deemed necessary. As for Cuba's five points, they merely said that those demands were not included in the agreement, their government could not discuss them, and it would be a waste of time to pursue this.[19]

The following day, Mikoyan went to Washington to meet with President Kennedy and go through the proposals from both parties in the negotiating process. During the meeting, the issue of the draft statements was brought up once again. Mikoyan expressed dissatisfaction with the U.S. proposal, because it nullified the obligations that the United States had agreed to. For his part, Kennedy said that the idea of reconciling the three statements was not viable, because the U.S. would not vote for the Cuban statement and the Cubans were not going to agree with theirs. It would be better, he said, for U Thant to simply make note of these statements, without putting them to a vote in the Security Council.[20]

This latest maneuver by the United States was aimed at blocking Cuba's direct participation in the negotiations, since the only option left to Cuba was to discuss its views in the Security Council. Although Mikoyan rejected the U.S. plan, Kennedy persisted, arguing that his options were constrained by the U.S. Constitution.

This meeting also took up the issue of reconnaissance flights over Cuban territory. Kennedy said that these flights would be carried out at high altitude as a way of directly monitoring compliance with the agreements, since in his country there was a strong campaign questioning whether the withdrawal of "offensive" weapons would actually be completed. Mikoyan replied that these overflights, whether at high or low altitude, were in violation of international law. If the U.S. government suspected that the agreements were not being fulfilled, he added, then it should accept multilateral inspection. He then said, "It seems that the United States does not want to put out all the sparks from the fire. But we want to resolve this matter as soon as possible, so that we may move onto other matters and resolve them as well. What can I tell Khrushchev? Do I tell him that you are willing to fulfill the obligations you've taken on, or that you are not willing to do so?"[21]

On December 3, representatives from the Soviet Union and the United States resumed negotiations, during which neither country changed its position in the least. That same day, Assistant Secretary of Defense Arthur Silvester told a news conference that the Soviet Union had begun removing its IL-28 bombers from Cuba. As soon as this dispute was resolved, the United States tried to exert pressure for the withdrawal of Soviet troops. Secretary of State Dean Rusk stated on December 10 that the presence of these troops in Cuba was cause for concern.

This position stood in contrast with that of the Soviets during the negotiating process. In his letter to Kennedy dated December 11, Khrushchev urged the U.S. president to wrap up negotiations on the basis of the agreements on Cuba, since dragging them out would only complicate matters further, at a time when it was necessary to turn to other pending issues.

In a session of the Supreme Soviet of the USSR on December 12, Nikita Khrushchev issued a report in which he sternly warned the United States to meet its obligations under the agreements it had made to resolve the crisis. "The Soviet government is confident that the obligations assumed by the United States of America concerning Cuba will be strictly met, as the failure to do so would prove dangerous—and not only for that region, since it would inevitably cause another sharp conflict and create a new threat to peace." He continued, "These obligations are in effect as long as the other party is fulfilling the agreement. If the other party does not carry out its obligations, we will be forced to undertake whatever actions the new situation requires."[22]

That same day, in response to rumors spread by the U.S. far right that the Soviets had not removed all their missiles from Cuba, President Kennedy stated that withdrawal of the weapons had been verified and that the United States was continuing to monitor the situation by its own means to ensure that Cuba did not acquire dangerous military capacity. Similarly, he said that the U.S. was drafting further regulations to ban the shipment of nonstrategic items from Western nations to Cuba.

Meanwhile, at a NATO ministerial meeting held in Paris December 13–15, the United States was praised for the position it maintained throughout the Cuban crisis. Defense Secretary Robert McNamara told the meeting it would be useful to replace the obsolete Jupiter missiles deployed in Italy and Turkey with submarines equipped with Polaris missiles. It seems that these were the first steps toward carrying out the agreement that had been secretly reached between the Soviet Union and the United States as part of resolving the crisis.*

At the United Nations, the U.S. government continued to refuse to consider any issue contained in the five-point Cuban demands, and avoided making any statements in the Security Council that would lead to a discussion in which Cuba would participate. This refusal was based, among other reasons, on domestic politics, because even though there was great relief in the United States at having avoided a serious military confrontation, the agreements between Khrushchev and Kennedy were questioned in certain political circles. Some even considered the agreements a failure, because they thought the government had, in effect, been forced to recognize as legitimate the existence of a communist regime only a few miles from its shores. Cuban counterrevolutionaries based in the United States viewed these

---

* The withdrawal of the Jupiter missiles stationed in Italy and Turkey was completed in late April 1963. They were replaced by submarines with Polaris missiles stationed in the Mediterranean.

agreements as a betrayal that dimmed their hopes of destroying the revolution.

On December 24, President Kennedy met with the main leaders of the mercenary brigade that had been defeated at Playa
Girón. Five days later, he presided over a ceremony at the Or-
ange Bowl in Florida to officially welcome the captured mercenaries who had been released by Cuba under agreements that
had been reached. At this event, Kennedy accepted a flag from
the brigade that, according to them, they had hidden after their
defeat at the Bay of Pigs. In his speech, the U.S. president assured them that this flag would be returned to them in a "free
Havana"—thus placing in doubt his promise not to invade Cuba.

By the end of the year, both the Soviet Union and the United States were looking to wrap up the negotiations, because both
powers were satisfied with the solution that had been reached.
For Cuba, however, the danger and aggression had not ceased:
the economic blockade persisted, along with all kinds of subversive actions, as well as the U.S. naval base at Guantánamo—a
source of repeated dangerous provocations.

On January 7, 1963, the negotiations concluded with two
notes sent to the secretary-general of the United Nations: one
submitted jointly by the Soviet Union and the United States,
and the other one by Cuba. The U.S.-Soviet document, signed
by Vasily V. Kuznetzov and Adlai Stevenson, said: "While it has
not been possible for our Governments to resolve all the problems that have arisen in connection with this affair, they believe
that, in view of the degree of understanding reached between
them on the settlement of the crisis and the extent of progress
in the implementation of this understanding, it is not necessary
for this matter to occupy further the attention of the Security
Council at this time." The statement maintained that both governments "express the hope that the actions taken to avert the
threat of war in connection with this crisis will lead toward the
adjustment of other differences between them and the general
easing of tensions that could cause a further threat of war."[23]

The note from the Cuban government, for its part, reiterated its opinion that the results arrived at did not constitute an effective agreement that could permanently guarantee peace in the Caribbean and eliminate external tensions. "No agreement acceptable to Cuba has been reached," the note said, "because the United States government, far from renouncing its aggressive and interventionist policy toward Cuba, has maintained its position of force in flagrant violation of international legal standards." Cuba stood by its conviction that no agreement would be effective unless it included the five points, because the mere promise from the U.S. government not to invade—which, furthermore, had not even been made official—constituted no guarantee whatsoever for Cuba. Furthermore, the document reaffirmed Cuba's sovereign right not to accept unilateral foreign inspections in its territory. The note also denounced the fact that the U.S. government "refuses even to give assurances that it will never again violate the United Nations Charter by invading the Republic of Cuba under the pretext that our country has not agreed to international inspections." Furthermore, it stated that "it is absurd insolence to offer a promise of non-invasion—which is equivalent to promising not to commit an international crime—on the condition that the country that is the target of possible invasion accept inspection of its territory."

The note went on to recall that the Soviet Union had complied with the verification requirement accepted by Premier Khrushchev in his October 28 letter to President Kennedy, in which Khrushchev agreed to have withdrawal of the missiles and IL-28s verified at sea. The note emphatically rejected the U.S. assertion of a right to use its own means to inspect Cuban territory, which represented an alarming defiance of the United Nations and an intolerable violation of Cuba's sovereignty. Finally, it restated Cuba's policy of peace and its desire to find peaceful solutions, and underscored its position of principles by stating: "To their positions of force, we shall respond with our firmness. To their attempt to humiliate us, we shall respond with our dignity. To their aggression, we shall respond with our determination to fight to the last combatant."[24]

By way of an epilogue

Thus concluded one of the most dangerous and dramatic episodes of the Cold War years. Looking closely at the events four decades later allows us to objectively weigh their lessons and significance.

For the Cuban revolutionary leadership, two key aspects of overall national policy were clarified. First, events reaffirmed the concept that the country's security depends above all on the courage, determination, and will of the entire people to participate in its defense. External support may be subject to various conjunctural factors of international politics, even though worldwide solidarity was always expected to play a significant role—one that would increase in proportion to the Cubans' own ability to resist foreign aggression.

Second, the events of those days left behind feelings of disillusionment and bitterness due to the poor political role of the Soviet Union in accepting all U.S. demands to put an end to the conflict. That left Cuba in a very complicated situation, since it had to firmly oppose the humiliating U.S. demand for on-site inspection to verify withdrawal of the weapons. Even worse was the public handling of the proposed swap of missiles in Cuba for the U.S. missiles in Turkey.

In any proposed exchange, it would have been more honorable for the Soviets—and a matter of elementary justice for the Cubans—to have demanded first of all the return of territory illegally occupied by the Guantánamo naval base and the withdrawal of U.S. troops stationed there.

After this bitter but instructive experience—in which Cuba was neither consulted nor taken into account as it should have been—Cubans never again had the same trust in the Soviet political leadership's ability to handle international problems.

On the other hand, there is no doubt that reaching a negotiated solution of the conflict between the Soviet Union and the United States made it possible to prevent a confrontation. It also helped develop consciousness regarding the apocalyptic consequences that such a war could have for humanity.

Unfortunately, however, this dangerous experience did not translate into the beginning of a worldwide process of disarmament. Nor did it lead to a political dialogue seeking solutions to the serious problems that afflict humanity, based on a shared interest in the survival and common development of all states and peoples. What happened was just the opposite: the arms race escalated considerably, and new conflicts turned into devastating confrontations in different parts of the world.

As for the confrontation between the United States and Cuba, the solution to the October Crisis did not go to the root of the problem. Even though it pushed back the danger of direct military aggression, it left intact the main causes that could unleash aggression at any time. A significant opportunity was lost to resolve the dispute between the two countries concretely and satisfactorily.

For the United States, the conflict with Cuba always went beyond its confrontation with the Soviet Union and the socialist bloc, although from the very beginning that was made into the main excuse for U.S. hostility to the revolution. "The fear of Communist expansion in the United States"—a U.S. Senate document states—"sharpened particularly when Fidel Castro emerged as the Cuban leader in the late 50s. His rise to power was considered the first significant penetration of Communists in the Western Hemisphere. U.S. leaders, including most members of Congress, demanded vigorous action to eliminate the Communist infection in this hemisphere."[1] Yet that aggressive policy toward Cuba did not end with the collapse of the Soviet Union, because what was really at stake was maintenance of the system of U.S. hegemony in Latin America.

Some have sought to limit the causes of the crisis to the Cold War period that humanity lived through following World War II. A world came into being that was divided into geopolitical spheres of influence and blocs of antagonistic countries, impossible to escape, while the specific problems of dependent and underdeveloped countries were ignored. In the final analysis, this confrontation on the international level left the Cuban government no alternative but to accept installation of nuclear weapons on its territory.

The U.S. government saw the impact of that decision on the military balance and other areas of foreign relations as jeopardizing its role as leader of the Western world. The reaction went beyond the bounds of international law and tried to impose conditions, such as the naval blockade, by means of force.

But this explanation alone is insufficient. To find a truly coherent explanation of the causes that gave rise to the crisis of 1962, one must also take into account another question that was present in that conflict and in all international politics at the time—the relations of the great powers with the dependent and underdeveloped countries. This is what can explain the fact that even though the resolution of the October Crisis initiated a process of détente between the two superpowers, the same did not occur between the United States and Cuba.

It is a proven fact that fear of the missiles was not what determined U.S. policy, since its intransigence toward the Cuban Revolution began earlier—even before Cuba established relations with the USSR. The reasons for Washington's stance must be found in a doctrine that dates back long before the Cold War, before the existence of the USSR and the European socialist camp.

The Cuban Revolution has been an especially sharp expression of contradictions in U.S. relations with Latin America that go back as far as 1823, when James Monroe laid the basis of U.S. political doctrine toward the rest of the continent. Perhaps what has most infuriated successive occupants of the White House since 1959 has been the survival of the Cuban Revolution despite their persistent efforts to overthrow it. This is why the hostile U.S. policy still prevails, as expressed—among other actions—in the expanded economic blockade, the Torricelli and Helms-Burton Acts,* and international anti-Cuba slander campaigns.

These reasons can provide the answer to questions that many honest persons in the world ask themselves. Why could the United States come to agreement with the Soviet Union—its main enemy—in 1962, while with Cuba it was unwilling to take a single step toward solving an apparently much simpler dispute? Why, after all these years, has Washington decided to improve its relations with countries such as Vietnam—with which it waged a bloody war that eroded its internal stability and international prestige—while on the contrary it maintains a belligerent stance toward Cuba?

Another point to think about concerns the sharp disagreements provoked by the U.S.-Soviet agreement, which disregarded the interests and opinions of the Cuban government. This undoubtedly reflected an attitude that tends to discount the rights of small countries to participate in solving international conflicts. Even more representative of that mentality was Washington's refusal to allow Cuban participation in negotiations to settle the conflict. This was not an isolated case; it has been the habitual practice of the powerful throughout history.

* See footnote on pages 57-8.

With the end of the Cold War—in which the world had found an unstable equilibrium in the division into antagonistic blocs—and the disappearance of the socialist regimes in the countries of Eastern Europe and in the Soviet Union itself, we are now forced to take up the theoretical and practical challenge of predicting what will be the future sources of international stability, because the military conflicts that have taken place in the last decade show a tendency to increase.

Today new variables are present: the military predominance of a single superpower for which arms production is one of its main sources of wealth, but which no longer has the objective basis that once justified that monumental enterprise; the proliferation of new nuclear states; the formation of large economic blocs that make it even more difficult for underdeveloped countries to participate in the world market; social and political conflicts that have given new life to nationalism, and that have generated the conditions of extreme poverty in which the majority of humanity lives; environmental problems that affect the rich and poor alike; and the absence of international mechanisms capable of regulating and balancing these contradictions, among other problems.

The responses to these great challenges have not been encouraging. The United States and its NATO allies continue opting for military force to solve problems arising from poverty and marginalization, and they try to legitimize their actions through theories of humanitarian intervention and limited sovereignty.

International organizations, regulated by antidemocratic and often outdated mechanisms, have turned into instruments of intervention. A globalized international economy controlled by transnational capital applies neoliberal schemes to underdeveloped countries, tending to perpetuate dependency and misery.

In today's world, the rich countries—particularly the United States—try to impose an international order based on ideological and political intransigence, seeking to impose their own institutions as the only ones and the universal ones, regardless of each nation's particular characteristics, interests, traditions, and culture.

But these realities should not give rise to pessimism about the future. History shows that noble and just causes have triumphed no matter how strong the forces opposing them. The example of the Cuban people during the days of the crisis proves it. They faced the danger of nuclear annihilation, but did not let themselves be intimidated. With courage and resolution they defended their sovereign principles. That stance is what prompted Commander Ernesto Che Guevara to declare on December 7, 1962, at a rally commemorating the death in combat of Antonio Maceo, deputy general of the Cuban Army of Liberation:

"Our entire people were a Maceo. All of our people vied to be in the front lines of combat, in a battle whose lines might not even be defined, a battle where the front lines were everywhere, where we were going to be attacked from the air, from the sea, from the land. . . .

"That is why his words, his phrases so dear to us, resound so deeply in the hearts of Cubans. . . . 'Whoever tries to take over Cuba will reap nothing but the dust of its blood-drenched soil, if he doesn't himself perish in the struggle.' That was the spirit of Maceo, and that was the spirit of our people.

"In these recent difficult moments, in this confrontation where we were perhaps only millimeters away from atomic catastrophe, we have been worthy of him."[2]

Documents
of the Cuban government

Artículo 3

Las Fuerzas Armadas Soviéticas destacadas en el territorio de la República de Cuba respetarán plenamente su soberanía.

Igual respeto ~~hacia las~~ observarán hacia las leyes de la República de Cuba, todas las personas pertenecientes a las Fuerzas Armadas Soviéticas o sus familiares

Artículo 4

El Gobierno de la Unión de Repúblicas Socialistas Soviéticas se hará cargo de los gastos de mantenimiento de las Fuerzas Armadas Soviéticas destacadas en el territorio de la República de Cuba en virtud del presente Acuerdo

Artículo 5.

A fin de no afectar los suministros de la población cubana, los artículos de consumo, diferentes materiales, maquinarias, aparatos y otros fines, destinados a las Fuerzas Armadas Soviéticas, serán suministrados desde la Unión Soviética. ~~Dichos~~ suministros, los equipos y municiones, destinados a las Fuerzas Armadas Soviéticas, así como los barcos asignados a su transporte tendrán libre entrada en el ~~país~~ territorio de Cuba.

A page from the Cuba-USSR mutual defense pact drafted in longhand by Fidel Castro and delivered to the Soviet leadership in that form by Ernesto Che Guevara and Emilio Aragonés.

Draft agreement between Cuba and the USSR on military cooperation and mutual defense

August 1962

In response to a military assistance pact proposed by Soviet premier Nikita Khrushchev, Cuban prime minister Fidel Castro prepared the following revised draft in August 1962. It was hand-delivered to Khrushchev by Ernesto Che Guevara and Emilio Aragonés in Moscow later that month.

Agreement between the Government of the Republic of Cuba and the Government of the Union of Soviet Socialist Republics on military cooperation for the defense of the national territory of Cuba in the event of aggression.

Agreement between the Government of the Republic of Cuba and the Government of the Union of Soviet Socialist Republics on military cooperation and mutual defense.

Agreement between the Government of the Republic of Cuba and the Government of the Union of Soviet Socialist Republics on military support by the Soviet Armed Forces in defense of the national territory of Cuba in the event of aggression.

(Any of the above three titles is suggested)

The Government of the Republic of Cuba and the Government of the Union of Soviet Socialist Republics,

Guiding themselves by the principles and objectives of the United Nations Charter,

Reiterating their desire to live in peace with all states and peoples,

Determined to make all possible efforts to contribute to the preservation and strengthening of world peace,

Anxious to establish and develop friendship, collaboration, and mutual aid between all peoples on the basis of the principle of respecting the sovereignty and independence of states as well as nonintervention in their internal affairs,

Faithful to a policy of principles based on friendship and solidarity between peoples defending a common cause, of which the fundamental pillars are peaceful coexistence between states with different social systems, legitimate defense against aggression, the right of every people to the form of government it deems appropriate to its aspirations of well-being and progress and to live in peace without being bothered or attacked from abroad, and the recognition of the historic prerogative of every nation, when it so desires, to break the binds that tie it to any form of domination or economic exploitation,

Determined to take the necessary steps to jointly defend such legitimate rights of the people of Cuba (if preferred, this could say the peoples of Cuba and the Soviet Union),

Taking into account, moreover, the urgency of taking measures to assure mutual defense against possible aggression against the Republic of Cuba, the USSR,

Desiring to reach agreement on all questions relating to the support that the Soviet Armed Forces will provide in defense of the national territory of Cuba in the event of aggression,

has agreed to subscribe to the present agreement.

Article 1

The Soviet Union will send to the Republic of Cuba armed forces to reinforce its defenses against the danger of foreign aggression and to contribute to preserving world peace.

The type of Soviet troops and the areas of their stationing in the territory of the Republic of Cuba will be set by the representatives named in accordance with Article 11 of this agreement.

Article 2

In the event of aggression against the Republic of Cuba or against the Soviet Armed Forces on the territory of the Republic of Cuba, the Government of the Union of Soviet Socialist Republics and the Government of the Republic of Cuba, making use of the right to individual or collective defense, provided for in Article 51 of the United Nations Charter, will take all necessary measures to repel the aggression.

Any information regarding an act of aggression and the actions taken in fulfillment of this article will be presented to the Security Council in accordance with the rules of the United Nations Charter.

The above-mentioned actions will be suspended once the Security Council takes the measures necessary to reestablish and preserve world peace.

Article 3

The Soviet Armed Forces based in the territory of the Republic of Cuba will fully respect its sovereignty.

All personnel attached to the Soviet Armed Forces and their family members will likewise observe the laws of the Republic of Cuba.

Article 4

The Government of the Union of Soviet Socialist Republics will assume the maintenance costs of the Soviet Armed Forces based in the territory of the Republic of Cuba by virtue of this agreement.

Article 5

So as not to affect supplies to the Cuban population, consumer goods, various materials, machinery, equipment and other goods destined for the Soviet Armed Forces will be supplied by the Soviet Union. Such supplies, equipment, and munitions destined for the Soviet Armed Forces, along with the ships assigned to transport them, will have free entry into the territory of Cuba.

Article 6

The Government of the Republic of Cuba, in agreement with the Government of the Union of Soviet Socialist Republics, will provide the latter's Armed Forces with everything necessary for their installation, stationing, communications, and mobility.

The transportation of personnel of the Soviet Armed Forces, the use of electrical energy and means of communications, along with other public services, provided to the Soviet Armed Forces will be paid by them, in accordance with the rates applicable to the Armed Forces of the Republic of Cuba.

The sites and land on which they will be installed and based will be provided, free of charge, by the Republic of Cuba. Their adaptation and repair will be assumed by the Soviet Armed Forces.

Article 7

In areas assigned to the Soviet Armed Forces, the construction of buildings, airfields, roads, bridges, permanent radio-communication facilities, and other types of installations will be undertaken using means and materials of the Soviet Armed Forces and with prior coordination with the competent organ of the Republic of Cuba in charge of such matters.

Article 8

In the event that the Soviet Armed Forces cease using them, the military barracks, airfields, and other constructions, along with permanent installations, will be turned over to the Government of the Republic of Cuba without any compensation.

Article 9

Matters of jurisdiction relating to the presence of the Soviet Armed Forces personnel in the territory of the Republic of Cuba will be governed by separate agreements based on the principles enunciated in Article 3 of this agreement.

Article 10

Both parties agree that the military units of each state will be under the command of their respective governments who, in coordination with each other, will determine the use of their respective forces to repel foreign aggression and restore the peace.

Article 11

In order to adequately regulate daily matters deriving from the presence of the Soviet Armed Forces in the territory of the Republic of Cuba, the Government of the Republic of Cuba and the Government of the USSR will name their respective representatives.

Article 12

This agreement will be submitted for ratification by the respective governments and will enter into effect on the day of the exchange of letters of ratification, which will be on _____.

Article 13

This agreement is valid for a five-year term. Either party may annul the agreement, notifying the other party at least one year prior to the expiration date of this agreement.

In the event that the five-year term is concluded without either party requesting its annulment, this agreement will be in effect for an additional five years.

Article 14

Upon termination of the agreement's validity, the Soviet Armed Forces will abandon the territory of the Republic of Cuba.

The Soviet party reserves the right to evacuate from the territory of the Republic of Cuba materials, munitions, equipment, machinery, mechanisms and all war matériel and other goods that are the property of the Soviet Armed Forces.

The Government of the Republic of Cuba will furnish all the aid necessary for the evacuation of the Soviet Armed Forces from the territory of the Republic of Cuba.

This agreement has been drafted on _____, 1962, in two copies, one in the Spanish language and the other in the Russian language, each of equal value.

Certifying the above, the heads of Government of both states have sealed and signed this agreement.

PRIME MINISTER OF THE PRESIDENT OF THE COUNCIL
REPUBLIC OF CUBA   OF MINISTERS OF THE UNION
         OF SOVIET SOCIALIST REPUBLICS

Fidel Castro Ruz   *Khrushchev N.S.*

'The imperialists will find a people willing to defend the nation house by house, inch by inch'

Declaration by the Council of Ministers
September 29, 1962

The following Cuban government statement was issued in response to a Joint Resolution by the U.S. Congress adopted by the Senate on September 20 by a vote of 86-1, and by the House of Representatives on September 26 by a vote of 384-7. It was signed into law by President Kennedy on October 3. The resolution stated "that the United States is determined (a) to prevent by whatever means may be necessary, including the use of arms, the Marxist-Leninist regime in Cuba from extending, by force or the threat of force, its aggressive or subversive activities to any part of this hemisphere; (b) to prevent in Cuba the creation or use of an externally supported military capability endangering the security of the United States; and (c) to work with the Organization of American States and with freedom-loving Cubans to support the aspirations of the Cuban people for self-determination."

The Council of Ministers of the revolutionary government of Cuba, meeting in special session to familiarize itself with and consider the Joint Resolution of the U.S. Congress, has agreed to issue the following declaration:

In an international situation laden with dramatic tension,

Cuba faces the risks of a direct armed attack by the U.S. government. With a display of official formality, the Joint Resolution of the U.S. Congress has now been added to the repeated statements and pronouncements by congressmen and leading figures of U.S. policy—including those by the secretary of state and by President Kennedy himself—and to the campaigns, tendentious information, and editorials by that country's press. This Joint Resolution summarizes, in an offensive and outrageous way, the entire policy of aggression and subversion that has characterized the international conduct of the U.S. government toward Cuba. It constitutes the open proclamation, without pretense or scruple, of a course based on aggression and force that the imperialist government of the United States—in violation of the most elementary principles of international law and the Charter of the United Nations—is carrying out against the Republic of Cuba.

The resolution of the U.S. Congress states that the United States is determined to use whatever means may be necessary—including armed action—to prevent the Cuban regime from extending by force its alleged aggressive or subversive activities to any part of this hemisphere; to prevent Cuba from establishing or exercising, with foreign support, a military capability that puts in danger the security of the United States; and to cooperate with the Organization of American States and with Cuban counterrevolutionaries for subversion in our country.

Such pronouncements have been formulated in the heat of the climate of hysteria that dominates the U.S. political scene these days. They are incited by the cynical accumulation of falsehoods, slanders, and distortions about Cuba's international conduct. In face of all this, the Council of Ministers wishes to establish clearly, before all the peoples of the world, the position of the Cuban people and the revolutionary government of Cuba on each of the questions referred to in the course of that campaign, whose aim is to psychologically prepare U.S. public opinion for the planned aggression. Likewise, the Council of Ministers wishes to formulate, categorically and clearly, the response by the people and the revolutionary government of Cuba to the Joint Resolution of the U.S. Congress—a response with a spirit of serenity, but with energetic and irrevocable determination.

The revolutionary government of Cuba declares once again that our country's foreign policy is based on the principle of nonintervention, on the right of nations to free self-determination, on recognition of the equal sovereignty of all states, on freedom of trade, on solving international disputes through negotiations, and on the will to live together peacefully with all peoples of the world. Faithful to those positions of its international policy and to the principles that underlie the Charter of the United Nations, Cuba constitutes no danger to the security of any country of the Americas. Cuba has never harbored, nor does it now harbor, aggressive aims toward any country. Rather, Cuba upholds the most absolute respect for a policy of nonintervention, convinced, as our own national history teaches, that each people has the sovereign right to decide its own historic course without hateful foreign interference. Far from having violated that international norm since the triumph of our revolution, Cuba, to the contrary, has been a constant victim of interference in its internal affairs, whose painful consequence has been loss of life and resources. It is Cuba that has been the victim of aggression coming from the territory of other countries of the Americas. Such aggression comes not only from the United States, but also from some Latin American countries whose governments, with open or secret complicity, behind the backs of their people and in opposition to their genuine feelings, have joined the U.S. government's chorus of imperialist smears.

The recent history of our continent includes the shame of Playa Girón, for which the president of the United States officially assumed responsibility, and for which the U.S. government used the territories and received the cooperation of the governments of other countries of the Americas. This history proves who has violated the principle of nonintervention and the right of self-determination of the peoples. In face of the abomination of false accusations contained in the Joint Resolution of the U.S. Congress, we proclaim once more that our doctrine is absolute observance of the sovereignty of the other states of the Americas. We also proclaim that Cuba will never seek to extend aggressive or subversive activities by force to any country of this hemisphere.

This Council of Ministers, expressing a truth that only the bad faith of the U.S. government and Congress dares to ignore, declares equally that Cuba will never use its legitimate means of military defense for aggressive purposes endangering the security of the United States.

The consistent conduct of the revolutionary government of Cuba, with the noble desire to carry forward its plans for development and for the work of revolutionary and socialist creativity, has proven its peaceful intentions. It has aspired, with legitimate historical right, only to develop Cuba's national life under the social and political system chosen by its people, exercising their absolute sovereignty. Far from having achieved this aspiration, however, Cuba has suffered constant interference in its internal affairs and the most cynical and intolerable aggression by the U.S. government, which, with stubborn international misdeeds, has fruitlessly sought to push Cuba back into the conditions of servitude, misery, backwardness, pillage, and oppression in which it lived during half a century of fictitious sovereignty and political pseudodemocracy. It is not the revolutionary government of Cuba that threatens the security of the United States and other countries of the hemisphere. It is the imperialist government of the United States, with its aggressive, interventionist, and provocative policy, that is putting in grave danger the security of Cuba, the whole hemisphere, and the world. This policy is carried out with the clear complicity of some Latin American satellite regimes, but in opposition to the positions of other Latin American governments that defend the principle of nonintervention and the right of nations to free self-determination—principles rooted in our common history and the immortal legacy of Bolívar, Juárez, and Martí.*

While it tries to present Cuba as a threat to its security and a danger to other countries of the hemisphere, the U.S. government has resorted to every possible means to overthrow the revolutionary government and to destroy the political, economic, and social order that the Cuban people—exercising the authority inherent in their self-determination, independence, and sovereignty—are building. It has carried out a campaign of slanders. It eliminated the Cuban sugar import quota into its market. It engaged in diplomatic conspiracy. It stopped the supply of oil. It burned cane fields, infiltrated CIA agents, and supported counterrevolution. It enacted an economic embargo. It murdered workers, farmers, teachers, and militia members. It clandestinely infiltrated explosives and weapons. It systematically violated Cuba's airspace and territorial waters, sponsored pirate attacks, and sabotaged production centers, violating both its own laws and international justice. It trained, organized, funded, led, and provided armed protection to the mercenary invaders of Playa Girón. And it used the Guantánamo naval base as a refuge for spies, provocateurs, terrorists, counterrevolutionaries, and fugitives from Cuban justice.

The U.S. government has not only committed the most brutal economic aggressions against our country. It has also unleashed a policy of pressuring all Latin American capitals to break relations with Cuba, trying to isolate it from the nations with whom it shares similar economic and social problems, ties of blood, and a common language and culture. The U.S. government instigated international meetings to condemn our country, forced our ex-

---

* Simón Bolívar led an armed rebellion that helped win independence from Spain for much of Latin America in the early nineteenth century.

Benito Juárez was a leader of the Mexican republic in the nineteenth century and led the fight against the French occupation in the 1860s. He was Mexico's president in the late 1860s and early 1870s.

José Martí, a noted poet, writer, speaker, and journalist, is Cuba's national hero. He founded the Cuban Revolutionary Party in 1892 to fight against Spanish rule and oppose U.S. designs on Cuba. In 1895 the party helped initiate a war of independence against Spain, and Martí was killed in battle the same year.

clusion from the Organization of American States, and imposed diplomatic and economic sanctions, although it failed to get the results it sought. It did not think out how these policies would seriously undercut the prestige of the governments. Or how they would deeply offend the anti-interventionist feelings, the independent spirit, and the principle of self-determination that are so deeply rooted among our peoples.

The United States has gone after our trade relations in every corner of the world where its influence reaches, interfering with and sabotaging sales of our goods and promoting a real international boycott against our economy. It is no secret to anyone that the U.S. government is now exerting powerful pressure on countries such as Britain, Norway, Greece, and others for whom maritime traffic is a vital necessity, so that their ships will not transport merchandise—including food and medicine—to Cuba. The U.S. obtained the desired prohibition from the West German government. This policy interferes with and disrupts the norms of international commerce and activities that are essential for the life of countries. In the process it has serious negative economic effects on the shipping lines of other nations, which, in order to protect their place in world trade, have had to withstand competition from the heavily subsidized U.S. merchant marine.

The U.S. secretary of state, making use of the fact that heads of UN missions are present at the United Nations General Assembly, has devoted entire weeks exclusively to promoting these plans against Cuba and to preparing the secret conference to be held with Latin American foreign ministers—right in the State Department offices in Washington—in open conspiracy against our country. He publicly declares the U.S. aim of enlisting Latin American ships and aircraft to "watch Cuba's shores." All this is done in the name of the military security of the United States and the political security of Latin American governments in face of the threat of subversion. Meanwhile, the very same congressional resolution declares they will support the counterrevolutionaries. In other words, they officially proclaim a policy of subversion against the government of Cuba and furthermore proclaim a policy of force that hints at military action.

Who carries out subversion, and who is the victim of subversion? Who constitutes a danger for the security of another country, and who could be the victim of this danger? The United States, which organized the invasion of April 1961? Guatemala, where the mercenaries were trained? Nicaragua, where they embarked from? Or Cuba, where they landed?

How can the United States justify its deeds, its threats, and its policy before the eyes of the world?

Equally absurd is its threat to launch a direct armed attack should Cuba strengthen itself militarily to a degree the United States takes the liberty to determine.

We have not the slightest intention of rendering accounts or of consulting the illustrious members of the U.S. Senate and House of Representatives about the weapons we find it advisable to acquire, nor the measures to be taken to fully defend our country just as we did not consult or request authorization about the type of weapons and the measures we took when we destroyed the invaders at Playa Girón.

Do we not have the rights that international norms, laws, and principles recognize for every sovereign state in any part of the world?

We have not surrendered nor do we intend to surrender any of our sovereign prerogatives to the Congress of the United States.

If the U.S. government harbored no aggressive intentions toward our country, it would not care about the quantity, quality, or type of our weapons.

If the United States could give Cuba effective and satisfactory guarantees with respect to our territorial integrity and would cease its subversive and counterrevolutionary activities against our people, Cuba would not need to strengthen its defenses. Cuba would not even need an army, and we would be happy to invest all the resources this implies in the nation's economic and cultural development.

Cuba has always been ready to hold discussions with the U.S. government and to do everything possible on our part, if only we were to find a reciprocal stance by the U.S. government of reducing tensions and improving relations.

In April of last year—even after the invaders' attack—we publicly repeated this willingness. The U.S. government turned a deaf ear and continued its policy of hostility and aggression. But the revolution has not been weakened; the aggression and harassment have made it stronger. To crush it is impossible. All of Washington's gold, its power, and its long subversive experience have run up against this immovable reality. It would have been far more intelligent to understand that.

Cuba could even have compensated U.S. citizens and interests affected negatively by laws of the revolution had it not been for the economic aggressions, and had the U.S. government been willing to negotiate on the basis of respect for our people's will, dignity, and sovereignty.

It was the U.S. government that chose the path of arrogance and disregard for the rights of a small state: hostility, economic aggression, subversion, terrorism, commercial blockade, indirect attack, political isolation, and the raised dagger of direct aggression.

The fruits of that policy have been utterly disastrous for its prestige. It is Goliath defeated by David.

The Joint Resolution of the U.S. Congress constitutes a barefaced admission that it will again resort to its pernicious policy, with such serious implications that the Council of Ministers of the revolutionary government of Cuba is today obliged to issue this emergency warning to the conscience of the world, given the danger that criminally threatens peace in the Americas and worldwide.

In the face of that painful reality and imminent danger that we denounce, Cuba proclaims its right to defend its sovereignty. To defend its independence against imperialist aggression, Cuba has been forced to strengthen its military defense capability, using human and material resources we would have preferred to direct toward social and economic progress. The revolutionary government of Cuba, in fulfillment of its duties, has taken and will take all the measures necessary to strengthen the military defense of our homeland.

Facing the certain danger of direct military aggression by the U.S. government, which the Joint Resolution of Congress authorizes, the Cuban people are preparing once again to confront it.

We warn the U.S. government, its Congress, and its president that they will not find a people unprepared. Rather, they will find a people who are alert, steadfast in their combat positions, willing to defend the nation's independence and sovereignty house by house, inch by inch.

The Cuban people are prepared to fight to the last man for their revolution, firmly convinced of the justice of the great historic work they are carrying out. So compelling are the motives that inspire the Cuban people to accomplish this work that no threat or aggression, no matter how powerful, will ever break their fighting spirit or diminish their will to resist.

The Joint Resolution of the U.S. Congress sharply reveals the irresponsibility of its leaders, its unprincipled policy, its reactionary and fascist concept of international relations—symptoms of the degeneration and decline of a system and of its public figures that recalls nothing of the greatness of the North Americans who once drafted the historic Declaration of Philadelphia, or the legacy of the man who spoke the immortal words at Gettysburg.

The same U.S. politicians and aggressive imperialist circles that pushed President Kennedy to go through with the adventure at Playa Girón, prepared by the previous administration, are now encouraging him in a new adventure of aggression, even though the disaster that only yesterday left him facing failure and ridicule ought to serve as a persuasive warning to use good sense.

The U.S. Congress forgets that the relationship of forces in the world has changed substantially. The imperialist countries today can no longer repeat with presumed impunity the policy of conquest, genocide, and barbarism that Hitler attempted with his delirious ambitions of domination.

The U.S. Congress likewise disdains the scope and the sincerity of the acts of solidarity Cuba has received—solidarity both for the creative work of the Cuban people and for the dramatic and glorious hour of the people's final struggle for independence. The U.S. Congress not only proposes to ignore the Cuban people's heroic determination and their ability to defend themselves, but also seems to dismiss the real, concrete content of the solidarity received. It underestimates the cogent force of the Soviet government's declaration that it will provide the assistance needed by Cuba or any other peaceful state in case of aggression. The U.S. Congress confuses the courage of a policy based on principles—which is what underlies the declaration of the Soviet government—with the demagogic and outright blackmailing posture of imperialist politicians who, with the worst aims, including for electoral gains, incite the U.S. government to put world peace at risk by aggression against our country.

The U.S. rulers also ignore the fact that new armed aggression against our nation would have consequences beyond our territory alone. This time, an armed invasion of Cuba would unleash a conflict of catastrophic results for the United States.

In response to the Joint Resolution, the Council of Ministers of the revolutionary government of Cuba asserts once again the peaceful intentions that motivate the Cuban people, and warns that neither our people nor the government of Cuba will be to blame for whatever may happen as a consequence of the aggression being authorized against our nation.

It is the president of the United States, its Congress, the imperialist policy makers, the Pentagon, and the international conspirators of the CIA who will have to bear—before history and the world—the grave responsibility for whatever happens as a result of the criminal aggression they propose to launch against Cuba. The weight of that responsibility bears down on their deadened consciences today.

The Cuban people wish to live in peace with the rest of the

Americas, but at the same time, alert and steadfast, they are prepared to defend the nation's independence and safeguard its territorial integrity. We therefore respond to the threatening and insolent resolution by stating that the Cuban people will resist, that they are prepared to resist, that they will not be alone in their resistance, and that they are willing to resist by any means necessary.

The U.S. Congress may dictate standards within its own borders. But as far as we are concerned, its resolution has as much value as a piece of wastepaper destined for the trash bin of history.

Patria o muerte!
Venceremos!

'Anyone who tries to inspect Cuba better come in full combat gear'

Address by Fidel Castro to the Cuban people
October 23, 1962

The following address by Cuban prime minister Fidel Castro was broadcast over Cuban television and radio the day after President John F. Kennedy's televised speech publicly launched the crisis.

DR. LUIS GÓMEZ WANGÜEMART: Good evening, television viewers. All of Cuba's radio and television stations have been hooked up this evening to carry the address of the prime minister of the revolutionary government and the general secretary of the ORI, Commander Fidel Castro, at a particularly delicate moment in world history.

As all of you know, the United States has established a naval blockade of the Cuban archipelago, using as a pretext the arms acquired by Cuba for the sole purpose of assuring its defense against U.S. aggression.

Cuba has replied to this aggressive act by issuing the order sounding the combat alarm, which in a matter of hours has put our people on a war footing.

Today the Soviet Union replied to Kennedy's speech with a measured and firm statement rejecting the assertions of the president of the United States and denouncing the war danger created by the U.S. aggression.

Today in Washington and New York, the Council of the OAS was convened by the United States. In addition, the United Nations Security Council met, upon the request of Cuba, the Soviet Union, and the United States.

What can you tell the people of Cuba concerning this new U.S. aggression, Dr. Castro?

FIDEL CASTRO: All these events are really the culmination of a policy pursued by the United States—not the United States, but the imperialists, the warmongers, the most reactionary circles of the United States—against our country since the triumph of the revolution.

None of these measures surprise us. Measures of this type, and others we have had to endure, are things that were to be expected from a government as reactionary and as disrespectful of the rights of other peoples and other nations as is the U.S. government.

All the people are familiar with this history. Ever since day one, since the very day of triumph—a triumph that cost our people so many sacrifices—our people could begin seeing what U.S. government policy toward us was going to be. This is apart from the fact that our people, or part of our people—those with the greatest political consciousness—clearly knew the history of relations between the United States and Cuba going back to the end of the last century. Our progress, our independence, and our sovereignty were always undercut by the policy of the Yankee governments, that is, intervention for imperialist ends. Going back to the Platt Amendment;* the successive interventions; the seizure of our country's wealth; the support they gave

---

* The Platt Amendment, named after U.S. senator Orville Platt, was a provision imposed on the Cuban government established during the U.S. military occupation following 1898. Under the terms of that amendment—incorporated in Cuba's new constitution—Washington was given the "right" to intervene in Cuban affairs at any time and to establish military bases on Cuban soil. These provisions were eliminated from the constitution in the wake of the 1933–34 revolutionary upsurge in Cuba.

to the worst, most reactionary, and most thieving governments. And finally, the support given to Batista. For we cannot forget, nor will we ever forget, that all the bombs they dropped on us, and on the people in the Sierra Maestra, were U.S.-made.

Our people are familiar with the whole process up to the present.

What is the current situation? The current situation is that this whole struggle has been a futile battle by an empire against a small country. It has been a futile, sterile, and failed struggle by an empire against a revolutionary government and against a revolution that is occurring in a small, underdeveloped country, a country that until recently was exploited.

Why has the situation been sharpened? Why has it reached critical proportions? Simply because the United States has failed in all its attempts against us up until now. In short, they have been defeated.

With each defeat, they've aggravated the situation further. They had to choose between two things: either resigning themselves and leaving the Cuban Revolution in peace, or else continuing their policy of aggression, with consequences that could be very bad for them. Up to now these have been bad, quite bad for their prestige. I believe they have lost a great deal of prestige in this sterile battle against us. As unfavorable as this battle has been for them; however, it could have been even more so.

All their attempts failed. U.S. governments are accustomed to solving the problems of Latin America by very simple means: above all, by coup d'états carried out by reactionary military cliques controlled by their embassies—that is, whenever the embassies could not solve the problems by simple orders through their ambassadors. Other procedures include promoting rebellions, revolutions, interventions, and so on. The interventions in our continent are well known—the intervention in Haiti, in Santo Domingo, in Nicaragua, in Mexico*—from which

---

* U.S. military forces had occupied Nicaragua from 1912–25, and again from 1926–33; Mexico from 1916–17; Haiti from 1914–34; and the Dominican Republic from 1916–24.

they wrested the part richest in minerals and oil, which the Yankees pirated. The history of Mexico is the history of a country filled with heroism. A good part of that heroism was expended in fighting for its independence against U.S. invasions. This history is well known.

The tactics they used to solve the problem of Guatemala[*] was that of a Playa Girón–type invasion. They also employed propaganda campaigns and promoted subversion. In other words, no government in Latin America was able to withstand the opposition of the U.S. government.

Things occurred exactly this way up until the triumph of the Cuban Revolution. When the Cuban Revolution triumphed, they began to try out all their methods against us. They began with slander campaigns, attempts to divide the people, to weaken the revolution through division, making use of that whole tremendous campaign launched inside and outside our country. They began with those futile campaigns. They continued with maneuvers of a political type in the OAS, in all those countries. Futile. They continued with economic aggression. This was one of the weapons I failed to mention: economic aggression as a weapon of pressure to control the situation in a given country. They continued with economic aggression—with oil, sugar— until they came to a total embargo. But economic aggression also failed.[†]

---

[*] Seeking to crush political and social struggles in Guatemala that accompanied a limited land reform initiated by the regime of Jacobo Arbenz, mercenary forces backed by the CIA invaded the country in 1954. Arbenz refused to arm the people and resigned, and a right-wing dictatorship led by Col. Carlos Castillo de Armas took over.

[†] In June 1960 U.S. refineries in Cuba began refusing to refine crude oil that Cuba had purchased from the Soviet Union. The revolutionary government responded by taking over the management of the Texaco, Esso, and Shell refineries. A few weeks later, in early July, Washington slashed Cuba's sugar quota by 95 percent. The quota was the amount of Cuban sugar Washington allowed to be imported into the U.S. market. In response, the revolutionary government authorized the nationalization of the holdings of the principal U.S. companies in Cuba. On October 19, 1960, Washington declared a partial embargo on trade with Cuba. A total embargo was imposed in February 1962.

They organized a Guatemala-type invasion: the invasion at Playa Girón. That failed too. They organized new maneuvers in the OAS, the breaking of diplomatic relations with Cuba, the Punta del Este agreements.* Because everything that has happened in Latin America since the triumph of the Cuban Revolution is connected precisely to the Cuban Revolution.

It's not funny. I can't call it funny, because it's ridiculous. It shows the mental poverty of the U.S. leaders. For example, in his speech at the Security Council today, [Adlai] Stevenson stated that what Cuba could not be forgiven for was not its communism, not its socialism, not its revolution, but rather the fact that it introduced these problems into Latin America at a time when the most extraordinary effort was being made for progress. He was referring to the Alliance for Progress.

As if anyone didn't know the Alliance for Progress—that facade, that fradulent policy—is neither progress, nor an alliance, nor anything like it, but simply another case of pulling our leg. In short, with all the agreements, all the steps, and even all the credits, very little of which have been distributed—yet even this little bit took place after the Cuban Revolution.

Thus we can say that without the Cuban Revolution, the imperialists would not have made the slightest effort to conceal their policy of exploitation. The Alliance for Progress is nothing more than a way to conceal their system of exploitation in Latin America. Because for every dollar they take from us, they lend one. It's a total failure.

To sum up, all these things—all this concern about Latin America—came about after the triumph of the Cuban Revolution. All those agreements, the isolation of Cuba, all those battles.

Simultaneously with this policy came more economic aggression, a total blockade. Futile. By blockade I mean a complete ban on the purchase of Cuban products and the sale of products to Cuba, despite the fact that all our factories and transportation required spare parts made in the United States.

---

* See the account of this meeting on pages 50–55.

That was not enough for them. All that was futile. They then began an even more aggressive policy. It was no longer a matter of banning the sale of our products in the United States, but of chasing our products all over the world, and, at the same time, attempting to prevent all the capitalist countries from selling to us.

They then attempted another type of blockade—to exert pressure by the threat of not permitting ships carrying products bound for Cuba to enter U.S. ports. They tried to impose a blockade on us by means of blackmailing even countries that were their allies, countries that lived off their merchant marine. Because there are a number of countries in which the merchant marine represents something very important to their life: Greece, Norway, Britain. There are others such as Panama and Nigeria, and countries such as Honduras, that have no ships of their own but lend their flags to foreign ships. Many of these are North American, seeking in this way to evade income tax laws and all the rest. This is a custom, one of the many "healthy" customs of Yankee imperialism.

So what happens? This means that the U.S. merchant marine is being subsidized one way or another, and it conducts a ruinous competition with the ships of all those countries. Because U.S. policy always has a double aim: the aim of harming Cuba, naturally; but it also aims to eliminate competition from other merchant marines. So it bans them from coming to Cuba. They sell to Cuba, and it's understandable that these countries are interested in trade with Cuba and the Soviet Union, trade with the socialist camp. Why? Because the socialist camp consists of one-third of humanity, and a very high percentage of world production.

They threaten these countries, that the ships of these countries won't be permitted to enter U.S. ports, that they'll be boycotted. That they'll be ruined. Futile attempts, futile. Because it can be said that they have tried every weapon, and every weapon, one after the other, has failed.

They began with *La Coubre*, in an attempt to prevent us from preparing ourselves.* The explosion of the ship *La Coubre*. The purpose of this was to prevent us from acquiring weapons from Belgium. Later they exerted pressure on Belgium.

They wanted us to be without weapons, at their mercy—naturally so they could attack us whenever they wanted. They thought that if we were disarmed, then a little-bitty invasion of the Playa Girón type would resolve everything for them.

This effort culminates now with a new adventure, which is truly dangerous to world peace. They are even trying to prevent us from arming ourselves with the assistance of the socialist camp.

To sum up, this has been the story of an uninterrupted chain of failures leading imperialism—which has not resigned itself and will never resign itself, despite the fact that it has no choice but to resign itself—to a series of steps that are more and more adventurous, more and more aggressive, with the single aim of destroying the Cuban Revolution.

But in the Cuban Revolution's four years of vigorous and healthy life, they have not been able to make a dent in it. If one analyzes the situation of our country and our people, it's clear that the revolution is stronger than ever at this moment. What has led them to this latest step is their failure to destroy the Cuban Revolution.

What is this latest step? It is an adventure, undoubtedly the most reckless adventure, and the most dangerous to world peace since the last world war.

The people were informed of the declaration Mr. Kennedy made yesterday. During the day we had been receiving a series of reports about unusual meetings, about unusual goings-on in Washington—meetings with an officer from the Pentagon, meetings with political leaders of both parties, and meetings of their Security Council. Movements of planes, ships, a whole

* *La Coubre,* a French ship carrying Belgian arms, exploded in Havana harbor on March 4, 1960, under suspicious circumstances, killing 101 people and injuring 200.

series of reports. We knew it had something to do with us. We knew because of everything that had come before in their policy since the revolution, the warmongering campaign, the hysteria, the Joint Resolution, all those things.

We realized that anything could happen from one moment to the next. They will never catch us unprepared and by surprise. They have not caught us by surprise up to now, nor will they ever catch us by surprise. When Girón occurred, they didn't catch us by surprise, and they'll never catch us unprepared and by surprise. When we realized that a series of movements were occurring and that some sort of action was imminent—we didn't know concretely what it was going to be or where it would come from—then we came to the conclusion, after discussing the situation with the compañeros, to put our forces on alert.

That is why yesterday, at 5:40 P.M., the order was given sounding the combat alarm. The combat alarm is the highest degree of alert and readiness in the armed forces. We wanted to avoid having to take this measure unless we were facing a very clear danger, because naturally all our efforts, the efforts of our country, have for many months been devoted almost exclusively to increasing production and solving problems of an economic character. And our country really has progressed and is advancing very much in this field.

Naturally, every time a mobilization of this type is made, it implies sacrifices in the field of production, no matter how much one tries to reconcile one thing with the other. And even though we're much better organized and have much more experience, it of course affects us in any case. In face of this situation, the order was decreed, and naturally all instructions related to the combat alarm were carried out, in anticipation of an aggression and against the danger of a surprise attack. At this moment, therefore, they cannot catch us by surprise.

Since we must always distrust these gentlemen, we felt the same thing might occur here, in line with the movements they've been carrying out. That is, the military landing maneuver—supposedly a maneuver—on the island of Vieques in Puerto Rico, might be redirected against Cuba, we felt, as in fact was done.* They suspended the maneuvers, and we were on alert, because one of the methods they can utilize is to simulate a maneuver and launch an attack, to try to obtain their proposed objectives through surprise.

The maneuvers were in progress, and in anticipation that something might occur, such as a sudden surprise attack, the combat alarm order was given. Later, Kennedy's statement was published, which simply confirmed and justified the measures we had taken. Why was this? Simply because an imperialist adventure of this type is fraught with such dangers that it is necessary to be on a state of total alert.

After some preliminary words of attempted self-justification—in which all the reasons invoked are absolutely unfounded—he says that the weapons received by Cuba "constitute an explicit threat to the peace and security of all the Americas in flagrant and deliberate defiance of the Rio Pact of 1947."† This is an act that might have validity for those who remain in the fold of imperialism, but not us.

What are "the traditions of this nation and hemisphere"? What are "the traditions of this nation"? What are they? The traditions of imperialist exploitation. The pirate-like sacking of our wealth and the exploitation of our workers? The tradition of submission and exploitation? According to him, then, we violate the traditions of this continent, the Joint Resolution of the 87th Congress. What do we care about any resolution of the 87th Congress—or the 7th or the 587th, for that matter? [*Applause*]

He speaks of the United Nations Charter precisely at the moment they are about to violate it. They invoke the United Nations Charter against us. We have not committed the slight-

---

* The U.S. Navy took over the island of Vieques, Puerto Rico, at the beginning of World War II to use as a military base. On October 21, 1962, the *Washington Post* ran a front-page story reporting that the mobilization of U.S. troops, planes, and ships south of Florida, allegedly for training exercise in waters around Vieques, was really aimed at Cuba.

† See footnote on page 89.

est violation of any of its articles—not the slightest. No one can show that we have violated a single article, not a single one. At the very moment they are about to commit a flagrant and bare-faced violation, they invoke the United Nations Charter.

He refers finally to "My own public warnings to the Soviets on September 4 and 13." What do we care about Mr. Kennedy's personal warnings? They might be important to him and the people around him, but they don't concern us in the least.

These are nothing less than the legal pretexts he uses. They are his basis for adopting a measure, which goes as follows:

"First, a strict quarantine on all offensive military equipment under shipment to Cuba is being initiated. All ships of any kind bound for Cuba from whatever nation or port will, if found to contain cargoes of offensive weapons, be turned back. This quarantine will be extended"—note this well—". . . this quarantine will be extended, if needed, to other types of cargo and carriers. We are not at this time, however"—at this time—". . . denying the necessities of life, as the Soviets attempted to do in their Berlin blockade of 1948."

Note well between the lines how it says that "this quarantine will be extended, if needed, to other types of cargo and carriers," but that we are "not at this time denying"—*at this time!*

"Second: I have directed the continued and increased close surveillance of Cuba and its military buildup. The foreign ministers of the OAS in their communiqué of October 6, rejected secrecy on such matters in this hemisphere. Should these offensive military preparations continue, thus increasing the threat to the hemisphere, further action will be justified."

"I have directed"—this gentleman has turned into a director!—". . . the Armed Forces"—the Armed Forces!—". . . to prepare for any eventualities." We are prepared just in case. "And I trust that in the interest of both the Cuban people and the Soviet technicians at these sites, the hazards of all concerned of continuing this threat will be recognized."

"Fourth: As a necessary military precaution, I have reinforced our base at Guantánamo"—they are shameless—". . . and evacuated today the dependents of our personnel there, and ordered additional military units to be on a stand by alert basis."

"Fifth: We are calling tonight for an immediate meeting of the Organ of Consultation under the Organization of American States, to consider this threat to hemispheric security and to invoke Articles 6 and 8 of the Rio Treaty in support of all necessary action. The United Nations Charter allows for regional security arrangements, and the nations of this hemisphere decided long ago against the presence of outside powers. Our other allies around the world have also been alerted." Yes, but they were alerted after the decision was taken. They did not consult any of them beforehand. We can talk about this later.

And "Sixth: Under the Charter of the United Nations, we are asking tonight that an emergency meeting of the Security Council be convoked without delay to take action against this latest Soviet threat to world peace. Our resolution will call for the prompt dismantling and withdrawal of all offensive weapons in Cuba, under the supervision of UN observers, before the quarantine can be lifted."

You can see how each one of these articles implies an aim— like the one I referred to where he said that "at this time" the quarantine applied to armaments; later it can be extended to other things.

Regarding the question of surveillance of Cuba, their surveillance has consisted of violating our airspace and territorial waters every day. They themselves admit it, because they're now talking of alleged photographs their planes took. How could their planes take photographs unless they violated Cuban airspace?

So each one of the points, each one of those actions involves an act of illegality.

They assembled the foreign ministers at Washington's State Department behind closed doors, in secret, and today they speak of that meeting.

They then speak of the Guantánamo base. What right do they have to speak of the Guantánamo base? That is, a base they hold in our territory, which they took by force and maintain against the will of our people. So, calmly, in a document of this type, they speak of the Guantánamo base, which is located in our territory, and shamelessly say they are utilizing this base, that they have reinforced it in order to utilize it against Cuba. This is a magnificent warning they are making to all countries where they currently have military bases!

They call for a meeting of the OAS. For what reason? To defend a Latin American country from aggression? No! To ratify and support aggression against a Latin American country.

Finally, he speaks of the United Nations for no other reason than to suggest sending observers to Cuba to supervise the measures we have taken for our defense.

Perhaps the most insolent thing in this entire declaration of Mr. Kennedy are the paragraphs he addresses to the people of Cuba. I'm going to read them, because one can see the extent of this man's cynicism and shamelessness.

He says: "I speak to you as a friend." He says: "Finally, I want to say a few words to the captive people of Cuba"—those people who are armed and have hundreds of thousands of men under arms, very good arms at that, are called "captive people." He might better have said "the captive *and armed* people of Cuba," ". . . to whom this speech is being directly carried by special radio facilities." The words "special facilities" means all their radio stations beamed to us.

I'll continue to read: "I speak to you as a friend"—a friend!—"as one who knows of your deep attachment to your fatherland." We don't deny it; I imagine he is well aware of our deep attachment to the fatherland. ". . . As one who shares your aspirations for liberty and justice for all. And I have watched with deep sorrow, and the American people have watched with deep sorrow that your nationalist revolution was betrayed"—if it had been betrayed, we would now be the best allies of imperialism in the world—". . . and how your fatherland fell under foreign domination. Now your leaders are no longer Cuban leaders inspired by Cuban ideals."—what are we then, Martians?—". . . They are puppets and agents of an international conspiracy which has turned Cuba against your friends and neighbors."—It is they who have compelled these neighbors to break with us; that is, to turn them into our enemies—". . . against your friends and neighbors and turned them into a target for nuclear war—the first Latin American country to have nuclear weapons on its soil.

"These new weapons are not in your interest. They contribute nothing to your peace and well-being. They can only undermine it. But this country has no wish to cause you to suffer"—listen well—". . . or to impose any system upon you. We know that your lives and land are being used as pawns by those who deny you freedom.

"Many times in the past, the Cuban people have risen to throw out tyrants who destroyed their liberty. And I have no doubt that most Cubans today look forward to the time when they will be truly free—free from foreign domination, free to choose their own leaders"—I don't know who chose us!— ". . . free to select their own system, free to own their own land." Get this: "free to own their own land"—the land we have taken away from the American companies and the big plantation owners and that we've put in the hands of the people—the same land that the peasants used to have to pay one-third, one-fourth, one-half of their income to rent.

And then notice how—I don't know, these things are really hard for me to understand, when this gentleman says "free to own their own land." This is a promise he makes, "free to speak and write"—what do you think of that?—"Free to speak and write." This gentleman is talking to a people, one million of whose sons and daughters have learned to read and write in the course of the revolution because the revolution has taught them. ". . . And worship without fear or degradation." No one here prohibits anyone from going to churches or anywhere else.

But it must be their own God—that is, the "golden calf," because these imperialist gentlemen have no God other than gold. ". . . To the society of free nations and to the associations of the hemisphere"—meaning Guatemala, Nicaragua, Paraguay, Peru, Venezuela, the "gorillas" of Argentina. In other words, he invites us to join the "society of free nations." Some society!

"Let no one doubt that this is a difficult and dangerous effort on which we have set out." No, we do not doubt it at all. It is difficult and dangerous. And if he understands this well, possibly he won't embark on such an "effort."

"No one can foresee precisely what course it will take or what costs or casualties will be incurred." Could this gentleman be so insolent as to speak of "casualties" that humanity might suffer? To teach our people to read and write, to make the peasants owners of their land, or to make people the owner of their land?

Anyone reading this speech has the strange sensation that this gentleman is either ill-informed, or else he has lost the last ounce of shame. Or it could mean something else: that this is solely for public consumption, a public that has been told all those things, a public intoxicated by lies and slander.

Of course, all these things seem totally ridiculous to our people. And Mr. Kennedy, in reality, is the ridiculous one.

There is another point in the argument of these gentlemen, when they say: "If they continue these preparations for a military offensive, thereby increasing the threat against this hemisphere, we will be justified to take additional measures." You all remember how World War II began. You remember how the invasion of Poland began, by a Hitler "communiqué." Hitler issued a communiqué that his troops, beginning at 3:00 A.M.—I don't remember what time—or 6:00 A.M., had begun to reply to Polish fire. They were not the ones attacking; Hitler was simply replying to Polish fire. All the campaigns of aggression, all the wars of aggression begun by Nazism and fascism—and Yankee imperialism is the most complete embodiment of fascism in the contemporary world—all their aggressions were always begun by speaking of the threat of aggression. In other words, they use the pretext of the danger of aggression to initiate their action.

Finally, because he is so "good," so "saintly," after writing all these criminal things, this gentleman repeats something that is a violation of law and morality. He says: "Our goal is not the victory of might, but the vindication of right. And it is not peace at the expense of freedom, but both peace *and* freedom, here in this hemisphere, and, we hope, around the world. God willing, that goal will be achieved." He even asks God to bless all the foul deeds he proposes to commit and has been committing.

That, in summary, is Mr. Kennedy's statement. To me and to our people, it is not the declaration of a statesman but of a pirate. Consider the following: The measure he is taking as a result of all this is a complete violation of international law. No state can do that. No state can stop the ships of another state on the high seas. No state can blockade another state. It is as if we were to send our ships with the following aim: "The United States cannot send such-and-such arms to Guatemala or Venezuela." Or as if any country were to place its warships around another country and blockade it. That goes against every international law, and it also goes against the ethics of international relations, against the most basic right of the peoples.

In the first place, it's a flagrant violation of law. Two violations are being committed: one, against our sovereignty in that it attempts to blockade our country; and, second, against the rights of all countries because it says that ships "from whatever nation" can be searched. Where? In North American waters? No. On the high seas; that is to say, in international waters! A violation is being committed here against the rights of all other nations, not just Cuba.

Of course, this is a deed that will very soon begin to have repercussions throughout the world, because every country sees what it means when one nation takes upon itself the right to blockade another nation.

And the more than 100 independent nations—and even those that are less independent—have to view with justified fear the fact that one country takes upon itself the right to blockade another nation, to prevent that country from freely acquiring and receiving the arms or the products it believes are necessary.

So the U.S. government violates the sovereign right of our

country and it violates international law. That is to say, it violates the right of all nations and establishes a precedent that has to be alarming for all the peoples of the world.

That, first of all, is what Mr. Kennedy's act involves.

Secondly, they list another series of measures, and I'll examine how they're going to carry these measures out. Because it's one thing to do x, and another thing to do y. They raise here the support of the OAS. In other words, they seek the complicity of the governments of Latin America to commit a crime against a Latin American country.

The governments that have let themselves be dragged along by that policy are undoubtedly committing the greatest act of betrayal any government of Latin America could commit. To lend oneself to an aggression like that against our country, to serve as puppet of the imperialists to commit this crime against a sister Latin American country, is the greatest act of betrayal that a government could commit.

This is a betrayal that the peoples will never commit. The imperialists want Latin American soldiers to come along with them to fight their Cuban brothers, to fight men who have the same problems, the same traditions, the same culture, and the same language. The imperialists do not want to come alone. In their adventure they want to make cannon fodder of the peoples of Latin America—peoples who will never agree to this aggression.

It will not be we alone—we will defend ourselves on our shores—it will be the peoples who will be charged with punishing the traitors. Because by doing this these traitors only bring closer the hour of revolution in Latin America. With the aggression against Cuba, by serving as puppets of the imperialists against Cuba, the only thing they are doing is bringing closer the day when their respective peoples will settle accounts with them. And the revolution arrives when one least expects it. That's especially the case the more abject, the more servile, and the more sell-out a government is. So this is what they try.

They also ask the United Nations that we disarm ourselves—

with the sending of observers, of course. With regard to this question, there is something very curious. The imperialists have now invented the terms "offensive" weapons and "defensive" weapons. Which weapons are offensive? And which are defensive? The rifles that came to Playa Girón were offensive weapons; the bazookas, the grenades, the mortars, the bullets, the knives they landed at Playa Girón were offensive weapons. But our rifles, mortars, and tanks were defensive weapons. Our tanks were defensive, while the Sherman tanks they landed were offensive.

What determines the offensive or defensive character of weapons is not their shape but their use, their employment. And since our weapons were used to defend ourselves, then our rifles, our cannons, our tanks were defensive. And the rifles, the weapons, the tanks they brought were offensive. That is not debatable anywhere. Nevertheless, the imperialists have now invented the category of "offensive weapons" and "defensive weapons." That is a pure invention of theirs, with the aim of keeping the people disarmed.

What have we said about this? What have we always said? At the time of the Joint Resolution of the U.S. Congress, which was another Yankee resolution—and I say Yankee because of its contradictions and its absurdities—because in this very resolution of the Congress it says: "Resolved by the Senate and House of Representatives of the United States of America, meeting in Congress assembled, That the United States is determined: (a) to prevent by whatever means may be necessary, including the use of arms, the Marxist-Leninist regime in Cuba from extending, by force or the threat of force, its aggressive or subversive activities to any part of this hemisphere; (b) to prevent in Cuba the creation or use of an externally supported military capability endangering the security of the United States; and (c) to work with the Organization of American States and with freedom-loving Cubans to support the aspirations of the Cuban people for self-determination." So at the very moment in which they say they are going to take measures of force "against subversion," they shamelessly speak of employing

¡ALARMA DE COMBATE!

Extra *REVOLUCION* **SEGUNDA EDICION** **Extra**

LA NACION EN PIE DE GUERRA

Ordena el Primer Ministro Fidel Castro ante el peligro de la agresión dispuesta por Kennedy

An hour and a half prior to Kennedy's speech on October 22, Fidel Castro gave the order mobilizing Cuba's military forces. **Top,** the Cuban daily *Revolución*, October 23, 1962, ran the headline: "Nation on War Footing." **Bottom,** Castro addressing the Cuban people the same day.

FIDEL CASTRO

BOHEMIA

" We know how to defend our integrity and sovereignty. Anyone who tries to come and inspect Cuba should know he'd better come in full combat gear! "

FIDEL CASTRO, OCTOBER 23, 1962

BOHEMIA

" More and more
Cubans, men
and women of
all ages and
professions,
were asking to
take their place
in defending
the country. "

BOHEMIA

GRANM

BOHEMIA

VERDE OLIVO

This page top, members of the Federation of Cuban Women work in the fields filling in for farm workers who were mobilized. **This page, bottom,** hundreds of thousands of militia combatants were mobilized.
Top left, women were part of the defense mobilization throughout the country. **Center left,** noted poet Manuel Navarro Luna reads poetry to mobilized troops.
Bottom left, in anticipation of an invasion, thousands of troops took up positions along the coast.

" We do not believe in mere promises of nonaggression; we need deeds. Those deeds are set forth in our five points. "

CUBAN GOVERNMENT STATEMENT
NOVEMBER 25, 1962

CESE DEL BLOQUEO ECONOMICO
CESE DE TODAS ACTIVIDADES SUBVERSIVAS
CESE DE LOS ATAQUES PIRATAS
CESE DE TODA VIOLACION AEREO - NAVAL
RETIRADA DE LA BASE NAVAL DE GUANTANAMO

5 PUNTOS DE CUBA POR LA PAZ Y CONTRA LA AGRESION

BOHEMIA

Above, on October 28, the Cuban government issued its "Five Points" as a basis for negotiations. These included a halt to all U.S.-organized acts of war and support to counterrevolutionary bands, an end to Washington's economic aggression, and return of the Guantánamo naval base.

Facing page, top right, in face of stepped-up spy flights violating Cuban air space, Fidel Castro ordered troops, beginning October 27, to open fire against all U.S. planes within range of their antiaircraft guns. At 10:17 a.m. that day, a Soviet missile crew shot down a U-2 outside Banes, in the present province of Holguín. U.S. pilot Rudolf Anderson was killed. **Bottom right,** during the crisis Castro visited artillery units.

" **Worldwide solidarity plays a significant role in the revolution's defense: one that increases in proportion to Cuba's own ability to resist foreign aggression.** "

GRANMA

GRANMA

"Starting on October 23, there were demonstrations in many countries against these U.S. actions, which endangered all humanity." **Clockwise from top right,** picket line at United Nations in New York City; in Algiers; in front of U.S. embassy in London (where cops attacked demonstrators); in Rio de Janeiro.

> " To their positions of force, we respond with our firmness. To their attempt to humiliate us, we respond with our dignity. To their aggression, we respond with our determination to fight to the last combatant. "

CUBAN GOVERNMENT DECLARATION
NOVEMBER 25, 1962

Top, at Indiana University in Bloomington, on October 24, 1962, a demonstration by 15–20 students organized by the Fair Play for Cuba Committee was attacked by a mob of several hundred. Carrying the "Hands Off Cuba" sign is Jim Bingham of the Young Socialist Alliance. Bingham and two other YSA leaders were accused of "inciting to riot" for organizing the demonstration. Seven months later they were indicted on charges of advocating the overthrow of the government of the United States and the State of Indiana. **Bottom,** counterrevolutionary Cuban exiles at training camp in the Florida Keys, October 1962.

Top, the Organization of American States—called by Che Guevara the "U.S. Ministry of Colonies"—approves resolution supporting "quarantine" of Cuba, October 23, 1962. **Center,** at the UN Security Council October 25, U.S. representative Adlai Stevenson displays photographs of the Soviet missile placements in Cuba. **Bottom,** U Thant, secretary-general of the United Nations (center), visits Cuba October 30–31, urging Cuba to accept foreign inspection on its soil as demanded by Washington and initially agreed to by the Soviet government. The Cuban government refused. Also in photo (from left to right) are Fidel Castro, Cuban foreign minister Raúl Roa, and President Osvaldo Dorticós.

" **The purpose of Kennedy administration policy was to strengthen the role of the United States as the leader of the capitalist world.** "

Above, Kennedy with U.S. Army officials during the crisis. **Top right,** James Meredith (center) is escorted by U.S. marshals and troops en route to classes at the University of Mississippi, October 2, 1962. Massive protests obliged White House to enforce Meredith's admission as first Black student, which was met by racist riots. **Center right,** peasants in Peru demand land, early 1960s. **Bottom right,** Algerian prime minister Ahmed Ben Bella arrives in Cuba on eve of crisis, October 15, 1962, in show of solidarity with Cuban Revolution. Eight days later, Washington suspends all economic aid to Algeria. Ben Bella is flanked by Fidel Castro and Osvaldo Dorticós.

" Not only was the decision to withdraw the missiles taken without consulting us, several steps were taken without informing us. The reaction of our nation was of profound indignation, not relief. "

FIDEL CASTRO

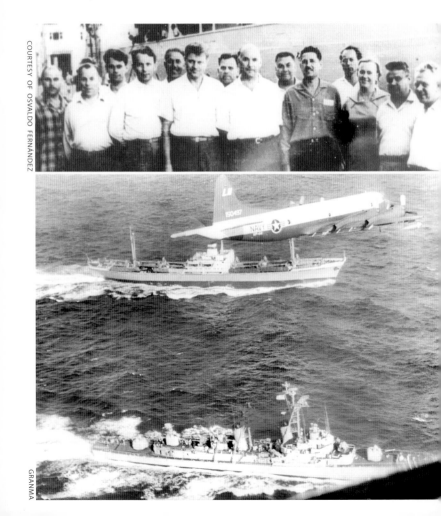

This page, bottom, following the unilateral Soviet decision to withdraw the missiles and agree to U.S. inspection, Vice Premier Anastas Mikoyan arrives in Havana, November 2. **This page, top,** discussions with the Cuban leadership. Clockwise from left, Raúl Castro, Fidel Castro, Osvaldo Dorticós, Emilio Aragonés, Carlos Rafael Rodríguez, interpreter, Anastas Mikoyan, Aleksandr Alekseev. **Bottom left,** a U.S. warship (in foreground) and plane monitoring one of the Soviet ships transporting withdrawn Soviet missiles on the high seas, November 1962. **Top left,** departure of the Soviet personnel of the missile division on November 29, 1962. In the front row center, in white shirts, are the head of the Soviet troops in Cuba, Gen. Issa A. Pliyev, and the head of the missile division, Maj. Gen. Igor D. Statsenko.

> " For Cuba the danger and aggression had
>   not ceased: the economic blockade persisted,
>   along with all kinds of subversive actions,
>   as well as the U.S. naval base at Guantánamo,
>   a source of repeated dangerous provocations. "

AP / WIDE WORLD PHOTOS

Above, Robert Kennedy (center) meets with leaders of Bay of Pigs
mercenaries freed by Cuban government in December 1962. He
immediately helped set them up as a mercenary force to once again
attack Cuba. **Inset,** the Zenon Viera naval base compound at Monkey
Point, Nicaragua, base of counterrevolutionary Cuban exiles until 1965.
Bottom right, Washington helped organize and arm hundreds of bands
of counterrevolutionaries inside Cuba, centered in the Escambray
mountains. In the photo are U.S.-made weapons seized from the bands,
the last of which were defeated by Cuban forces in 1965. **Top right,** the
U.S. naval base in Guantánamo, maintained in violation of Cuban
sovereignty and against the will of the Cuban government and people.

" We possess moral long-range missiles that cannot be dismantled and will never be dismantled. This is our strongest strategic weapon. "

FIDEL CASTRO, NOVEMBER 1, 1962

Since the January 1959 victory, the Cuban Revolution has supported national liberation struggles throughout the world. **Top,** Cuban internationalist volunteers in Angola in 1970s. Following a 13-year effort, in 1988 Cuban forces, and Angolan troops routed the U.S.-backed invasion by the South African apartheid regime. **Bottom,** Cubans and Vietnamese work on a stretch of the "Ho Chi Minh Trail" during war of national liberation against U.S. aggression, early 1970s.

subversion against the Cuban Revolution.

But when they stated "to prevent in Cuba the creation or use of an externally supported military capability endangering the security of the United States," we announced that our aim was not to attack any country, much less any Latin American people, nor was it to attack the United States.

That would be absurd. There is nothing more ridiculous than to attribute to us aggressive intentions against the United States. After four years of *them* attacking *us*, it now turns out, according to them, that *we* are the ones with aggressive intentions against these gentlemen. That really takes it to the limit.

What did we say in regard to this question of weapons? We said, "Equally absurd is its threat to launch a direct armed attack should Cuba strengthen itself militarily to a degree the United States takes the liberty to determine. We have not the slightest intention of rendering accounts or of consulting the illustrious members of the U.S. Senate and House of Representatives about the weapons we find it advisable to acquire, nor the measures to be taken to fully defend our country—to fully defend our country!—just as we did not consult or request authorization about the type of weapons and the measures we took when we destroyed the invaders at Playa Girón."*

Do we not have the rights that international norms, laws, and principles recognize for every sovereign state in any part of the world? What part of the world, what country, is denied the right to arm itself? What part of the world, what country, is asked to give an accounting of the weapons it arms itself with? What part of the world, what country? What makes the imperialists think we are the only such country, in the only such part of the world? Why, when we are a sovereign state, just as sovereign as they are—and even more so, because we are not the slaves of exploitation, the slaves of imperialism, the slaves of the war-making policy they follow! [*Applause*]

* See the Cuban government's September 29 declaration in reply to the Joint Resolution by the U.S. Congress, on pp. 213–23.

We are not sovereign by the grace of the Yankees, but by our own right. We are not just sovereign in words, we are sovereign in deeds. And we are true to our status as a sovereign state, so to take away our sovereignty it will be necessary to wipe us off the face of the earth! [*Applause*]

Our declaration in reply to the Joint Resolution went on to state: "We have not surrendered nor do we intend to surrender any of our sovereign prerogatives to the Congress of the United States. If the U.S. government harbored no aggressive intentions toward our country, it would not care about the quantity, quality, or type of our weapons. If the United States could give Cuba effective and satisfactory guarantees with respect to our territorial integrity and would cease its subversive and counterrevolutionary activities against our people, Cuba would not need to strengthen its defenses. Cuba would not even need an army, and we would be happy to invest all the resources this implies to the nation's economic and cultural development."

Is this clear enough? Who are the ones who forced us to arm ourselves?

They do not renounce their policy of hostility. They do not renounce their policy of aggression and subversion. They proclaim it. And while they are proclaiming that they are trying to destroy the revolution, they tell us what measures we should take; what steps we should take to defend ourselves. The victim has to consult the victimizer as to how he is going to defend himself!

That basically is what those super-mistaken gentlemen are suggesting. Because to say this is one thing. But to believe that we're going to pay attention to them—if they believe that, they're crazy.

We said: Cuba has always been ready to hold discussions with the U.S. government and do its share, were it to find a reciprocal stance by the U.S. government of reducing tensions and improving relations. This is what Cuba suggested in all frankness and sincerity. Through the voice of our president, the Cuban

Revolution presented this view at the United Nations.[*]

"Cuba has indeed been arming itself. It has the right to arm and defend itself. The important question is the following: Why has Cuba been arming itself? There is no doubt that we would have liked to channel all these human and material resources, all the energies we've had to use in strengthening our military defenses, toward the development of our economy and our culture. We have armed ourselves, contrary to our own wishes and desires, because we have been forced to strengthen our military defenses so as not to endanger the sovereignty of our nation and the independence of our homeland.

"We have armed ourselves because the people of Cuba have the legitimate right granted them by history to defend their sovereign decisions, to lead the country along the historic paths that our people have chosen in the exercise of that sovereignty. I ask you to answer sincerely, guided by your consciences, the following question: What would have happened had we not strengthened our military defenses when a division, armed and trained by the U.S. government, invaded our country at Playa Girón?

"Our revolution would not have been defeated, of course, nor would our historical progress have been reversed. But there is no doubt that it would have been a long and bloody fight, and many more human lives and greater amounts of wealth would have been destroyed.

"We quashed that invasion in seventy-two hours. That unjustified and arrogant invasion of our country was quashed in seventy-two hours because we exercised in time the right to strengthen our defensive military capability in order to safeguard our sovereignty, our independence, and our revolution."

Our people will never forget that "friend" Kennedy gave the orders for the attack [on Playa Girón], an attack that cost our people so many lives, that left so many widows and orphans. It

---

[*] Cuban president Osvaldo Dorticós addressed the UN General Assembly on October 8, 1962.

did not cost tens or even hundreds of thousands of lives, of course, because it was rapidly defeated.

But what would have happened had they seized the [Zapata] Swamp, that piece of our territory that could be reached only by two narrow roads through marshland? What would have happened had they begun to operate their bombers from there, attacking our cities, our transportation lines, and our factories every night? How much misery, how much destruction, how much killing, how many problems would this have created for the country?

Because all that was the intention of "friend" Kennedy, like his intention in everything else: to deprive our country of food, trade, spare parts, raw materials. There was the economic blockade. There was the subversion. There were the thousands of weapons dropped into the mountains of our country to organize bands of mercenaries, counterrevolutionary bands. There were the pirate attacks they made of all types, beginning with the planes that in the first days of the revolution came here to burn our sugar estates, to drop incendiary bombs upon our canefields, up to the attack on Havana in the middle of the afternoon during the first year of the revolution, an attack that cost dozens of victims.

Then came attacks like the one on the oil refinery in Santiago de Cuba* prior to the invasion of Girón. The treacherous Pearl Harbor–type bombing carried out on April 15, two days before the invasion, during which women and children were hurt and there were all kinds of victims.†

When you watch the documentaries of those days, you can see the bodies of women murdered by the homicidal bullets of our "friend" Kennedy's bombers.

---

* On March 13, 1961, a U.S.-organized sabotage team attacked the nationalized Texaco refinery in Santiago de Cuba. A Cuban sentry was killed, another seriously injured, and fire damage was done to the refinery.

† As a prelude to the Bay of Pigs invasion, eight planes attacked airfields at Santiago de Cuba, San Antonio de los Baños, and Havana on April 15, 1961, in an attempt to destroy Cuba's air force planes on the ground. The attack, which killed seven and wounded fifty-three, had been authorized by Kennedy the day before.

There were the many pirate attacks, such as the last one, in which a small unarmed launch was attacked by a U.S.-armed PT boat. And not only was it attacked, but it was sunk, and two of the crew members were captured and taken to the United States.* These were revolutionaries, from revolutionary families, and they had them there, kidnapped, cynically and shamelessly. These are the acts and the crimes that the imperialists have constantly been committing since the triumph of the revolution, long before we began arming ourselves.

When the CIA agents blew up the ship *La Coubre*, which was carrying weapons, costing us close to 80 lives, we did not even have relations with the Soviet Union. And we were arming ourselves, because after the agrarian reform law they began preparations in Guatemala for the expedition. When was this? Ever since the first year of the revolution, five months after the triumph of the revolution, simply because the revolution had decreed an agrarian law. For this sole reason they began to prepare the expedition, and they began their war on us.

What were the aims? To destroy the revolution, to condemn the people once again to the miseries and injustices of the past. Those are the objectives they have been pursuing since the first moment.

What did we do? Defend ourselves. What did we do other than defend ourselves? Or did the imperialists think that after their first attack on us, after their first action they would have a people on their knees, a government on its knees, and a legion of revolutionaries carrying a white flag?

Did they think that we revolutionaries would surrender, that the people of Cuba would surrender? Was that what they were expecting? That apparently is what they were expecting. So what we did was defend ourselves. And for each measure they took against us, we took others. They were the ones who decreed this

---

* On October 13, 1962, counterrevolutionaries aboard a PT boat opened fire on a small unarmed pleasure craft with four Cuban civilians aboard. Two of the Cubans, who were wounded, were taken to Miami.

policy of aggression, of enmity toward us, of breaking relations with our country. They were the ones.

If they failed, the blame is theirs, not ours. They were the ones who time and again rejected the proposals by the Cuban Revolution, the words of friendship of the Cuban Revolution, the repeated offers to negotiate, from the beginning up until the time of the compañero president's appearance at the United Nations. Of course, they could not reply to these words. Why don't they want to negotiate? Why did they not respond to the call for negotiations made by the government of Cuba, presented there before the representatives of all the countries of the world?

Our opinion on weapons is clearly set forth. We acquire the weapons we want for our defense, and we take the measures we deem necessary for our defense. This is what we have done. What are these measures? We do not have to tell the imperialists what these measures are, nor do we have to tell them what weapons these are. Who says that we are obliged to render accounts to the imperialists, the aggressors, as to the measures and the weapons we have for our defense?

Up until now none of our weapons has been of the offensive type. Why? Because we have never harbored aggressive intentions against anyone. We have never pursued an offensive policy against the rights of any people of any country. We will never change this policy. We will never be the aggressors. That is why our weapons will never be offensive weapons.

We can clearly state that all countries can rest easy, every country in Latin America, every country of America—the United States—because we shall never be the aggressors. We shall never be the ones to take the offensive.

But in the same way as we declare this clearly and honestly, we also declare that neither shall we be easy victims of any aggression. And we also declare, with the same determination and the same certainty, that we will know how to defend ourselves and we will repel any aggressor. That is what our weapons are for.

That is precisely what I said on July 26 in Santiago de Cuba: That we knew the intentions of our enemies, their plans, and that we had to take the appropriate measures, not only to resist, but to repel them. That is simply what has happened: We have taken the appropriate measures to resist and—listen carefully—to repel any direct aggression by the United States. [*Applause*]

We reject definitively any attempt at monitoring, any attempt at inspection of our country. Our country will not be inspected by anyone. No one will be able to come and inspect our country, because we will never authorize anyone to do so. We will never renounce our sovereign prerogatives. Within our borders, we are the ones who rule, and we are the ones who do the inspecting—nobody else. That is all there is to it. We therefore reject definitively any attempt to investigate our country in any way, no matter where it comes from.

Cuba is not the Congo. Imperialist forces went to the Congo flying the banner of the United Nations. They assassinated the leader of the Congo. They divided it, they muzzled it, and they killed the independent spirit of that nation.*

Cuba is not the Congo. No one can come under that banner or any other banner to inspect our country. We know what we are doing, and we know how we must defend our integrity and our sovereignty. [*Applause*]

Anyone who tries to come and inspect Cuba should know that he'd better come in full combat gear! That is our definitive

---

* After the Congo won its independence from Belgium in June 1960, Washington and its allies moved quickly to destabilize the new government headed by Prime Minister Patrice Lumumba, who had been the leader of the independence struggle. In July 1960, Moise Tshombe began a war against the new regime by declaring the secession of the southern province of Katanga (today Shaba), with himself as president. Lumumba's government appealed to the United Nations for help, and the UN sent "peacekeeping" troops. Washington and its allies moved swiftly to disarm Lumumba's forces, sending Belgian and UN troops into the capital, Léopoldville. They also backed Tshombe's proimperialist breakaway regime in Katanga.

The U.S.-led intervention succeeded by late 1960 in winning over a faction within the Congolese government, headed by army chief of staff Joseph Mobutu, and Lumumba was deposed in September. As UN troops stood watch, he was later arrested and handed over to Tshombe's forces, who murdered him in January 1961.

answer to the illusions and to the proposals for carrying out inspections in our territory.

In the same way that we are not interested in inspecting anyone else's territory nor are we concerned over what anyone does in their own territory, we do not accept inspections of our territory of any kind. Of course, new, ever more aggressive statements are being made. And we have one here made by Mr. Dillon. Dillon is the secretary of the treasury who was in Mexico attending a meeting of the ministers. He is the man who makes others believe he is giving them money.

It reads as follows: He told the Latin American finance ministers today that a new action against Cuba will be fully justified if the offensive preparations on the island are not checked immediately. Dillon said the following during a speech he made at this meeting:

"I can assure you that the United States is determined to continue on the path it has chosen until the offensive weapons now in Cuba are withdrawn or are neutralized effectively." In other words, he is saying: I can assure you that the United States is determined to continue on the path it has chosen—that is, that the United States is resolutely determined to commit suicide. [*Laughter*]

He continues: "We hope that this will be realized." Listen to this: "We hope that this will be realized by the immediate . . ."—right now, right here and now— ". . . by the immediate acceptance by Cuba of the resolution which we have proposed to the UN Security Council requesting the immediate dismantling of offensive arms in Cuba under the supervision and inspection of the United Nations."

This gentleman proposes that we disarm. We are sorry to tell him that his hopes are mistaken, because not now, not ever, will we disarm as long as the U.S. policy of aggression and hostility against us persists.

What is our principled position regarding the arms buildup or regarding disarmament? We are decidedly in favor of disarmament. What is our policy on military bases? We are decidedly in favor of dismantling all military bases. What is our policy on the presence of troops in various countries? We are in favor of a peace policy. We maintain there should be no troops or military personnel from one country in the territory of another country. That is our principled position. If the United States desires disarmament, that is magnificent. Let us all disarm. Magnificent! Let us all support a policy for the dismantling of bases, of troops throughout the world. Magnificent! We agree with that policy.

But we do not agree with a policy that calls for disarming ourselves in the face of the aggressors. That is so stupid, so ridiculous, and so absurd, that it's not worth wasting any more time thinking about such idiocy. [*Applause*] It's idiocy for one of two reasons, either because they believe it—which isn't possible—or because they think they're going to scare us.

Here we are all cured of fear. It may be—and this is the most probable—that they do it as a pretext. All U.S. policies are riddled with contradictions, with lack of sense, lack of principles, and lack of morality. That is what characterizes U.S. policies. That's why it can be said that it is a policy of pirates, of filibusters.

What is the latest step? Reporting on this declaration, we have here an AP cable dispatch, which says:

"President John F. Kennedy proclaimed a blockade of Cuba today to go into effect tomorrow at 9:00 A.M. He ordered the Defense Department to adopt the measures necessary to implement it, including the use of force if necessary. The U.S. Commander in chief signed this document in his office. It is called 'The banning of offensive weapons to Cuba.' He listed the offensive weapons: ground-to-ground missiles, bombers, air-to-ground missiles, nuclear warheads, electronic equipment for such weapons, and anything else that might later be added by the Defense Department.

"Kennedy granted the necessary powers to Defense Secretary Robert McNamara to use the army in any form necessary, as well as any other force that might be supplied by any other Latin American nation. However, he explained that force, as well as any other force that might be supplied by another Latin American nation, is to be used only when it becomes necessary. He explained that force is to be used only when it becomes necessary and only in the event that vessels carrying cargo for Cuba refuse to heed orders.

"The Defense Department will establish the restricted or prohibited areas for vessels going to Cuba." They own the seas already. Morgan is the owner of the seas. I don't say [Sir Frances] Drake, because Drake was a person of some renown.* The proclamation says that any vessel will be stopped and will be detained, if necessary. Anyone refusing to heed orders will be taken into U.S. custody and sent elsewhere. The text of the declaration was not immediately released for publication.

White House press secretary Pierre Salinger only read the clear passages. This is the decree. In other words, tomorrow, we will have the little American ships. We have always had them around the island, really, but now they possibly will make their displays of force more clearly visible, and they will be inspecting vessels. What right do they have to do this? They have no right. They can search through the archives, or anywhere else they want, but in the history of piracy they will not find a precedent of any kind for this sort of action. It is an act of war in time of peace! This is pure Yankee, ladies and gentlemen. And they claim they are at peace.

They might find precedents for all these acts in the history of fascism. They cannot deny it, because the United States today is unfortunately the refuge of world reaction, of fascism, of racism, and of all the most retrograde and most reactionary currents in the world. This is a historical fact. Once it was a country of liberty. Once it was a country that had the sympathy of the entire world. But those days of Lincoln are gone—from Lincoln to Kennedy is quite a long stretch. In that country the worst and the most reactionary things in the world find asylum, to the misfortune of humanity.

---

* Henry Morgan was a seventeenth-century pirate who, with tacit backing from the British throne, operated in the Caribbean, preying on Spanish targets in particular. Sir Frances Drake performed similar services for the crown in the previous century.

Very well, this is the situation at the moment: threats, and threats of taking measures. Let us look at what these are and how they are to be taken, and what is to happen. Because it is not the same to be surrounded by little ships in the water—there are none as yet—as it is to try and impose those things here in our territory. Threats of new measures. What they say here in the first part in this gentleman's speech would not be unusual: "This quarantine will be extended, if needed, to other types of cargo and carriers." It would not be unusual if they tried to extend it at a given moment to other types of cargo, including food and everything. In other words, a total blockade.

We can state that if there is a total blockade, we will be able to resist it.

All these things simply serve to reduce that country in stature, and to magnify in stature the grandeur of our homeland. At this moment a wave of repudiation is sweeping the world, despite the reactionary press and the attempts at keeping appearances. It is clear that they have tried to dress up the doll, but the doll is losing its clothing, leaving only the skeleton.

There are already a few U.S. embassies that have been attacked, among them the one in London. A demonstration of 2,000 persons broke through a cordon of 100 police and penetrated the embassy in London.

In other words, this action has provoked world repudiation—and it will do so more and more. If they add other articles to the blockade and try to starve our people into submission, that repudiation will multiply. We will see what withstands the most—their shame or our honor, their cowardice or our courage.

If they blockade us, they will magnify the grandeur of our homeland, because our homeland will be able to resist. There is no doubt that we will resist any cowardly blockade. What might happen—a total blockade or a direct aggression? Those are the alternatives. They have already established what they call a quarantine. They are so shameless that they themselves say they are calling it a quarantine even though it is actually a blockade.

The alternatives are a total blockade or aggression. In the face of that, what can we tell the people? We will adopt in a timely manner the necessary measures, and if a total blockade comes about, we will be able to resist it. That will simply sink imperialism into the deepest abyss of discredit, while elevating our country to unimagined heights of heroism and grandeur. We will not die of hunger.

If it comes to direct attack, we will repel it! That is what I can tell you. If there is a direct attack we will repel it. I think that is sufficient. The people should know the following: we have the means with which to repel a direct attack. This is clear as clear can be. [*Applause*]

So they threaten us with being the target of nuclear attacks? They don't scare us. I would like to know if the senators, the imperialists, the Yankee millionaires possess the frame of mind of our people, the calmness of our people. Because to be fully convinced you are defending a just cause is not the same thing as being a pirate. And they are pirates.

I would like to know if at the present time they are as calm and serene in facing this as we are. We are not intimidated. We are calmed somewhat by knowing that the aggressors will not go unpunished. We are calmed by knowing that the aggressors will be exterminated. Knowing that makes us calm.

We are running risks that we have no choice but to run. They are the risks run by humanity. And we, who are part of humanity—and a very worthy part to be sure—know how to run these risks calmly. We have the consolation of knowing that in a thermonuclear war, the aggressors, those who unleash a thermonuclear war, will be exterminated. I believe there are no ambiguities of any kind.

Humanity must face this danger. It must fight for peace. It is not for nothing that peace is a basic aspiration of humanity. That is why humanity must mobilize itself against those who promote war and aggression, against those who place the world on the brink of war, against those who follow this policy of playing with fire, the fire of war and nuclear war, which would cause such frightful harm to all humanity.

We, as part of humanity, run those risks, but we are not afraid. We must know how to live in the era that has fallen to us, and with the dignity required.

Who are the ones making threats? These gentlemen. But whom do they threaten? Those who cannot be intimidated. It is possible that those who threaten, these gentlemen who threaten us, are victims of fear. What a sad truth it is, incredibly. It turns out now that in their obsession the imperialists have ended up inventing and creating a kind of fear of Cuba. The shark is frightened, and it is calling on the other little sardines to try to devour the ex-sardine, Cuba.*

And the others go scurrying. Some governments go and give support. So much more shame and infamy for them, and so much more glory for our people, for our revolution, and for us all. When our country decided to be free and to make a revolution, it knew that it had to face the consequences, to confront many enemies. We were no longer the puppet, no longer the flock of sheep; the sheep following along behind, obedient to the voice and whip of the master. Not us. And when the reactionaries of this continent unite together against our glorious revolution and our heroic people, this only serves to ennoble our people, to raise the merit, the prestige, and the heroism of our people, who are confronting the reactionaries alone on this continent.

Those agreements do not worry us. We know how they are obtained, how they are demanded, how they are extracted. And we know the infinite amount of mud it involves, mud of which we are clean. These are meaningless agreements, furthermore, since to crush the revolution they would have to come destroy it by force, and they cannot destroy it by force. All the rest is just verbiage.

Against that policy of provocation and violence is our firm and calm position of defending ourselves. What is the position

* This analogy comes from the book, *The Fable of the Shark and the Sardines: The Strangulation of Latin America,* by Juan José Arévalo, president of Guatemala from 1945 to 1951.

of the Soviet Union? A calm, exemplary position. The Soviet response has been a real lesson to imperialism: Firm, calm, full of arguments, full of reason, all of which strip the aggressive policy of Mr. Kennedy to its skeleton. History will note this all down, the position of one camp and of the other, the position of the imperialists and of the defenders of peace, of those who fight to prevent the world from suffering the tragedy of a war. History will have to note this down.

Humanity must struggle with the hope of peace. That hope is based precisely on the fact that the imperialists today are not the all-powerful lords and masters of the world. The imperialists cannot launch a war without suffering the consequences of the war they provoke, which is extermination. That is what may stop them. Since they are no longer lords and masters, humanity must maintain the hope that there will be peace. With firmness, with resolution, and with a policy of principles.

That policy of principles gains more sympathizers in the world every day. And that policy of provocation and war, of piracy and arbitrary acts, is repudiated more and more in the world every day. History will note the responsibility falling to each and every one.

If the imperialists, against the most basic interest of humanity, force things to the point of unleashing a war—an exceedingly painful war for humanity—the historic responsibility will be theirs. And on their shoulders—or better said, on their ashes—they will have to bear the tremendous and staggering responsibility of the harm they may cause the world.

Our policy is one of respect for principles, of respect for international norms, and of peace. We can say this because it is true; we can speak this way without any ulterior motive. We can speak this way because we are convinced of the cause we defend, we are convinced that justice and right are on our side, and because we know that our people are running these risks not because we are a corrupt, vile, abject people, or a people who live in the muck of injustice and exploitation. Our people have unfurled a banner of justice. Our people have freed themselves of vice, depravity, exploitation, and the moral and material poverty of the past. And our people are convinced of what they are doing. This is the source of our people's strength. They are convinced of the historic role they are playing, convinced of the prestige they enjoy, of the faith that other peoples of the world have placed in them. And because they are convinced of this, they are able to look ahead calmly.

All of us, men and women, young and old, are united together in this hour of danger. And our fate, the fate of all revolutionaries and patriots, will be shared by all of us together. And victory, too, will be shared by all of us together!

Patria o muerte!
Venceremos!
[*Ovation*]

'Our five points are minimum conditions to guarantee peace.'

Discussions with UN Secretary-General U Thant
October 30–31, 1962

The following are transcripts of two meetings between Fidel Castro and U Thant, secretary-general of the United Nations. Gen. Indar Jit Rikhye, U Thant's military adviser, also participated in the first meeting. In addition to Castro, the Cuban delegation consisted of President Osvaldo Dorticós, Foreign Minister Raúl Roa, and Carlos Lechuga, who returned to New York on the same plane as U Thant to take up the post of Cuba's permanent representative to the UN. The talks took place in Havana's Presidential Palace.

OCTOBER 30, 1962

(3:10 P.M.)

U THANT: There is one point I would like to mention. In the discussions I held in New York with representatives of both the Soviet Union and the United States, General Rikhye was always present. In my opinion his presence would be useful in this meeting with the prime minister.

FIDEL CASTRO: We have no objection.

(General Rikhye is called to participate in the meeting.)

U THANT: First of all, Mr. Prime Minister, I want to thank you and your government for the invitation extended to me to come to Cuba, not only for this mission but also for the invitation made to me earlier.

As I said when accepting your invitation, I have come as quickly as I could. I am sure that today and tomorrow we will have fruitful talks to find a solution that respects Cuba's sovereignty and independence.

CASTRO: We are ready to discuss for as long as necessary. Our time is freely available to meet with you.

U THANT: As you know very well, the problem of Cuba was put forward last week in meetings of the Security Council. Meanwhile, meetings were held of the forty-five neutralist [Nonaligned] countries, primarily those which had participated in the Bandung and Belgrade conferences.* Two meetings were held, and they sent representatives to confer with me—because I too come from a neutralist country [Burma] and I participated in the two meetings—asking me to take an initiative that could contribute to the peaceful solution of this problem.

On October 24 I decided to take this initiative.

After hearing statements from the three delegations at the Security Council, I concluded that the immediate problem was to make an appeal to the three powers. I called on Premier Khrushchev to suspend weapons shipments to Cuba, voluntarily, for two or three weeks. I called on President Kennedy to voluntarily suspend the quarantine. And now I appeal to you, Your Excellency, to voluntarily suspend construction of missile bases, to give us an opportunity to discuss this problem calmly.

CASTRO: Excuse me, it is not "now," it was then . . .

TRANSLATOR: Indeed. "I appealed to you, Your Excellency, to voluntarily suspend construction of missile bases . . ."

---

* In April 1955 representatives of twenty-nine countries from Africa and Asia met in Bandung, Indonesia. The conference approved a final communiqué declaring colonialism "an evil which should speedily be brought to an end." The Belgrade conference of 1961, attended by representatives of twenty-five countries including Cuba, founded the Movement of Nonaligned Countries.

U THANT: Immediately after my request, the Security Council suspended its meetings to give me an opportunity to carry out my proposals.

The next day I learned that Soviet ships were approaching the quarantine zone. I addressed a second appeal to Premier Khrushchev and to President Kennedy, asking them to avoid a direct confrontation over this matter, so as to allow me the few days necessary to try to deal with the issue. That day I also sent you a letter, to which you responded very kindly asking me to visit Cuba. The substance of that letter involved suspending construction of missile bases in Cuba.

Since then, there have been communications between Premier Khrushchev and President Kennedy, between Premier Khrushchev and me, between President Kennedy and me, and naturally Your Excellency responded to my letter of October 27. The content of this letter is publicly known already, since it has been published.

As I see it, Excellency, the problem has two parts: one immediate and the other long-term. For now the Security Council wants to take up the solution of the immediate problem.

The purpose of my negotiations with the three powers, about which I have been speaking, naturally concerns only the immediate problem. But the United Nations will have to be involved in some way in solving the long-term problem.

The immediate problem has several factors. The first is that Premier Khrushchev has responded to my request, giving instructions to the captains of Soviet ships to keep their distance for now from the quarantine zone, for several days.

President Kennedy responded that he was willing to avoid a direct confrontation with Soviet ships so long as they were not transporting weapons, and Premier Khrushchev has told me very explicitly that Soviet ships are not transporting weapons at this time. If the two powers agree, for two or three weeks no arms will be sent to Cuba, and then in two or three weeks, if there are no weapons being shipped, the United States would suspend the quarantine.

The United States wishes to be certain that Soviet ships are not carrying weapons. What the United States wants is a UN mechanism or device that could assure them that no arms enter Cuba during this period of two or three weeks.

The Soviet Republic does not agree with this proposal.

Yesterday the Soviet government proposed a new solution, which is that Soviet ships would allow inspection by the Red Cross, a verification on the part of the Red Cross that the Soviets are not transporting weapons. This response by the Soviet government was communicated to the United States last night.

We made contact by phone yesterday with the Red Cross in Geneva, and the Red Cross has responded that it would agree—in the interests of world peace and international cooperation—to take charge of this task, either on the high seas or in the ports of disembarkation, provided that the government of Cuba agrees.

My stance cannot in any way be that of a direct participant. It is not my place to associate myself with any of the proposals. All I have said to the Red Cross, the Soviet Union, and the United States is that—with due consideration to Cuba's sovereignty—I would ask this of the Red Cross, always subject to the consent of the Cuban government.

This was explained to the three parties, and they were informed that it would be transmitted to the Cuban government.

Therefore the first point, Your Excellency, which would help very much in my work, would be to know the attitude of the Cuban government to the idea that the Red Cross would verify the transport of weapons in Soviet ships during the next two or three weeks.

The question is: What would be Cuba's position on this proposal?

OSVALDO DORTICÓS: Do you mean on the high seas or in Cuba?

U THANT: Of course, I have made this Red Cross proposal known to the Soviet and U.S. governments. The Soviet government responded that this issue is a matter of Cuban sovereignty. I have not received a reply from the U.S. government on the matter.

Does Your Excellency wish to discuss point by point, or all together?

CASTRO: I prefer that you continue your presentation.

U THANT: The United States tells me—and it has said the same thing in negotiations and in Security Council meetings—that it is more concerned about the launch platforms than the weapons. Its main concern is the missile launchers.

As is well known, last Sunday Premier Khrushchev instructed Soviet technicians to dismantle the missile launchers and return the missiles to the Soviet Union. He also said he would ask the United Nations to send a team to verify whether this has really been done.

I replied to the Soviet representatives that before sending a verification team, the most important point was to obtain the prior consent of the Cuban government. This matter was not to be put forward without the knowledge and consent of the Cuban government, and no actions were to be taken that would trample on Cuba's sovereignty. I also told both the Soviet representatives and the U.S. government that I would come to Cuba to present this point of view to Prime Minister Castro and his colleagues. Of course, both the Soviet and U.S. governments agree that if the missile launchers are withdrawn, tensions will diminish.

What the United States seeks, through myself, is a temporary agreement, pending the completion of dismantling the launchers.

I have asked the Soviet representatives how long this will take, and I kept on asking Moscow, but as of this morning I still have not received a reply.

What the United States seeks is a temporary agreement with the United Nations—subject, naturally, to the authorization and consent of the Cuban government.

Nobody knows, of course, how much time this will take: one or two weeks, perhaps more.

So if the Cuban government agrees, the first proposal of the United States is that a team of UN representatives would be suggested, made up of persons whose nationalities are acceptable to the Cuban government. The second proposal would be a UN reconnaissance plane with a crew of persons acceptable to the Cuban, Russian, and U.S. governments. It has been suggested to have a plane whose crew would consist of one Cuban, one Russian, and one U.S. representative during the week or two this might take.

I have replied to the United States that this proposal would also be presented to Prime Minister Fidel Castro.

The United States has told me that once these mechanisms have been put into effect, it would make a public declaration, at the Security Council if necessary, that it will not harbor aggressive intentions against the Cuban government and that it will guarantee the territorial integrity of the nation. I have been asked to tell you this.

The most important thing—as I have replied to the United States and to everyone—is that all these agreements cannot be taken without the consent of the Cuban government. They have replied to me that if this agreement is carried out with the concurrence of the Cuban government and of the United Nations, not only will the United States make such a declaration at the Security Council but it will also lift the blockade.

Yesterday I raised with the United States that it would look very bad if the blockade were maintained while I was consulting with Prime Minister Fidel Castro and the Cuban leadership, and I asked that it be suspended. This morning the news was announced that the blockade was to be suspended for forty-eight hours during my visit to the Republic of Cuba.

As you know, Your Excellency, I said at the Security Council that such a blockade has been something extremely uncommon, very unusual, other than in times of war. That's what I said at the Security Council. This viewpoint is shared by the forty-five countries that met and addressed their request to me. Two of these forty-five, which also have seats on the Security Council at this time—that is, the United Arab Republic and Ghana—made statements to this effect in a meeting of the Security Council.

Others of the forty-five neutralist countries, especially those that participated in the Belgrade conference, will make similar statements if the opportunity arises. All this has to do with the immediate problem.

Your Excellency, the Security Council has not authorized me to deal with the long-term problems, even though this is something that will have to be taken up later in the Security Council.

For purposes of this first discussion, Your Excellency, that is everything I have to tell you.

CASTRO: There is one point I find confusing—the proposals for inspection. They talk about two points here: about a team, and about a plane. I would like you to elaborate on that—the part that refers to proposals for inspection. Please repeat that.

U THANT: Both proposals would involve the United Nations. It would consist of two units: one on the ground and the other from the air, for as long as it takes to dismantle the bases, that is, around two weeks.

CASTRO: I don't understand why they ask these things of us. Could you explain a little better?

U THANT: The explanation the United States gives is that it wants to make sure that the launchers are really being dismantled and that the missiles are being returned to the Soviet Union.

CASTRO: What right does the United States have to ask this? Is this based on a genuine right, or is it a demand imposed by force, made from a position of force?

U THANT: My viewpoint is that this is not a right. Something like this could be undertaken only with the approval and acceptance of the Cuban government.

CASTRO: What we do not understand is precisely why this is asked of us. We have not violated any law. Nor have we carried out any aggression against anybody whatsoever. All our actions have been based in international law; we have done absolutely nothing outside the norms of international law. To the contrary, we have been the victims, in the first place, of a blockade, which is an illegal act. And secondly, we have been victims of another country's claim to determine what we have the right to do or not do within our own borders.

It is our understanding that Cuba is a sovereign state, no more and no less than any other member state of the United Nations, and that Cuba has all the attributes inherent to any of those states.

Moreover, the United States has been repeatedly violating our airspace without any right to do so, thereby committing an act of intolerable aggression against our country. It has tried to justify this by referring to an agreement of the OAS, but so far as we are concerned that agreement has no validity. We were expelled from the OAS, in fact.

We can accept anything that respects our rights, anything that does not imply a reduction in our status as a sovereign state. But the rights that have been violated by the United States have not been restored. And we accept nothing imposed by force.

As I see it, all this talk about inspection is one more attempt to humiliate our country. We do not accept it.

This demand for inspection aims to validate the U.S. presumption that it can violate our right to freely act within our borders, that it can dictate what we can or cannot do within our borders. And our line on this is not only a line for today; it is a view we have always maintained, without exception.

In the revolutionary government's reply to the joint resolution of the U.S. government, we said the following:

"Equally absurd is its threat to launch a direct armed attack should Cuba strengthen itself militarily to a degree the United States takes the liberty to determine. We have not the slightest intention of rendering accounts or of consulting the illustrious members of the U.S. Senate and House of Representatives about the weapons we find it advisable to acquire, nor the measures to be taken to fully defend our country. . . . Do we not have the rights that international norms, laws, and principles recognize for every sovereign state in any part of the world?

"We have not surrendered nor do we intend to surrender any

of our sovereign prerogatives to the Congress of the United States."

That view was repeated by the president of the Republic of Cuba at the United Nations, and also in numerous public statements I have made in my capacity as prime minister of the government. This is the firm position of the Cuban government.

All these steps were taken for the sake of the country's security, faced with a systematic policy of hostility and aggression. They have all been taken in accordance with the law, and we have not renounced our decision to defend those rights.

We can negotiate with full sincerity and honesty. We would not be honest if we agreed to negotiate away the sovereign rights of our country. We are willing to pay whatever price is necessary to uphold these rights. And that is not a mere formula, mere words; it's the deeply felt stance of our people.

U THANT: I understand perfectly Your Excellency's feelings. That is why I clearly said to the United States and others: "Any action of the United Nations in Cuban territory can be undertaken only with the consent of the people and government of Cuba." I told them so in the name of peace, which all the world and all the peoples of the world ardently wish for. I told the forty-five countries that I agreed to come to Cuba without having commitments from either side.

Some press reports last night and this morning, before I left on this trip, said I was coming to arrange details of a UN presence in Cuba. That is totally erroneous—that would constitute a violation of the sovereignty of the Republic of Cuba. I have come here solely to present the viewpoints of the other side and to explore the options of finding a peaceful solution.

As well, the forty-five countries that asked me to come know which position is legal and which one is not.

But in the name of world peace—and for a period of only one or two weeks, perhaps three—they have asked me to come and try to find a possible solution.

Your Excellency, my conscience is clear on this issue—the United Nations can undertake an action of this kind only when it has the consent of the government involved. This is not the first time this has happened. In Laos, when a situation arose that threatened international peace, the United Nations went into that country only after obtaining the consent of the government of Laos. In 1956 a situation arose in Egypt, in the United Arab Republic, and the United Nations went into Egypt—and is still in Egypt—always with the consent of the government. Similarly in 1958, another situation that threatened world peace arose in Lebanon, and the United Nations went in there after obtaining the consent of the government of Lebanon.[*]

One condition is absolutely necessary in order to undertake this kind of action: the consent of the government involved. . . .

CASTRO: In the case of the Congo . . .

U THANT: There was also the case of Somalia.[†]

CASTRO: In the case of the Congo, my understanding is that they requested the United Nations come in.[‡]

U THANT: In the Congo the request was made by the government of the Congo.

CASTRO: In the Congo, the government that made that request is now dead and buried!

Our government has not the slightest doubt that the present secretary-general of the United Nations is acting with good

[*] In Laos, a civil war pitted liberation forces against the pro-imperialist monarchy backed by Washington. In July 1962 an agreement was reached in Geneva, calling for creation of a coalition government. The agreement rapidly fell apart and the civil war resumed.

Egypt was invaded in October 1956 by British, French, and Israeli troops in response to that country's nationalization of the Suez Canal in July. In November the United Nations sent a "peacekeeping" force, which remained until Egypt asked them to leave in 1967.

In Lebanon, a popular rebellion broke out in early 1958 against the pro-imperialist government. In June the United Nations sent troops to protect the regime under the guise of preventing "illegal infiltration of personnel or supply of arms" from Syria. In July the U.S. government too sent in 10,000 troops, ostensibly to "protect U.S. citizens."

[†] In 1949 the United Nations established a trusteeship over Somalia to be administered by Italy, its former colonial master. The country did not become independent until 1960.

[‡] For the Congo, see note on page 247.

intentions, impartiality, and honesty. We have no doubt about your intentions, your good faith, and your extraordinary interest in finding a solution to the problem. We all have a high regard for your mission and for you personally. I say this with all sincerity.

I understand that we must all take an interest in peace. But sacrificing the rights of the peoples, violating the rights of the peoples, is not the road to peace; that is precisely the road that leads to war. The road to peace is to guarantee the rights of the peoples, and the willingness of the peoples to resist and defend those rights.

In all the cases cited by Mr. Secretary—Laos, Egypt, Lebanon, the Congo, which I mentioned—in all those cases, what has been seen is nothing but a chain of aggressions against the rights of the peoples. It all has been caused by the same thing.

The road to the last world war was the road that included toleration of German imperialism's annexation of Austria and its dissolution of Czechoslovakia—that is what led to war. These dangers are a warning to us. We know the course that aggressors like to follow. In our own case, we can foresee the course that the United States wants to follow.

That is why it is really difficult to understand how one can speak about immediate solutions without speaking of future solutions. What interests us most is not paying whatever price to achieve peace today. Rather, we are interested in definitive guarantees of peace. What interests us is not having to pay every day the price of an ephemeral peace.

Of course Cuba is not Austria, or Czechoslovakia, or the Congo. We have the firmest intention to defend our rights and surmount all the difficulties, all the risks. In order for your mission to be successful, Mr. Secretary-General, you must be aware of our determination, so that you can work fully informed of these circumstances.

U THANT: I am fully aware of the sentiments and the points of view that Your Excellency has expressed.

Concerning the point of immediate and long-term solutions,

I wish to say that the Security Council has authorized me to look for the means by which peace can be obtained for this region.

I understand that immediate and long-term solutions are closely linked; and we must explore the possibilities for long-term solutions in light of the situation as it is now. That is what the Security Council has authorized me to do. In practice it is very difficult to separate these things.

I believe that if we can find an immediate solution, doing so would lead us toward a permanent solution, not only for the United Nations but for all interested parties.

In citing Laos and the other cases where the United Nations has gone in, I agree with you, but I also wish to say that in those places the United Nations has been able to avoid or prevent outside aggression.

Please consider this: the presence of the United Nations in Cuba for a period of three weeks, perhaps more, would also be able to eliminate or make more remote the danger of aggression.

I am of the opinion that now and in the coming period, the presence of the United Nations in some countries will especially serve to push back and prevent aggression.

DORTICÓS: I would like to say something. I share the view expressed by our prime minister concerning our full appreciation for the mission that Mr. Secretary-General is undertaking with great nobility. That mission, of course, is none other than seeking ways to guarantee peace in this crisis situation.

It seems there is a question to be answered: Wherein lies the danger of war? Is it perhaps in the weapons of one kind or another that Cuba possesses, or is it in the aggressive intentions of the United States against Cuba?

We believe it is aggression that can lead to war. The weapons that exist in Cuba, no matter what they may be, will never initiate aggression. Therefore we ask ourselves this question: Why is inspection and our agreement to inspection a requirement to guarantee peace? In order to guarantee peace, it would be enough for the United States to pledge, with all necessary assurances through the United Nations, not to attack Cuba.

That is why we have stated—as our prime minister has repeated here with absolute clarity—that matters involving a long-term solution, if they can be called that, are inseparably linked to the immediate solution to the crisis. The immediate solution of the crisis would occur the moment the United States offers guarantees not to attack Cuba. The minimum conditions are those contained in the statements that our prime minister made October 28, with which I am sure Mr. Secretary-General is familiar.*

The stationing of United Nations inspection troops in Cuba—which the revolutionary government of Cuba does not accept, for the reasons the prime minister has expressed—would mean at best the guarantee for two or three weeks of a peace that the prime minister has justly characterized as "ephemeral." The danger of war would be renewed immediately afterwards, because the conditions that lead to U.S. aggression against Cuba would still remain.

Let the United States give the assurances that we consider the minimum ones, and that will begin resolving the immediate problem. I would say in the last instance, that in the interests of achieving peace now, it is not a question of discussing immediate or long-term questions. We believe the five points contained in the declarations of our prime minister are ingredients that are part of the immediate discussion geared toward guaranteeing peace.

These five points are not to be relegated to a long-term discussion. Rather, circumstances demand they should be part of the immediate discussion, because in our judgment they are minimum conditions for guaranteeing peace.

I repeat: peace is not endangered by our weapons. Peace is endangered by the aggressive conduct of the United States. Negotiation and discussion around these five points are what will make the danger of war disappear in short order.

That's how we see the problem.

---

* For the five points outlined on October 28, see pages 179–80.

U THANT: In the first place I wish to thank Your Excellencies, Mr. President and Mr. Prime Minister, for your words regarding me personally and the position I occupy. I fully agree with both of you that the solution we find for short-term agreements must also include negotiations for long-term agreements. But in terms of the United Nations, I believe that the best solution— and I think that the 110 member nations will agree on this—is that through the Security Council UN representatives should be provided to set about looking for and finding a long-term solution. But for now, at this moment, I do not think that the United Nations, its Security Council, can reach a positive and acceptable long-term solution that is in the best interests of the whole world and of world peace. If a long-term solution is found, that will be in the best interests of the whole world and of world peace, but I believe it is difficult to achieve that in the United Nations at this time.

CASTRO: As I see it, if the short-term solution that Mr. Secretary talks about is not achieved, it will simply be because the United States does not want it, because the U.S. persists in demanding inspection as an act of humiliation against Cuba. To achieve the unilateral security that the U.S. requires, it ought to have been enough for them that the Soviet government decided to withdraw the strategic weapons that it had brought here for the defense of the Republic of Cuba.

The Cuban government has placed no obstacles in the way of the withdrawal of those weapons. The decision by the Soviet government inherently involves a public decision; and the mere fact of being adopted in that way in front of everyone has had repercussions on world opinion. The United States knows that this decision was adopted by the Soviet Union seriously and that the strategic weapons really are being withdrawn.

But if, in addition to this, what the United States is actually seeking is to humiliate our country, it will not succeed!

We have not vacillated for even one minute in our determination to defend our rights. We cannot accept conditions of the kind imposed only on a defeated country. We have not relinquished our decision to defend ourselves. Our determination is such that they will never be able to impose conditions on us, because first they would have to destroy us and annihilate all our people. And in that case they will find nobody here upon whom to impose humiliating conditions.

U THANT: Concerning the subject of the U.S. declaration, the United States has said that it will make a public statement of nonaggression and of respect for the territorial integrity of Cuba, once the missiles have been dismantled and withdrawn.

In my opinion there is no disagreement. I fully agree with Mr. Prime Minister that action by the United Nations involves an invasion of the rights of a member state. And in this case, speaking about Cuba, if you do not agree to accept UN action, then my duty, what I must do, is to report this back to those who made the proposal.

It is not my intention here to impose anything. My duty is solely to explain the possibilities of finding ways, means, or forms in which we could find a peaceful solution, without making specific proposals. I will take into account everything that has been said here this afternoon, and I will return to present my report to the interested parties.

I believe this meeting has been very useful, and if the prime minister agrees, we will meet again in the morning before I leave. Meanwhile, I will ponder what has been expressed on these matters by Mr. President and Mr. Prime Minister.

CASTRO: To conclude, I would like to respond on the matter of inspection by the Red Cross. We are equally opposed to such inspection in our ports. I ask myself: If the Soviet Union authorizes inspection of its ships on the high seas, then why would it be necessary to inspect them again in Cuban ports?

Secondly, I see that Mr. Secretary is focusing his attention on getting the United States to make a public statement, a pledge before the United Nations that it will not invade Cuba.

Let me say, first of all, that the United States has no right to invade Cuba. One cannot negotiate over a promise not to commit a crime, over the mere promise not to commit a crime. Faced with the threat of this danger, we have more confidence in our determination to defend ourselves than we do in words from the U.S. government.

But furthermore, if the United Nations puts such a high value on a public pledge made before it by the United States—the pledge not to invade—why does it not put the same value on the public pledge the Soviet Union made before the United Nations to withdraw the strategic weapons that the USSR sent to defend the Republic of Cuba? These would be two equally public commitments. If one of the two pledges—the U.S. pledge not to invade Cuba—does not need any additional guarantee, why then does the pledge by the Soviet Union to withdraw its strategic weapons require the additional guarantee of inspecting us?

We will meet again, with pleasure, as often as you wish and at any time you wish.

U THANT: Thank you very much, Your Excellency.

On the first point I just want to say that when the Soviet government declared its willingness to accept inspection by the Red Cross on the high seas, we reported this to the Red Cross. Initially they said yes, even though they had to submit the issue to their governing body; they had to vote on this and accept it. But they indicated to us that it would be simpler to do this at the ports of disembarkation rather than on the high seas. That is, it's not a question of inspecting again, it's only once.

Also, I am very pleased to have your response on this matter and to have talked about this.

DORTICÓS: We could reach some arrangement on the hour to meet tomorrow.

U THANT: I have some consultations to make here, particularly with the ambassador of Brazil.

CASTRO: As far as we're concerned, we can meet at any hour you wish. It is not necessary to set the time now. Simply contact our foreign ministry and say what time you wish to see us.

U THANT: Tomorrow, not today.

CASTRO: Whenever you wish.

OCTOBER 31, 1962*

(10:20 A.M.)

U THANT: I would like to thank the government and the people for the hospitality and kindness they have shown me in this country.

The purpose of this new meeting is to exchange ideas on some confidential matters I have in mind.

Of course, Excellency, I have studied the views you expressed yesterday. I appreciate them and understand them perfectly—that Cuba, as a sovereign country, cannot tolerate any foreign interference that would affect its independence. I understand this because it is a valid principle of the rights of sovereign states.

It is my understanding that Your Excellency is opposed to any kind of verification of any actions whatsoever by your country, and that your government—in accordance with the rights of a sovereign state—is opposed to any inspection.

The first point is the following. It is my responsibility to report to the Security Council on this difficult problem, and I would like to obtain some clarifications.

In the first place, I would like to learn more about this: As Your Excellency knows, last Sunday Khrushchev replied to Kennedy in a letter telling him that he had ordered the dismantling of the bases in Cuba and the return of the missiles to the Soviet Union. Also, that he accepted verification by UN observers of the dismantling effort.

What I want to know, in light of this statement by the Soviet Union, specifically, is what the Cuban government thinks about this Soviet declaration made by Khrushchev to Kennedy and to the Security Council, since the Soviet Union is also a member of the Security Council. What is Your Excellency's viewpoint?

CASTRO: It is our understanding that when the Soviet government decided to dismantle the bases and spoke about verification, they were referring to some type of inspection outside

---

* Participating in this session were U Thant, Castro, Dorticós, Roa, and Lechuga.

Cuba's national territory—inasmuch as the premier of the Soviet Union could not talk about verification on Cuban territory, since that is something that concerns only the revolutionary government of Cuba.

Therefore, I think that at no time did he refer to verification on Cuban territory, but rather to some type of verification outside the national territory.

U THANT: Thank you very much, Mr. Prime Minister. Tonight in New York, I of course have to report to the two parties what the prime minister has said, because I believe this information needs to be provided in the negotiations between the Soviet Union and the United States, if that is what you think.

CASTRO: We think more than that: we think we should report this publicly.

CARLOS LECHUGA: The prime minister will be speaking to the Cuban people tomorrow on radio and television.

U THANT: My primary goal in reporting to the Security Council is to reduce tensions and restore peace. If this problem is not resolved in good time, the United Nations will suffer a collapse that would jeopardize its future.

My colleagues and I believe—and I have let the United States know this—that the blockade is illegal, that no state can tolerate a blockade, whether military or economic. A blockade is an imposition of force by a large power against a small country.

I also told them that the reconnaissance flights being made over Cuba were illegal and unacceptable. These three things—economic blockade, military blockade, and aerial reconnaissance—are illegal, and I said so on Friday, privately of course.

In the United States there are three forces: the Pentagon, the Central Intelligence Agency, and the State Department. In my opinion, the Pentagon and the CIA have more power than the State Department. If the CIA and the Pentagon continue to wield that power, the future of the world looks very bleak to me.

I told the United States that if it were to take some drastic action, then I would not only report it to the Security Council, but I would accuse the United States in the Security Council;

and that even though the United States might have the votes and the veto, there could still be a moral sanction.

I also told them that I would resign from my position, that if the United Nations cannot stop a great power from committing an act of aggression against a small country, then I do not want to be secretary-general.

I have not taken off a single Sunday. My family is very unhappy because I have too much work. If I cannot achieve peace, then I have no business in this position.

On Saturday I repeated this again to the United States, and I warned them not to commit any aggression against Cuba, because that would be the end of the United Nations. The United Nations is the only intermediary acceptable to all the powers. My goal is to achieve peace and ensure that the United Nations will last.

Since this is my mission, I would like to tone down the reports to the Security Council, in order to alleviate tensions. In the United States, as you know, there is great hysteria; the press and radio are fostering that climate, and I believe this hysteria must be lessened.

The U.S. press has been saying that the secretary-general is coming to Cuba to inspect, but nothing can be done about that.

My mission is to explore the possibilities for a common agreement. If the prime minister is going to speak publicly about the matters that have been discussed here, I would have to wait until he speaks in order to make my report. But I would suggest—not that I want to influence your speech at all—but I would suggest that the speech be postponed until I speak with the Soviet Union and the United States, for the sake of the mission I am undertaking.

CASTRO: When will you speak with the United States and the Soviet Union?

U THANT: Tomorrow.

CASTRO: I will speak in the evening. I have to speak tomorrow, because I have already announced it, and because the people are very concerned.

U THANT: I understand the thinking of the prime minister. Before leaving New York I told the United States to suspend the blockade while negotiations were going on. I have been told that they suspended the reconnaissance flights last night, but I do not know whether this has actually been done.

When I get back, I will ask them to continue the suspension of the military blockade and the reconnaissance flights, but I will also ask them to suspend the economic blockade.

I am seeking a long-term solution, not only an immediate one, because I feel that the two go together. I do not know if I will get a quick response from the Soviet Union and the United States, since Moscow and Washington have to be consulted and that always takes time. I appeal to the prime minister not to make any statement until I have a response from Moscow and Washington. I do not know when that will be, but I believe it will take more than one day.

Of course, I will be in constant contact with the prime minister. Again, I would ask that no statement be made that could worsen the situation.

CASTRO: I have to speak to the people in any case, because they have been waiting for many days. In fact, I did not want to speak until after your visit, after talking with you.

What statements do you think would be harmful?

U THANT: I am thinking of the first response from Khrushchev, concerning the dismantling and inspection agreed to by the Soviet Union. Since Your Excellency believes that the Soviet Union meant that the inspection would be conducted outside Cuba, I think this could create some division or some misunderstanding between the Soviet Union and Cuba.

CASTRO: Do you feel it would be harmful to publicize the viewpoint that we expressed yesterday? Because we must explain to the people what our views are; this is a matter of basic necessity.

There are some matters—above all the things discussed today—that we could avoid revealing, if you wish.

U THANT: No, what was said yesterday would not tend to create difficulties.

CASTRO: In that case, I will explain that in today's meeting there were certain points of a confidential nature, which you asked me not to reveal.

U THANT: I think that would be helpful.

CASTRO: I agree.

U THANT: Thank you. I will not relate this discussion to my colleagues either.

CASTRO: No problem. I will explain to the people that some parts of the discussion were confidential.

U THANT: Thank you very much. My next appeal to Your Excellency is the following. I understand perfectly that the Cuban people feel aggrieved. I would feel the same way if my country, Burma, were threatened by a great power.

This crisis that we are going through is the biggest one since the Second World War. Just as I have appealed to the United States to curb both their words and their actions at this time, in order to see if something can be accomplished, I also make an appeal to the prime minister, not only for peace but also for the future of the United Nations—although it's not my place to recommend what Your Excellency should say in your speech—that tomorrow you not speak in a way that might create further problems and frictions.

I know that you have every right to react that way, but I make this second appeal for the sake of peace and the future of the United Nations.

As for the common points, I want to say this: Yesterday I had a long discussion with the Brazilian ambassador and the Brazilian general who is here.

I have become convinced that the best solution is not only to focus on the immediate problem, but on the long-term problem as well. I am fully convinced that this is the only solution: to deal with both problems at the same time. That is what I will report to the Security Council, and I will say that if the Security Council does not also deal with the long-term problem at the same time, it will not be able to solve the crisis. That will be one of my recommendations to the Security Council.

As Your Excellency knows, the long-term discussion will mean difficulties in the Security Council, due to the stance of the United States. Of course, a long-term solution will require reciprocal arrangements and concessions from both parties, undertaken of course through the United Nations.

For example, if the United States continues to insist on inspection, logically this will also hold things up.

CASTRO: We maintain the view that there will be no solution, that is, no definitive solution, if the five points Cuba put forward are not met. These points are very legitimate, they are unquestionably right.

We know, of course, that this involves difficulties; we know that. But in any case there will be no definitive solution without this solution.

We are willing, with all honesty, to seek definitive solutions and to reach a permanent resolution to the crisis. But what we will not accept is a solution to this crisis under conditions that imply some special status for our country, or that leave the Cuban state *capitis deminutio* [of diminished stature].

We can accept no solution that does not maintain unimpaired all—absolutely all—the sovereign prerogatives of our country. It is easy for us to come to an honorable agreement, because for our part we have no conflict with anyone, we harbor no aggressive intentions against anyone. We carry out a policy of absolute respect for international norms and for the rights of other states.

U THANT: We would like to know your view on just when I ought to report to the Security Council; if you have any definite idea on the moment when the Security Council should be informed.

CASTRO: So far as we are concerned, you could report to the Security Council whenever you consider most useful and appropriate for what you have to do. Could it nevertheless be early next week—Wednesday, for example? Is Wednesday possible?

U THANT: I think so, next Wednesday.

Of course, if discussions continue outside the Security Council, I expect to participate in them. But if discussions are held in the Security Council they will be very forthright; therefore, they should be held after the U.S. elections. Many delegations feel that a large part of this problem is caused by the domestic fray of the U.S. elections. Many feel we should get past that date in order to discuss under better conditions.

CASTRO: I understand that all these things cannot be made public.

U THANT: This is something that is being talked about at the United Nations.

CASTRO: Yes, but not in my speech.

U THANT: One other point. My visit has been very satisfactory. I would like to return to Cuba. But this is impossible because I have talks arranged for tomorrow with representatives of the Soviet Union and the United States, and there are many other things—such as problems of the Congo, China—and I'm obliged to have many meetings about these. My duties are so many that I don't see my family. I would therefore like to request that one or two persons whom I trust might remain here as my representatives in Havana, to maintain direct contact with the prime minister and the president.

CASTRO: We are very anxious to please you and help you in every way. But we cannot accede to this request, because such UN representatives might be seen by the people as some type of inspection officials; it could be misinterpreted by the people.

Precisely for this reason we have decided to send a new head of our UN mission. And if necessary, we will send the foreign minister to be in contact with you. Everything you may wish to communicate with us can be done through him; that is, through a compañero at the highest level.

In this way the United Nations—which has so much work—will not have to expend personnel, who can then be employed in some of its other tasks.

U THANT: I respect your viewpoint, and I will take all the personnel with me.

CASTRO: And you'll be taking some of our personnel too, because Ambassador Lechuga is leaving with you!

U THANT: Ah, yes, I have made the appropriate arrangements for his visa, and I hope he will have no difficulties with it.

LECHUGA: Thank you.

U THANT: I would like to make a personal appeal. The United States says that one of its aircraft—which was carrying out an illegal flight—has been lost. And it was announced over the radio and in the press that there was only one man in the plane. I think that for humanitarian reasons, and also as a way to facilitate negotiations and peaceful solutions, I would like to know whether the aircraft is in Cuba, or if it fell into the sea, whether the pilot is alive or dead, and if there is any possibility of returning the pilot to the United States as a conciliatory gesture by Cuba.

CASTRO: According to the news we have, the pilot was killed when the plane crashed. Had the pilot survived, we would very gladly have been willing to make a gesture of this kind.

U THANT: Can I give that news to the United States? Or has some means already been worked out to report it?

CASTRO: The plane was shot down by our antiaircraft forces many kilometers inside our national territory. We have not publicized that fact, but now we are letting you know. The pilot was killed when the plane was shot down; we have preserved the body. We are telling you everything we know so that you can make whatever use of the news you think best.

U THANT: The United States did not tell me that fact.

CASTRO: This is one of the worst problems: the violation of our airspace. We cannot accept their "officializing," as a privilege, flying into our airspace. We cannot accept that. As I see it, this is one of the problems that can create an incident at any time. We are trying to avoid that, but there is a limit.

The provocations are very great, and at any time another plane may be shot down. The crews of our antiaircraft batteries are outraged by these provocations. We cannot accept that situation indefinitely; it is one of the most delicate points.

U THANT: I agree with you that those flights are illegal. And so do the forty-five neutralist countries.

CASTRO: The blockade is taking place in international waters, but the flights take place in our airspace, over our territory. We will not tolerate this from the imperialists. It is the point that is closest to triggering a conflict.

U THANT: As I said yesterday, I have told the United States that this is a violation of Cuba's sovereignty. Last night they stated that flights had been suspended, but I do not know if they are going to be resumed.

CASTRO: I traveled through the interior of Havana province and I came across U.S. planes twice in one afternoon. It takes a lot of effort to keep the crews of the antiaircraft units calm. It's the hardest task for their commanders. The crews consist of youth, and they are very fired up.

U THANT: As a personal step—seeing that the flight was illegal and the plane was shot down in Cuba—I am going to report that to the United States, and with that motivation I am going to appeal to them not to resume the flights. Could I ask the prime minister's authorization to inform the U.S. government that the Cuban government will return the body to the family of the pilot, for humanitarian reasons?

CASTRO: Yes, through your offices. I can tell you that the plane was a U-2.

U THANT: That's a very famous aircraft.

RAÚL ROA: I should say so. It's quite famous as a plane for spying.

CASTRO: The pilot went down with the plane, it seems he could not release the parachute.

U THANT: If these negotiations are successful, I hope to continue talks in New York with the foreign minister or with the head of the diplomatic mission toward establishing a UN program of technical assistance in Cuba.

CASTRO: Thank you.

U THANT: I understand that you want to have discussion only on the five points.

DORTICÓS: They are the minimum conditions.

CASTRO: They are so reasonable that we cannot give up any

of those points. It is only logical, it is elementary, that if the weapons of our friends are removed from Cuba, then the weapons of our enemies cannot remain in our national territory.

The United States says that the [Guantánamo] base is there by virtue of a treaty. It recognizes that one government of Cuba was qualified to make that treaty. So why doesn't another government of Cuba have the right, by virtue of treaties, to have bases in the national territory? That is, why cannot another government of Cuba, also by virtue of treaties, accept friendly weapons into our national territory?

U THANT: I attended the Belgrade conference, not as UN secretary-general, and I signed the agreement that no country ought to have bases in other countries without the consent of the government and people of those countries.

DORTICÓS: The Belgrade conference took the same stand concerning the Guantánamo base.

CASTRO: As a matter of principle we support the removal of all bases on foreign soil.

U THANT: One last request, if it would not be considered an interference in what you are going to say over the radio tomorrow, is that your speech might appeal to the United Nations as an effective instrument of peace and to stop war.

I think that the United Nations should take definite steps to resolve this problem peacefully, and it would be very useful for my efforts if the prime minister were to say that he would like to see a strong United Nations for the prevention of war.

CASTRO: Even if you had not asked me to do so, our feelings were precisely to make reference to that mediation, and to express our confidence in your efforts. At the same time I want to express respectful recognition of the role the UN is carrying out at this time. I believe the United Nations is carrying out one of that institution's most appropriate roles, and is doing so successfully. It is making felt in the UN a collective opinion about this case; not the opinion of one bloc, but of an institution.

U THANT: Thank you, Mr. Prime Minister. I am finished now.

If you wish to pose any questions that might be useful for the report . . .

CASTRO: We have nothing more to ask. We feel very satisfied with the way in which you have put things forward. Please take back with you the certainty that our position is very firm: that we are fully determined to defend the sovereignty of our country.

I am thinking of using the transcripts of yesterday's discussion as a basis for how I explain matters tomorrow. Is it a problem for you if I speak broadly about that?

On that basis I will keep the second part secret. I can explain to the people that we discussed some confidential matters and that we responded on that basis. In other words, today's discussion is confidential, but not yesterday's. Is this your opinion?

U THANT: Yes, I agree with that. The talks yesterday expressed the viewpoints of Cuba, and I think it is very useful to say that. Without meddling in the substance of your speech, I reiterate my appeal to you concerning the language to be used, in deference to the success of the efforts I have undertaken.

CASTRO: Concerning the issues we discussed yesterday, I will use the same words tomorrow that I did yesterday. I understand them to be words suitable to the level and circumstances of the negotiations. Tomorrow we will try to be as careful as possible.

U THANT: Thank you, Mr. Prime Minister.

CASTRO: We would like for there to be a solution, but as a small country we wish to be respected, and we are willing to make whatever sacrifice it takes to uphold our sovereignty.

We are not a great power, we are a small country. We are convinced, however, that we are defending—with honor and great prestige—the rights of small nations, and ours is a trench where those rights are being defended. We will not abandon this trench; we would rather perish than abandon this trench.

U THANT: I too defend the rights of small countries, because I represent a small country. The job of the secretary-general is thankless. Several times I have wished to resign, but my friends have insisted that I continue for the future of the United Nations. My term of office expires in April; unfortunately, there is no other candidate so far. Last week I again raised the idea of resigning, but I am the candidate most accepted by everyone—by the big powers and by the nonaligned nations. As of now, no other candidate has emerged who brings together the support of everyone.

I have been away from my country for almost six years. I was back in my country only once, for ten days. The government of my country wants me to work there, but the future of the world is more important at this time than the future of a single country.

My wife is not happy in the United States.

CASTRO: Today there are several U.S. news dispatches that again speak of an invasion of Cuba, saying that the U.S. pledge is restricted to right now only, and that Cuba could be invaded for some other reason.

DORTICÓS: The dispatches today carry information along these lines: U.S. government spokesmen have said that just because they are not invading now—since the supposed missile bases are dismantled—this does not mean they won't use force tomorrow, under cover of the OAS and the Rio Treaty.

This makes it clear why for us it is fundamental to have discussions around the five points that we have referred to.

U THANT: The Pentagon is very strong.

CASTRO: And it must have come out of this crisis strengthened.

U THANT: I am convinced that many Americans—not the Pentagon, nor the CIA, nor Kennedy, of course—are against U.S. policy on Cuba, despite the poisoning of the press, radio, and daily propaganda.

The day after my report to the Security Council, I received 620 telegrams from Americans, appealing to me that the United Nations should peacefully resolve the problem of Cuba. Of those, only five asked the UN to stay out of the problem and allow the United States to invade Cuba.

On Monday I received 200 cables, most of them asking for a peaceful solution to the Cuban problem.

I thank you again for your hospitality and for these useful

exchanges of ideas. I understand the position of the government of Cuba and, of course, I assure you that I will make every effort to arrive at a peaceful solution.

In particular, the governments of the forty-five countries put their trust in the results of my efforts to reach a peaceful solution to the problem.

If you agree, I will bring in my colleagues for them to pay their respects.

CASTRO: With pleasure.

(11:58 A.M.)

'We have as little faith in Kennedy's words as we have fear of his threats'

Cuba's position on the Caribbean Crisis
November 25, 1962

The following statement by the National Directorate of the Integrated Revolutionary Organizations and the Council of Ministers of the Republic of Cuba was issued in response to new threats against Cuba made by U.S. President Kennedy during a November 20 press conference in Washington.

The National Directorate of the Integrated Revolutionary Organizations and the Council of Ministers, meeting in joint session to take up questions relating to the so-called Caribbean Crisis, hereby resolve to make known to the people of Cuba and the world the position of our party and the Cuban government.

In his latest public statement, President Kennedy announced the lifting of the blockade of Cuba in return for the withdrawal by the Soviet Union of the intermediate-range ballistic missiles and IL-28 medium-range bombers stationed in Cuba. Nevertheless, the statements by the president of the United States contain the seeds of a provocative and aggressive policy against our country, which must be denounced.

In one part of his speech, President Kennedy said: "As for our part, if all offensive weapons systems are removed from Cuba and kept out of the Hemisphere in the future, under adequate verification and safeguards, and if Cuba is not used for the export of aggressive Communist purposes, there will be peace in the Caribbean. And as I said in September, 'We shall neither initiate nor permit aggression in this hemisphere.' We will not, of course, abandon the political, economic, and other efforts of this Hemisphere to halt subversion from Cuba, nor our purpose and hope that the Cuban people shall some day be truly free. But these policies are very different from any intent to launch a military invasion of the island."

The position of force adopted by the U.S. government is wholly contrary to international legal norms. Above and beyond the outrages it has committed against Cuba, and that brought the world to the brink of war—an outcome avoided by means of agreements based on a commitment by the United States to abandon its aggressive and criminal policy against Cuba—it refuses even to give assurances that it will not again violate the United Nations Charter and international law by invading the Republic of Cuba, on the pretext that our country has not agreed to international inspection.

It is completely clear that Cuba has a sovereign right, based on the United Nations Charter, to agree or not to agree to inspection of its territory. Cuba has never offered or agreed to such verification.

The Soviet government, for its part, complied with the verification requirement it spoke about in its letter of October 28, by allowing the United States to verify on the high seas the withdrawal of the missiles. The United States agreed to this form of verification.

President Kennedy's claim is groundless. It is merely a pretext for not carrying out his part of the agreement and for persisting in his policy of aggression against Cuba. As if that were not enough, even if permission were given for inspection, carrying with it all the guarantees that the U.S. government might

see fit to demand, the peace of the Caribbean would still be subject to the condition that Cuba not be used for "the export of
aggressive Communist purposes."

What this means is that any effort by the peoples of Latin
America to free themselves from the imperialist yoke could
serve as a pretext for the U.S. government to accuse Cuba of
breaking the peace, and then to attack our country. Flimsier
guarantees would be difficult to imagine.

To all this must be added one additional fact that speaks to the
warmongering and domineering policy of the U.S. government.
In his latest statement, President Kennedy tacitly reasserted the
"right"—already claimed on several other occasions—for spy
planes to fly over the territory of Cuba and photograph it from
coast to coast. This too is a gross violation of international law.

Respect for international law is an essential condition if the
nations of the world are to live together regardless of their social or economic systems. The only effective guarantee that the
rule of law will be maintained in international affairs and that
the provisions of the law will be complied with is for all nations
to respect established norms. At this moment of sharp rivalry
between two conceptions of society, the United States has arro-
gated to itself the right to violate existing international norms
and to establish new formulas as it pleases.

It is our view that when such a dangerous situation is reached,
when one country decides, by and for itself, how law is to be
applied in its relations with other countries, there is no choice
but to firmly resist its claims.

The United States is trying to dictate what kind of arms we
should or should not have. The U.S. rulers, who compel us to
expend enormous resources in order to defend ourselves against
the aggression to which we have been subjected during the four
years of our revolution's development, also claim to be the
judges of what the limit should be on the armaments with which
we defend our freedom.

It was the U.S. government that, by its repeated and overt
attacks on our country, made it necessary for the Cuban people

to arm themselves. It was President Kennedy himself who ordered an army of mercenaries to land at Playa Girón. It was under his administration that thousands upon thousands of U.S. weapons were dropped on our country by parachute or unloaded by sea with the aim of encouraging and organizing bands of counterrevolutionaries, who committed the worst possible crimes against teachers, literacy volunteers, peasants, and workers.

The government of the United States—both the previous and present administrations—not only adopted criminal economic measures against Cuba, which confronted our people with harsh problems; in addition, their acts of military aggression forced us to devote great energies and resources to defense of our integrity. What would have become of our country and its revolution had our people not offered stubborn and heroic resistance to the actions of that powerful and aggressive country? The United States is guilty of a policy of economic strangulation and of violence against Cuba, a policy that has led to the Caribbean Crisis with all its consequences and dangers.

Furthermore, the United States violated the principle of freedom of the seas by establishing a blockade of Cuba; it violated the United Nations Charter by adopting unilateral measures against our country; and it now takes refuge in the Organization of American States, seeking official sanction for its acts of air piracy. The OAS expelled us from its ranks; it declared us to be outside Latin America. But the OAS has no jurisdiction whatsoever on our soil; its decisions have no validity for us; to cite them is arbitrary—it is pure sophistry on the part of the imperialist aggressor.

The U.S. government has reiterated its interventionist aims. It has stated that under no circumstances will it abandon its political, economic, "and other" acts of aggression. What is meant by "other" efforts against Cuba? Internal subversion? Sabotage? Acts of terrorism? Pirate raids? Infiltration by CIA agents? The landing and dropping of weapons in our territory? Invasions by mercenaries? All these things, in Pentagon jargon, are termed "paramilitary warfare."

If that is how matters stand, Cuba will have to defend itself by every available means. It reserves the right to acquire weapons, of whatever type, for its defense and will take such steps as it deems appropriate to strengthen its security in the face of this open threat.

After examining President Kennedy's statement, then, it can be said that armed conflict has been averted but peace has not been achieved.

For our people there has been no peace, but rather nonstop attacks. Many of their sons and daughters have died as a result of armed attacks, sabotage, murders, subversive acts, and raids by pirate aircraft and ships instigated by the U.S. government. President Kennedy's statement offers not peace but the continuation of such acts.

We therefore reiterate the five points that are essential to a genuine and definitive settlement of the crisis.

First: an end to the economic blockade and to all measures of commercial and economic pressure exercised against our country by the United States in every part of the world.

Second: an end to all subversive activities, to the bringing in of weapons and explosives by air and by sea, to the organization of mercenary invasions, to infiltration of spies and saboteurs, all these activities being conducted from the territory of the United States and a few countries that are its accomplices.

Third: an end to the acts of piracy carried out from bases in the U.S. and Puerto Rico.

Fourth: an end to all violations of our airspace and territorial waters by U.S. aircraft and warships.

Fifth: withdrawal from the Guantánamo naval base and the return of Cuban territory occupied by the United States.

These are not irrational demands; they do not go against the rights of anyone; they are claims so legitimate, and so clearly limited to the rights of the Cuban people, that no one can object to them.

The U.S. government demands that the United Nations should verify, in our territory, the withdrawal of strategic weapons. Cuba demands that the United Nations should verify, in the territory of the United States, Puerto Rico, and other places where attacks on Cuba are prepared, the following: the dismantling of the training camps for mercenaries, spies, saboteurs, and terrorists; of the centers where subversion is prepared; and of the bases from which pirate vessels set out for our coasts.

In addition, one of the necessary guarantees Cuba demands is that effective measures of oversight be established to prevent repetition of such acts in the future.

If the United States and its accomplices in aggression against Cuba do not agree to such inspection in their territories by the United Nations, then Cuba will under no circumstances agree to inspection of its own territory.

Only through reciprocal concessions and guarantees will it be possible to reach a broad and honorable agreement acceptable to all. If such an agreement is reached, Cuba will have no need for strategic weapons for its defense. The foreign military technicians on hand to instruct our armed forces would be reduced to the minimum, and the necessary conditions would be created for the normal development of our relations with the countries of this hemisphere.

A just and satisfactory solution to this crisis will without doubt help solve the other pending problems throughout the world. It would be a solid step forward along the genuine road of peace. And the world needs peace.

It is a legitimate aspiration of humanity that the enormous sums now being invested in the manufacture of costly and deadly armaments should be devoted to creating goods of use to man, especially for the benefit of the underdeveloped peoples whom the colonizing and imperialist countries have left mired in the greatest poverty. The war industry and arms trafficking can be of interest only to the monopolists whose business it is to stifle the most legitimate aspirations of the people and to profit, like birds of prey, from destruction and death.

As Marxist-Leninists, we defend peace by conviction and on principle. Weapons are to us a heavy burden imposed by the imperialists, which divert energy and resources from the creative tasks of the revolution. Our position is to obtain peace as the supreme aspiration of humanity.

We believe in the possibility of averting war, and we do not believe that war is a fatal and inexorable fait accompli. But this does not mean that the imperialists have a right to be pirates or aggressors, or to commit acts of genocide against any people.

The imperialists must not confuse a principled position with weakness in face of their acts of aggression. It must be made quite clear to them that today they are in no position to impose their law on the world, and they will not be permitted to do so.

Cuba stresses once again that there is no better solution than the road of peace and discussion between governments, but at the same time we repeat that we shall never give in to the imperialists. To their positions of force, we shall respond with our firmness. To their attempt to humiliate us, we shall respond with our dignity. To their aggression, we shall respond with our determination to fight to the last combatant.

We do not believe in mere promises of nonaggression; we need deeds. Those deeds are set forth in our five points. We have as little faith in President Kennedy's words as we have fear of his veiled threats.

Patria o muerte!
Venceremos!

Osvaldo Dorticós
PRESIDENT OF THE REPUBLIC

Fidel Castro
PRIME MINISTER AND GENERAL
SECRETARY OF THE INTEGRATED
REVOLUTIONARY ORGANIZATIONS

Notes

Chapter 1

1. Dino A. Brugioni, *Eyeball to Eyeball: The Inside Story of the Cuban Missile Crisis* (New York: Random House, 1990, 1991), p. 69.

2. U.S. Department of State, *Foreign Relations of the United States, 1961–1963*, volume X, *Cuba, 1961–1962* (hereinafter *FRUS*, vol. X) (Washington, D.C.: United States Government Printing Office, 1997), pp. 459–75.

3. Ibid., p. 459.

4. Ibid., p. 460.

5. Ibid., p. 461.

6. Ibid., p. 462.

7. Ibid.

8. Ibid., pp. 462–63. Emphasis in original.

9. Ibid., p. 466. Emphasis in original.

10. Ibid., p. 466. Emphasis in original.

11. Ibid., pp. 467–68.

12. Ibid., pp. 468–75.

13. Ibid., p. 475.

14. See "Notes of the 483d Meeting of the National Security Council," *FRUS*, vol. X, pp. 479–81; "Record of Actions at the 483d Meeting of the National Security Council," *FRUS*, vol. X, pp. 481–83; "Memorandum for the Record," prepared by Admiral Burke, *FRUS*, vol. X, pp. 484–88.

15. Footnote to "Cuba and Communism in the Hemisphere," *FRUS*, vol. X, pp. 466–67.

16. Ibid.

17. "Record of Actions at the 483d Meeting of the National Security Council," *FRUS*, vol. X, p. 482.

18. Ibid.

19. Maxwell D. Taylor, *Swords and Plowshares* (New York: W.W. Norton, 1972), p. 180.

20. General Anatoli I. Gribkov and General William Y. Smith, *Operation Anadyr: U.S. and Soviet Generals Recount the Cuban Missile Crisis* (Chicago: Edition Q, 1994), p. 87.

21. Arthur M. Schlesinger, Jr., *A Thousand Days: John F. Kennedy in the White House* (Boston: Houghton Mifflin, 1965), p. 295.

22. Brugioni, *Eyeball to Eyeball*, p. 60.

23. Theodore C. Sorensen, *Kennedy* (New York: Harper & Row, 1965, 1988), p. 347.

24. Gribkov and Smith, *Operation Anadyr*, p. 86.

25. *FRUS*, vol X, pp. 576–606.

26. Ibid., p. 606.

27. Ibid., p. 605.

28. Ibid., p. 603.

29. "Program of Covert Action Aimed at Weakening the Castro Regime. Washington, May 19, 1961," *FRUS*, vol. X, p. 555.

30. Ibid., p. 556.

31. Ibid.

32. See *Playa Girón: La gran conjura* [Playa Girón: the great plot] (Havana: Editorial Capitán San Luis, 1991), pp. 25–30; and Fabián Escalante Font, *Cuba: La guerra secreta de la CIA, 1959–1962* [Cuba, the CIA's secret war, 1959–1962] (Havana: Editorial Capitán San Luis, 1993), pp. 110–19.

33. See *Noticias de Hoy*, Havana, August 12, 1961, second edition, pp. 1, 5–8.

34. "Memorandum From the President's Special Assistant (Schlesinger) to the President's Assistant Special Counsel (Goodwin). Washington, D.C. July 8, 1961," *FRUS*, vol. X, p. 621.

35. "Memorandum for the Record. Washington, July 19, 1961. U.S. Government Relations with Cuban Revolutionary Council," *FRUS*, vol. X, pp. 627–28.

36. "Memorandum for the Record. Washington, July 20, 1961. Minutes of Meeting of Special Group," *FRUS*, vol. X, p. 632.

37. "Paper Prepared in the Central Intelligence Agency," *FRUS*, vol. X, pp. 636–37.

38. See Ramón Torreira and José Buajasán, *Operación Peter Pan: Un caso de guerra psicológica contra Cuba* [Operation Peter Pan: an example of psychological warfare against Cuba] (Havana: Editora Política, 2000).

39. See "Ley de la circulación de nuevos billetes cubanos" [Law on the circulation of new Cuban banknotes], *Obra Revolucionaria* No. 27, Havana, August 10, 1961, pp. 19–21.

40. "Acerca de la captura de los impresores de la falsa ley sobre la patria potestad" [On the arrest of the printers of the fake parental custody act],

Noticias de Hoy, Havana, September 22, 1961, p. 6.

41. "Memorandum for the Record. Washington, October 5, 1961," *FRUS*, vol. X, p. 660.

42. Ibid., footnote summarizing Barnes memorandum.

43. See Escalante Font, *Cuba: La guerra secreta*, pp. 116–21.

44. Ernesto Guevara de la Serna, August 8, 1961, speech, in *Ernesto Che Guevara: Obras 1957–1967*, vol. II (Havana, Casa de las Américas, 1970), pp. 423, 438. This speech is available in English in *Che Guevara and the Cuban Revolution* (Pathfinder, 1987).

45. "Memorandum from the President's Assistant Special Counsel (Goodwin) to President Kennedy. Washington, August 22, 1961," *FRUS*, vol. X, p. 640.

46. Manuel Tello, *Mexico: una posición internacional* [Mexico: an international policy] (Mexico City: Editorial Joaquín Muztiz, 1972), p. 109.

47. Carlos Lechuga, *Itinerario de una farsa* [Itinerary of a farce] (Havana: Editorial Pueblo y Educación, 1991), p. 187.

48. "Memorandum of Conversation Between President Kennedy and President Frondizi. New York, September 26, 1961, 9 a.m.," *FRUS*, vol. X, pp. 657–58.

49. For more information on the process leading up to the call for this meeting of the OAS foreign ministers, and on the meeting itself, see Lechuga, *Itinerario de una farsa*.

50. Lechuga, *Itinerario de una farsa*, p. 212.

51. José Miró Cardona, *Renuncia ante el Consejo Revolucionario de Cuba* [Resignation from the Cuban Revolutionary Council]. (Miami, April 1963), p. 5.

52. *Chronology of the Cuban Missile Crisis*. Edited by The National Security Archive, Washington, D.C., 1989, p. 51.

53. "Memorandum from the Officer in Charge of Cuban Affairs (Hurwitch) to the Chief of Operations, Operation Mongoose (Lansdale). Washington, January 16, 1962," *FRUS*, Vol. X, p. 705.

54. Decree No. 3447. Washington, D.C., February 6, 1962, (Source: *American Foreign Policy, Current Documents, 1962* [Washington D.C.: U.S. Government Printing Office], pp. 338–39). The resolution went into effect at 12:01 a.m., Eastern Standard Time, February 7, 1962.

Chapter 2

1. *Defensa de Cuba* [Defense of Cuba], pamphlet (Havana: Universidad Popular, second cycle, 1960), p. 6.

2. "Informe sobre el estudio de las Fuerzas Armadas Revolucionarias y proposiciones nuestras para su mejoramiento. Estrictamente Secreto" [Report on the study of the Revolutionary Armed Forces and our proposals for its improvement. Top secret]. Prepared by the Chief of Organization and Mobilization of the General Staff, Captain Emilio Aragonés, for the Chief of the General Staff, Commander Sergio del Valle. December 29, 1961. Archives of the Defense Information Center of the Revolutionary Armed Forces (hereinafter CID-FAR Archives). Among the proposals in this document was a reduction in the number of personnel for peacetime to an estimated figure of 98,000 by 1962.

3. "Resumen de las plantillas de las FAR para el año 1962" [FAR personnel summary for 1962], signed by the chief of staff, Commander Sergio del Valle. Havana, February 7, 1962. CID-FAR Archives.

4. Walfrido La'O Estrada, interview by the author, May 1999. Estrada headed up the Political Section in the early days of the Eastern Army.

5. FAR personnel summary for 1962.

6. Ibid.

7. Ibid.

8. Cuban-Soviet agreements signed on August 4 and September 30, 1961, respectively. CID-FAR Archives.

9. Cuban-Soviet agreement, July 13, 1962. CID-FAR Archives.

10. Agreements of August 4 and September 30, 1961. CID-FAR Archives.

11. Fidel Castro. Order no. 1 by the Commander in Chief of the FAR for the 1962 instructional year. CID-FAR Archives.

12. Fidel Castro. Appeal to combatants of the FAR, December 18, 1961. CID-FAR Archives.

13. Raúl Castro. Order no. 2 by the minister of the FAR on the second semester of instruction of the FAR, June 1, 1962. CID-FAR Archives.

14. Raúl Menéndez Tomassevich, "Ni un minuto de tregua" [Not a minute of truce]. Interview by José Cazañas Reyes, *Verde Olivo*, special issue, December 1986, p. 38.

15. Alberto Edel Morales, "El mecanismo de respuesta de la Revolución contra el bandidismo" [The revolution's response mechanism against banditry]. Unpublished essay. (Trinidad: Archive of the National Museum of the Struggle against Banditry), p. 8.

16. *Gaceta Oficial*, January 5, 1961. Laws 923 and 924.

17. For Law 988, see José Suárez Amador, *La Lucha Contra Bandi-*

dos en Cuba [The struggle against bandits in Cuba] (Havana: Editorial Letras Cubanas, 1981), pp. 78–79.

18. "Demanda del Pueblo de Cuba al Gobierno de Estados Unidos por daños humanos" [Lawsuit by the People of Cuba v. the U.S. Government for Human Damages), *Granma*, special supplement, June 1, 1999.

Chapter 3

1. "Memorandum from the President's Assistant Special Counsel (Goodwin) to President Kennedy. Washington, November 1, 1961," *FRUS*, vol. X, p. 665.

2. "Inter-Agency Staff Study: Plan for Cuba. Washington, undated," *FRUS*, vol. X, p. 677.

3. Ibid., p. 680.

4. Ibid., p. 681.

5. Ibid.

6. Ibid.

7. "Memorandum for the Record. Washington, November 22, 1961," *FRUS*, vol. X, p. 685.

8. "Memorandum from President Kennedy. Washington, November 30, 1961," *FRUS*, vol. X, p. 688.

9. "Draft Memorandum for the Record. Washington, December 1, 1961," *FRUS*, vol. X, pp. 690–91.

10. "Memorandum from the Chief of Operations, Operation Mongoose (Lansdale). Washington, December 7, 1961," *FRUS*, vol. X, p. 693.

11. "Memorandum for the Record. Washington, December 8, 1961. Subject: Minutes of Special Group Meeting," *FRUS*, vol. X, pp. 695–96.

12. "The Cuba Project: Program Review by the Chief of Operations, Operation Mongoose (Lansdale), Washington, January 18, 1962," *FRUS*, vol. X, p. 710.

13. Ibid., pp. 710–11.

14. "Memorandum from the Chief of Operations, Operation Mongoose (Lansdale) to the Members of the Caribbean Survey Group. Washington, January 20, 1962," *FRUS*, vol. X, p. 721.

15. U.S. Senate, *Alleged Assassination Plots Involving Foreign Leaders: An Interim Report of the Select Committee to Study Governmental Operations with Respect to Intelligence Activities*. November 20 (legislative day, November 18), 1975. United States Government Printing Office. Washington, vol. II, pp. K.10–K.11.

16. "Memorandum from the Chief of Operations in the Deputy Di-

rectorate for Plans (Helms) to Director of Central Intelligence McCone. Washington, January 19, 1962," *FRUS*, vol. X, p. 720.

17. "The Cuba Project Program Reviewed by the Chief of Operations of Operation Mongoose (Lansdale), Washington, February 20, 1962." FRUS, vol. X, p. 746.

18. Ibid., p. 746–47. See also Laurence Chang and Peter Kornbluh, *The Cuban Missile Crisis* (New York: A National Security Archive, Documents Reader, The New Press, 1992), pp. 26–37. And John Elliston, *Psywar on Cuba: The Declassified History of U.S. Anti-Castro Propaganda* (Melbourne and New York: Ocean Press, 1999), pp. 77–82.

19. Chang and Kornbluh, *The Cuban Missile Crisis*, p. 37.

20. Ibid.

21. "Guidelines for Operation Mongoose. Washington, March 14, 1962," *FRUS*, vol. X, p. 771.

22. Gribkov and Smith, *Operation Anadyr*, p. 93.

23. U.S. Senate, *Alleged Assassination Plots Involving Foreign Leaders*, op. cit.

24. "Memorandum from the Chief of Operations, Operation Mongoose (Lansdale) to the Special Group (Augmented). Washington, July 25, 1962," *FRUS*, vol. X, p. 884.

25. "Memorandum from the Department of Defense Operations Officer for Operation Mongoose (Craig) to the Special Group (Augmented). Washington, August 8, 1962," *FRUS*, vol. X, pp. 917–20.

26. "Memorandum from the President's Military Representative (Taylor) to President Kennedy. Washington, August 17, 1962," *FRUS*, vol. X, pp. 944–45.

27. "National Security Action Memorandum No. 181. Washington, August 23, 1962," *FRUS*, vol. X, pp. 957–58.

28. U.S. Senate, *Alleged Assassination Plots Involving Foreign Leaders*, op. cit., vol. II, p. K.16.

29. "Memorandum from Secretary of Defense McNamara to the Joint Chiefs of Staff. Washington, May 1, 1961," *FRUS*, vol. X, pp. 405–06.

30. Miró Cardona, *Renuncia*, p. 6.

31. Ibid.

32. "Cuba and Communism in the Hemisphere," *FRUS*, vol. X, pp. 467–68.

33. "Memorandum from Secretary of Defense McNamara to President Kennedy. Washington, June 8, 1961," *FRUS*, vol. X, pp. 571–72.

34. Department of Defense. Office of the Secretary of Defense. His-

torian's Cable Files, Cuba. January–August 1962. Retranslated from the Spanish.

35. In Elliston, *Psywar on Cuba,* p. 92.

36. *U.S. News & World Report,* September 24, 1962.

37. Ibid.

38. "Memorandum from the President's Special Assistant for Science and Technology (Wiesner) to the President's Deputy Special Assistant for National Security Affairs (Kaysen). Washington, September 25, 1962. Attachment," *FRUS,* vol. X, p. 1090.

Chapter 4

1. *Revolución,* May 30, 1962, pp. 1 and 5.

2. Sergo Mikoyan, speaking at the conference on the Cuban Missile Crisis held in Cambridge, Massachusetts, October 11–12, 1987. Transcription in James G. Blight and David A. Welch, *On the Brink: Americans and Soviets Reexamine the Cuban Missile Crisis,* 2nd ed. (New York: Hill and Wang, 1989, 1990), pp. 238–39.

3. Raymond L. Garthoff, *Reflections on the Cuban Missile Crisis,* revised edition (Washington, D.C.: Brookings Institution, 1989), p. 12.

4. Nikita S. Khrushchev, *Khrushchev Remembers* (Boston: Little, Brown, 1970).

5. A.A. Gromyko, "La Crisis del Caribe: sobre lo revelado ahora y lo oculto entonces" [The Caribbean Crisis: what has been revealed now and was hidden then], *Izvestia,* April 15, 1989. Printed in Spanish in *Comentarios, artículos y editoriales,* DOR-CCPCC, no. 22, June 21, 1989.

6. Ibid.

7. Aleksandr Alekseev, speaking at tripartite conference on the Cuban Missile Crisis held in Havana, January 9–12, 1992. Transcription in Blight et al., *Cuba on the Brink,* p. 77.

8. Aleksandr Alekseev, article published in *Ekho Planety,* no. 33, Moscow, November 1988, pp. 26–33.

9. Ibid.

10. Ibid.

11. Ibid. The U.S. congressional elections were actually November 4.

12. Sergo Mikoyan, "La Crisis del Caribe, en retrospectiva," [The Caribbean Crisis: a retrospective], *Revista América Latina,* no. 4, USSR, 1988.

13. Ibid.

14. Robert McNamara, speaking at tripartite conference on the Cu-

ban Missile Crisis held in Moscow, January 1989. Transcripts of sessions.

15. Transcripts of presentations at tripartite conference in Moscow, 1989.

16. Fidel Castro at the 1992 tripartite conference in Havana. A slightly different translation can be found in Blight et al., *Cuba on the Brink*, p. 202.

17. Mikoyan, "La Crisis del Caribe, en retrospectiva."

18. Alekseev, article published in *Ekho Planety*.

19. Fidel Castro at the 1992 tripartite conference in Havana. A slightly different translation can be found in Blight et al., *Cuba on the Brink*, p. 197.

20. Fidel Castro at the 1992 tripartite conference in Havana. In Blight et al., *Cuba on the Brink*, p. 206.

21. Minutes of the Central Committee of the Communist Party of Cuba, January 25, 1968. October Crisis Collection, Institute of Cuban History (IHC) Archives (hereinafter IHC Archives). A version in English of excerpts from this speech dealing with the October Crisis has been posted on the website of the National Security Archive.

22. Ibid.

23. Fidel Castro at the 1992 tripartite conference in Havana. In Blight et al., *Cuba on the Brink*, pp. 198–99.

24. Minutes of the Central Committee of the Communist Party of Cuba, January 25, 1968 (IHC Archives).

25. Fidel Castro at the 1992 tripartite conference in Havana. A slightly different translation can be found in Blight et al., *Cuba on the Brink*, p. 201.

26. Minutes of the Central Committee of the Communist Party of Cuba, January 25, 1968 (IHC Archives).

27. Fidel Castro at the 1992 tripartite conference in Havana. In Blight et al., *Cuba on the Brink*, pp. 83–85.

28. Minutes of the Central Committee of the Communist Party of Cuba, January 25, 1968 (IHC Archives).

29. Fidel Castro at the 1992 tripartite conference in Havana. In Blight et al., *Cuba on the Brink*, p. 84.

30. Transcript of presentation at tripartite conference in Havana, 1992. In Blight et al., *Cuba on the Brink*, pp. 56–60.

31. Gribkov and Smith, *Operation Anadyr*, pp. 23–24.

32. Transcript of presentation at tripartite conference in Havana, 1992.

In Blight et al., *Cuba on the Brink,* pp. 60–61.

33. Interview with retired Col. Mikhail I. Derkachev, who was former aide to Army General Issa A. Pliyev, June 1991.

34. Interview with retired Maj. Gen. Leonid S. Garbuz, who held the position of second-in-command to the head of the STF for combat preparation. General Garbuz was also directly in charge of the missile troops. He is now retired and chief of the Cuba group of the Russian Committee of Veterans of War and Work. He was interviewed in Cuba and Moscow, in December 1989 and May 1990 respectively (author's archives).

35. Ibid.

36. Ibid.

37. Interviews with Vice Adm. Aldo Santamaría Cuadrado, Pedro Oropeza del Portal, and Franco Lemus (author's archives).

38. Carlos Rafael Rodríguez, report on meeting with Nikita Khrushchev on December 11, 1962 (CID-FAR Archives).

39. Interview with retired Col. Victor Semykin, main engineer of the 43rd Missile Division, which served in Cuba during the 1962 missile crisis. Moscow, May 1990 (author's archives).

40. Interview with retired Col. Ivan Schishenko, who served in the warhead special unit. Moscow, May 1990.

41. Interview with retired Col. Aleksandr Kovalenko, who first was head of an R-14 regiment and later headed a similar R-12 unit. Moscow, May 1990.

42. Ibid.

43. Ibid.

44. Interview with Sgt. Aleksei F. Maslov, radar operator of an antiaircraft defense regiment stationed in Santiago de Cuba. Havana, December 1990.

45. Interview with Sgt. Victor Poletin, radar operator of antiaircraft defense missile troops. Moscow, May 1990.

46. Interview with Sergeant Maslov.

47. Interview with Colonel Kovalenko.

48. Interview with Colonel Semykin.

49. Interviews with retired Major General Garbuz and retired Rear Admiral Tikhonov.

50. Interview with retired Col. Osvaldo Fernández, FAR, whose assignment was to accompany Maj. Gen. Igor D. Statsenko, chief of the missile division.

51. Interviews with retired Lt. Gen. N.K. Beloborodov, commander of Warheads Special Unit, and with Colonel Shishenko.

52. Interviews with Lieutenant General Beloborodov, Major General Garbuz, Rear Admiral Tikhonov, Colonels Burkov, Kovalenko, and Schishenko.

53. Interview with Lieutenant General Beloborodov (author's archives).

54. Gribkov and Smith, *Operation Anadyr*, p. 4.

55. Interview with Lieutenant General Beloborodov.

56. Ibid.

57. Interviews with retired Cols. A.M. Burlov, first engineer of the R-12 missile regiment, and J.N. Schishenko, chief of the special missile warhead preparation brigade. December 1989.

58. Interview with Major General Garbuz.

59. Interview with Colonel Burlov.

60. Ibid.

61. Ibid.

62. Interviews with Major General Garbuz and Colonel Burlov.

63. Interview with Major General Garbuz.

64. Interviews with General Beloborodov, General Garbuz, and Colonel Burlov.

65. Transcript of presentation at tripartite conference in Havana, 1992. In Blight et al., *Cuba on the Brink*, pp. 76–77.

66. Minutes of the Central Committee of the Communist Party of Cuba, January 25, 1968 (IHC Archives).

67. Fidel Castro at the 1992 tripartite conference in Havana. A slightly different translation can be found in Blight et al., *Cuba on the Brink*, p. 86.

68. Ibid.

69. Transcript of presentation at tripartite conference in Havana, 1992. In Blight et al., *Cuba on the Brink*, p. 62.

Chapter 5

1. See John Prados, *Presidents' Secret Wars: CIA and Pentagon Covert Operations since World War II* (New York: William Morrow, 1986), pp. 132–33.

2. Sorensen, *Kennedy*, p. 669.

3. Fidel Castro at the 1992 tripartite conference in Havana. In Blight et al., *Cuba on the Brink*, p. 84.

4. Emilio Aragonés Navarro, interview with the author, January 17, 1989 (author's archives).

5. Ibid.

6. Ibid.

7. *Noticias de Hoy*, Havana, September 3, 1962.

8. *U.S. Policy toward Cuba*, part 1, p. 17.

9. Osvaldo Dorticós, speech delivered at the Twenty-sixth National Council of the Central Organization of Cuban Workers (CTC), September 7, 1962. *Obra Revolucionaria*, no. 26, 1962, p. 12.

10. Fidel Castro, speech delivered at the Third National Congress of Municipal Education Councils, September 10, 1962. *Obra Revolucionaria*, no. 26, 1962, pp. 24–25.

11. *Noticias de Hoy*, Havana, September 12, 1962, p. 2.

12. *New Times* magazine, no. 6, Moscow, 1989. Georgi Bolshakov: "Hot Line."

13. Fidel Castro at the 1992 tripartite conference in Havana. In Blight et al., *Cuba on the Brink*, pp. 207–9

14. Ibid., p. 208.

Chapter 6

1. Blight et al., *Cuba on the Brink*, p. 125.

2. Sorensen, *Kennedy*, pp. 673–76.

3. Sorensen, *Kennedy*, pp. 675–76.

4. "Summary of Agreed Facts and Premises, Possible Courses of Action and Unanswered Questions. Washington, October 17, 1962." Washington National Records Center, RG 330, OASD (C) A Files, FRC 71 A 2896, Historical, October 1962. Reprinted in Chang and Kornbluh, *The Cuban Missile Crisis, 1962*, pp. 114–15.

5. Nikita S. Khrushchev, *Khrushchev Remembers: The Glasnost Tapes*, translated and edited by Jerrold L. Schecter with Vyacheslav V. Luchkov (Boston: Little, Brown, 1990), p. 174.

6. Transcripts of tripartite conference in Moscow, 1989.

7. Robert F. Kennedy, *Thirteen Days: A Memoir of the Cuban Missile Crisis* (New York: W.W. Norton, 1969), p. 37.

8. Sorensen, *Kennedy*, p. 687.

9. Ibid., p. 691.

10. Blight et al., *Cuba on the Brink*, p. 142.

11. Department of State, *Foreign Relations of the United States, Cuban Missile Crisis and Aftermath*, vol. XI, (Washington, D.C.: United

States Government Printing Office, 1996), pp. 126–36.

12. ABC television program on the Cuban Missile Crisis, October 17, 1992.

13. Blight et al., *On the Brink,* p. 391, note 70.

14. "Notes on October 21, 1962 meeting with the President." Washington National Records Center, RG 330, OASD (C) A Files: FRC 71 A 2896, Misc. Papers Regarding Cuba. Top Secret. Reprinted in Chang and Kornbluh, *The Cuban Missile Crisis, 1962,* pp. 144–45.

15. Ibid.

16. Sorensen, *Kennedy,* p. 698.

17. Kennedy, *Thirteen Days,* p. 53.

18. Reprinted in Kennedy, *Thirteen Days,* pp. 163–64.

19. Ibid., p. 165.

20. Ibid., p. 166.

21. Ibid.

22. Ibid., pp. 167–69.

23. Garthoff, *Reflections on the Cuban Missile Crisis,* p. 75.

Chapter 7

1. Interview with Manuel de Jesús Quiñones *(Pedro Luis)*, December 1988. In 1962 he was in charge of military information for the General Staff of the FAR.

2. *Noticias de Hoy,* Havana, October 23, 1962.

3. "Letter from President Kennedy to Chairman Khrushchev, Washington, October 22, 1962." U.S. Department of State, *Foreign Relations of the United States, 1961–1963,* Volume XI, *Cuban Missile Crisis and Aftermath* (Washington: United States Government Printing Office, 1996), p. 163 (hereinafter *FRUS,* vol. XI).

4. Message from Nikita S. Khrushchev to Fidel Castro, October 23, 1962. Archives of the Office of Historical Affairs of the Council of State. An English translation is reprinted in Blight et al., *Cuba on the Brink,* pp. 212–13.

5. Fidel Castro at the 1992 tripartite conference in Havana. In Blight et al., *Cuba on the Brink,* p. 213.

6. For information on the resolution approved by the OAS on October 23, 1961, see *Bulletin of the Department of State,* November 12, 1962, pp. 720–22. See also *American Foreign Policy, Current Documents, 1962,* pp. 408–10.

7. *Noticias de Hoy,* Havana, October 25, 1962, p. 2.

8. Ibid.

9. "Expediente relativo a la alarma de combate del 22 de octubre de 1962. Documentos de la reunión del 24 de octubre." [Report on the combat alarm of October 22, 1962; Documents relating to the meeting of October 24], CID Archives; Military Unit 1081 Collection, Bundle 1, Inventory 1, Record 1.

10. Ibid.

11. Ibid.

12. Garthoff, *Reflections on the Cuban Missile Crisis*, p. 62, and Cagan Scott, "Nuclear Alert and Crisis Management," *International Security*, Spring 1985, p. 108.

13. Published in English in Kennedy, *Thirteen Days*, pp. 185–86.

14. Presentation by Georgi Kornienko, who was chief political adviser at the Soviet embassy in Washington during the crisis, at the tripartite conference on the Cuban Missile Crisis in Antigua, January 4–7, 1991.

15. "Telegram From the Department of State to the Embassy in Brazil, Washington, October 26, 1962," *FRUS*, vol. XI, pp. 228–29.

16. Fidel Castro at the 1992 tripartite conference in Havana. In Blight et al., *Cuba on the Brink*, p. 112.

17. Ibid., p. 111.

18. Fidel Castro to Nikita Khrushchev, October 26, 1962. Reprinted in full in Blight et al., *Cuba on the Brink*, p. 481. The letter is also reproduced in Chang and Kornbluh, *The Cuban Missile Crisis, 1962*, p. 189.

19. Georgi Bolshakov, "Hot Line," *New Times* magazine, nos. 4, 5, 6, Moscow, 1989.

20. "Telegram from the Embassy in the Soviet Union to the Department of State, Moscow, October 26, 1962, 7 P.M.," *FRUS*, vol. XI, p. 239.

21. See Khrushchev's message to Kennedy in *Noticias de Hoy*, October 28, 1962, p. 4. Published in English in Kennedy, *Thirteen Days*, pp. 196–201.

22. Kennedy, *Thirteen Days*, pp. 202–3.

23. Ibid., p. 204.

24. Fidel Castro at the 1992 tripartite conference in Havana. In Blight et al., *Cuba on the Brink*, p. 107.

25. *Noticias de Hoy*, Havana, October 28, 1962, p. 1.

26. General Anatoly Gribkov and General William Y. Smith, op. cit. p. 63.

27. Kennedy, *Thirteen Days*, p. 207.

28. Ibid., p. 213.

29. Ibid., p. 212.

30. Arthur M. Schlesinger, *Robert Kennedy and His Times* (Boston: Houghton Mifflin, 1978), p. 524.

Chapter 8

1. Printed in *Granma*, November 23, 1990. Reprinted in Chang and Kornbluh, *The Cuban Missile Crisis, 1962*, p. 239.

2. Fidel Castro at the 1992 tripartite conference in Havana. In Blight et al., *Cuba on the Brink*, p. 214.

3. Ibid., p. 215.

4. *Noticias de Hoy*, Havana, October 31, 1962, p.10. Reprinted as "Prime Minister Castro's 'Five Points' Letter to UN Secretary General U Thant, October 29, 1962," Chang and Kornbluh, *The Cuban Missile Crisis, 1962*, pp. 241–42.

5. Printed in *Granma*, November 23, 1990. Reprinted in Chang and Kornbluh, *The Cuban Missile Crisis, 1962*, p. 240.

6. Printed in *Granma*, November 23, 1990. Reprinted in Chang and Kornbluh, *The Cuban Missile Crisis, 1962*, p. 243.

7. Printed in *Granma*, November 23, 1990. Reprinted in Chang and Kornbluh, *The Cuban Missile Crisis, 1962*, p. 244.

8. Fidel Castro, "Informe al pueblo de Cuba sobre las conversaciones con el Secretario General de la ONU" [Report to the Cuban people on talks with the UN secretary-general], *Obra Revolucionaria*, no. 32, Havana, November 2, 1962.

9. Ibid.

10. Sorensen, *Kennedy*, pp. 720–21.

11. Fidel Castro, "Carta al Secretario General de las Naciones Unidas. Noviembre 19 de 1962" [Letter to the secretary-general of the United Nations. November 19, 1962], *Política Internacional*, no. 1, 1963, pp. 238–39. Reprinted in Chang and Kornbluh, *The Cuban Missile Crisis, 1962*, pp. 288–89.

12. "The President's News Conference of November 20, 1962," in *Public Papers of the Presidents of the United States: John F. Kennedy, Containing the Public Messages, Speeches and Statements of the President, January 1 to December 31, 1962* (Washington: United States Government Printing Office, 1963), pp. 830–38.

13. "Notas de la conversación entre Anastas Mikoyan y U Thant, efectuada el 26 de noviembre de 1962" [Notes from the talks between Anastas Mikoyan and U Thant held on November 26, 1962] (IHC Archives).

14. United States draft statement at the Security Council (IHC Archives).

15. USSR draft statement at the Security Council (IHC Archives).

16. "Observaciones del Gobierno Revolucionario de Cuba sobre los proyectos de declaración ante el Consejo de Seguridad de los gobiernos de Estados Unidos y la URSS" [Remarks of the Revolutionary Government of Cuba on Draft Statements of the Governments of the USSR and the United States at the Security Council] (IHC Archives).

17. "Proyecto de declaración del Gobierno Revolucionario de Cuba ante el Consejo de Seguridad" [Draft Statement of the Revolutionary Government of Cuba at the Security Council] (IHC Archives).

18. "Notas de la conversación de Anastas Mikoyan con el representante permanente de Estados Unidos ante la ONU, Adlai Stevenson, con fecha 28 de noviembre de 1962" [Notes from discussion between Anastas Mikoyan and the U.S. permanent representative to the United Nations, Adlai Stevenson, November 28, 1962] (IHC Archives).

19. Ibid.

20. "Mensaje confidencial del jefe de la Misión Permanente cubana en las Naciones Unidas al Ministro de Relaciones Exteriores de Cuba sobre notas de la entrevista de Mikoyan con Kennedy, fechado el 2 de diciembre de 1962" [Confidential message from the head of Cuba's Permanent Mission at the United Nations to the Cuban minister of foreign relations on notes from the meeting between Mikoyan and Kennedy, December 2, 1962] (IHC Archives).

21. Ibid.

22. *Noticias de Hoy*, Havana, December 13, 1962, p. 9.

23. *Política Internacional*, no. 1, 1963, pp. 146–47. Reprinted in Chang and Kornbluh, *The Cuban Missile Crisis, 1962*, p. 297.

24. Carlos Lechuga, "Carta al Secretario General de las Naciones Unidas. 7 de enero de 1963" [Letter from Carlos Lechuga, Cuba's permanent representative to the United Nations, to the UN Secretary General. January 7, 1963], *Política Internacional*, no. 1, 1963, p. 243.

By way of an epilogue

1. United States Senate, *Alleged Assassination Plots Involving Foreign Leaders*. Op. cit., p. B-1.

2. Ernesto Che Guevara, speech delivered at a rally in honor of Antonio Maceo, December 7, 1962. *Obra Revolucionaria*, no. 33, Havana, December 1962, p. 6.

Glossary of individuals

Abashvili, Vice Adm. Georgio S. – Second in command of naval forces for the Soviet Troop Force in Cuba.

Acheson, Dean – U.S. secretary of state, 1949–53. During the October Crisis, he was unofficial foreign affairs consultant to President Kennedy.

Achilles, Theodore C. – Special assistant to U.S. secretary of state Dean Rusk.

Ageyev, Gen. Pyotr V. – Senior official of the Directorate of Operations of the Central General Staff of the Soviet armed forces.

Akindinov, Maj. Gen. Pavel V. – Chief of staff of the Soviet Troop Force in Cuba.

Alekseev, Aleksandr – Soviet ambassador to Cuba beginning August 1962.

Almeida, Cmdr. Juan – Chief of Cuba's Central Army.

Amory, Robert – CIA deputy director for intelligence.

Anderson, Adm. George W. – Chief of U.S. naval operations beginning 1961.

Anderson, Maj. Rudolf – Pilot of a U.S. U-2 spy plane shot down over Cuba by a Soviet missile and killed October 27, 1962.

Aragonés, Capt. Emilio – Head of organization and mobilization of the general staff of Cuba's Revolutionary Armed Forces and organizational secretary of the National Directorate of the Integrated Revolutionary Organizations.

Ball, George W. – U.S. undersecretary of state for economic affairs, January–December 1961, and then undersecretary of state.

Bandilovsky, Lt. Col. A.Z. – Head of a regiment of the missile division of the Soviet Troop Force in Cuba.

Barnes, C. Tracy – CIA assistant deputy director for covert action.

Beloborodov, Lt. Gen. N.K. – Head of the special unit responsible for nuclear warheads for the Soviet Troop Force in Cuba.

Biryuzov, Marshal Sergei – Soviet vice minister of defense and head of the USSR's Strategic Missile Forces.

Bissell, Richard M., Jr. – CIA's deputy director for plans 1959–62, in charge of covert operations against Cuba.

Bolshakov, Georgi – Official at the Soviet embassy in Washington.

Brezhnev, Leonid – Secretary of the Central Committee of the Communist Party of the Soviet Union and member of its Presidium.

Bundy, McGeorge – Special assistant to the president for national security affairs.

Burke, Adm. Arleigh A. – U.S. chief of naval operations beginning August 1961.

Burlatsky, Fyodor – Official of the Central Committee of the Soviet Communist Party and a member of Khrushchev's personal staff.

Burlov, Col. Anatoly M. – Engineer of the missile division of the Soviet Troop Force in Cuba.

Butski, Maj. Gen. Aleksei S. – Representative of the Ministry of Defense within the Soviet Troop Force in Cuba.

Cabell, Gen. Charles P. – CIA deputy director until January 1962.

Castilla Mas, Cmdr. Belarmino – Chief of staff of Cuba's Eastern Army.

Castro, Fidel – Commander in chief of the Revolutionary Armed Forces and prime minister of the revolutionary government of Cuba.

Castro, Cmdr. Raúl – Minister of the Revolutionary Armed Forces of Cuba.

Cline, Ray – CIA deputy director for information.

Coerr, Wymberley DeR. – Deputy assistant secretary of state for inter-American affairs.

Cherkesov, Lt. Col. I.I. – Chief of a regiment of the missile division of the Soviet Troop Force in Cuba.

Dankevich, Col. Gen. Pavel B. – Second in command of the Soviet Troop Force in Cuba.

Davidkov, Col. Gen. Victor Y. – Second in command of air units of the Soviet Troop Force in Cuba.

Del Valle, Cmdr. Sergio – Chief of staff of the Revolutionary Armed Forces of Cuba.

Dementyev, Maj. Gen. Aleksei A. – Second in command of land forces for the Soviet Troop Force and head of the Soviet military specialists in Cuba.

Dennison, Adm. Robert L. – Commander of the U.S. Atlantic Command.

Derkachev, Col. Mikhail I. – Adjutant of Soviet general Pliyev.

Dillon, C. Douglas – U.S. secretary of the treasury.

Díaz, Higinio – Cuban counterrevolutionary. During the Bay of Pigs invasion, he headed a group of mercenaries that backed down from a planned landing at Baracoa in eastern Cuba.

Dobrynin, Anatoly – Soviet ambassador to Washington.

Dorticós, Osvaldo – President of the Republic of Cuba.

Dulles, Allen W. – CIA director until November 1961.

Eisenhower, Dwight D. – President of the United States until January 1961.

Eisenhower, Milton S. – Brother of Dwight Eisenhower and member of the U.S. Tractors for Freedom Committee, which negotiated for the release of the prisoners from the Bay of Pigs invasion.

Esterline, Jacob D. – Chief of Section 4 of the Western Hemisphere Division of the CIA's Directorate of Plans.

Fernández Mell, Cmdr. Oscar – Chief of staff of Cuba's Western Army.

Frondizi, Arturo – President of Argentina, 1958–62.

Garbuz, Maj. Gen. Leonid S. – Second in command for attention to the missile units and combat preparation of the Soviet Troop Force in Cuba.

García Incháustegui, Mario – Cuba's permanent representative to the United Nations at the opening of the October 1962 crisis.

García, Cmdr. Calixto – Second in command of Cuba's Eastern Army.

García, Cmdr. Guillermo – Head of Cuba's Western Army.

Gálvez, Cmdr. William – Head of the Isle of Pines Military Region of Cuba's armed forces.

Gilpatric, Roswell L. – U.S. deputy secretary of defense.

Goodwin, Richard N. – Assistant to the special counsel to the president of the United States and president of the Interagency Task Force on Cuba until November 1961; subsequently deputy assistant secretary of state for inter-American affairs.

Goulart, João – President of Brazil, 1961–64.

Grechko, Marshal Andrei – Deputy to the Soviet defense minister.

Grechko, Maj. Gen. Stepan M. – Deputy head of antiaircraft defense for the Soviet Troop Force in Cuba, 1962.

Gribkov, Gen. Anatoly I. – Official of the Main Directorate of Operations of the Soviet Central General Staff and representative of the Soviet Ministry of Defense within the Soviet Troop Force in Cuba in October 1962.

Gromyko, Andrei A. – Soviet foreign minister.

Guevara, Cmdr. Ernesto Che – Minister of industry, member of the Secretariat of the National Directorate of the Integrated Revolutionary Organizations, and commander of Cuban defense forces in western Cuba during the crisis.

Hayward, Rear Adm. John T. – Head of Task Force 135 during the U.S. naval blockade of Cuba, October 24–November 20, 1962.

Helms, Richard M. – Head of operations for the CIA's Directorate of Plans until February 1962; subsequently became director of plans.

Hurwitch, Robert A. – Officer in charge of Cuban affairs at the State Department until February 1962.

Ivanov, Col. Gen. Semyon P. – Head of the Main Directorate of Operations of the Soviet general staff and secretary of the Defense Council.

Johnson, Lyndon B. – Vice president of the United States.

Johnson, Gen. Max S. – Former commandant of the U.S. Army War College.

Johnson, U. Alexis – U.S. deputy undersecretary of state for political affairs beginning April 1961.

Kennedy, John F. – President of the United States, January 1961 to November 1963.

Kennedy, Robert F. – U.S. attorney general and top adviser and liaison to the president on Cuban affairs.

Khrushchev, Nikita S. – Soviet premier and general secretary of the Communist Party of the Soviet Union.

King, Col. J.C. – Head of the CIA's Western Hemisphere Division.

Kohler, Foy D. – U.S. ambassador to Moscow beginning September 1962.

Kornienko, Georgi – Chief political adviser in the Soviet diplomatic mission in Washington.

Kosygin, Aleksei – President of the Supreme Soviet of the USSR and member of the Presidium of the Central Committee of the Communist Party of the Soviet Union.

Kovalenko, Lt. Col. Aleksandr A. – Head of the R-12 missile regiment of the Soviet Troop Force in Cuba.

Kozlov, Frol R. – Secretary of the Central Committee of the Communist Party of the Soviet Union and member of its Presidium.

Kuznetzov, Vasily V. – Vice minister of foreign relations of the USSR.

Lansdale, Gen. Edward G. – Head of operations of Operation Mongoose beginning December 1961.

La'O Estrada, Walfrido – Chief of the Revolutionary Instruction Section of Cuba's Eastern Army.

Lechuga, Carlos – Cuba's representative to the Organization of American States until February 1962, then Cuba's ambassador to Mexico. Became Cuba's permanent representative to the United Nations in late October 1962.

LeMay, Gen. Curtis – Chief of staff of the U.S. Air Force.

Lemus, Capt. Franco – Second in command of Cuba's army corps in Pinar del Río.

Loginov, Evgenii – Soviet minister of civil aviation.

Loufti, Omar – Undersecretary-general of the United Nations.

McCloy, John J. – Presidential adviser and chairman of the Coordinating Committee for the negotiations between the U.S. and USSR on Cuba in the United Nations.

McCone, John A. – Director of the Central Intelligence Agency beginning November 1961.

McNamara, Robert S. – U.S. secretary of defense.

Malinovsky, Marshal Rodion Y. – Soviet minister of defense.

Martin, Edwin – U.S. assistant secretary of state for inter-American affairs.

Maslov, Sgt. Aleksei F. – Member of the antiaircraft missile troops of the Soviet Troop Force in Cuba.

Menéndez Tomassevich, Cmdr. Raúl – Chief of staff of Cuba's Central Army.

Mikoyan, Anastas – Vice premier of the Soviet Union.

Mikoyan, Sergo – Son and personal secretary of the vice premier of the Soviet Union.

Miró Cardona, José – President of the counterrevolutionary U.S.-based Cuban Revolutionary Council.

Nitze, Paul H. – Assistant secretary of defense for international security affairs.

Oropeza, Capt. Pedro E. – Chief of Cuba's antiaircraft defense units.

Parrott, Thomas A. – Assistant to President Kennedy's military representative.

Pelipenko, Maj. Gen. Nikolai R. – Second in command of the rear guard of the Soviet Troop Force in Cuba.

Petrenko, Gen. Pavel M. – Second in command of political work for the Soviet Troop Force in Cuba.

Pliyev, Army Gen. Issa Aleksandrovich – Chief of the Soviet Troop Force in Cuba.

Potelin, Sgt. Victor – Member of the antiaircraft missile troops of the Soviet Troop Force in Cuba.

Powell, Gen. Herbert B. – Head of the U.S. Unified Atlantic Command during the October Crisis.

Powers, Gen. Thomas – Commander of the U.S. Strategic Air Command.

Pujals Mederos, José – Cuban counterrevolutionary working for the CIA.

Quiñones, Manuel de Jesús (Pedro Luis) – Head of the Directorate of Military Intelligence of the FAR's general staff.

Rashidov, Sharaf – Alternate member of the Presidium of the Central Committee of the Communist Party of the Soviet Union and its general secretary in Uzbekistan.

Reuther, Walter P. – President of United Auto Workers and member of the U.S. Tractors for Freedom Committee, which negotiated for the release of the prisoners from the Bay of Pigs invasion.

Rikhye, Gen. Indar Jit – Military adviser of UN secretary-general U Thant.

Rivero, Rear Adm. Horacio – Head of Task Force 129 during the U.S. naval blockade of Cuba October 24–November 20, 1962.

Roa, Raúl – Cuba's minister of foreign relations.

Roca, Blas – Director of the newspaper *Noticias de Hoy* and member of the Secretariat of the National Directorate of the Integrated Revolutionary Organizations.

Rodríguez, Carlos Rafael – President of the National Institute of Agrarian Reform and member of the National Directorate of the Integrated Revolutionary Organizations.

Roosevelt, Eleanor – President of the U.S. Tractors for Freedom Committee, which negotiated for the release of the prisoners from the Bay of Pigs invasion.

Rusk, Dean – U.S. secretary of state.

Santamaría, Cmdr. Aldo – Head of Cuba's Armored Forces.

Schlesinger, Arthur, Jr. – Special assistant to President Kennedy.

Seleznyov, Maj. Gen. Victor P. – Second in command of missile armaments of the Soviet Troop Force in Cuba.

Semykin, Col. Victor – Officer of the Soviet Troop Force in Cuba.

Shishenko, Col. Ivan – Head of the warehouses storing nuclear warheads for the Soviet Troop Force in Cuba.

Sidorov, Lt. Col. I.S. – Head of a regiment of the missile division of the Soviet Troop Force in Cuba.

Silvester, Arthur – U.S. assistant secretary of defense.

Smith, Gen. William Y. – Assistant to General Maxwell D. Taylor.

Solovev, Lt. Col. Y.A. – Head of a regiment of the missile division of the Soviet Troop Force in Cuba.

Sorensen, Theodore C. – Special counsel to President Kennedy.

Statsenko, Maj. Gen. Igor D. – Head of the missile division of the Soviet Troop Force in Cuba.

Stevenson, Adlai E. – U.S. permanent representative to the United Nations.

Sweeney, Gen. Walter C. – Head of the U.S. Tactical Air Command.

Tavares de Sa, Hernane – Assistant secretary-general of the United Nations.

Taylor, Vice Adm. Edmund Battelle – Head of Task Force 83 during the U.S. naval blockade of Cuba, October 24 to November 20, 1962.

Taylor, Gen. Maxwell D. – President of the Cuba Study Group, April–June 1961. Military representative to President Kennedy from June 1961 to October 1962 and chairman of the Joint Chiefs of Staff in October 1962.

Thompson, Llewellyn – U.S. ambassador to the Soviet Union, 1957–62.

Thyraud de Vosjoli, Philippe – Head of French intelligence in Washington.

Tyree, Rear Adm. John A. – Head of Task Force 137 during the U.S. naval blockade of Cuba, October 24–November 20, 1962.

Ushakov, Gen. Sergei F. – Second in command of the Soviet Air Force general staff.

U Thant – Secretary-general of the United Nations.

Ward, Vice Adm. Alfred G. – Head of Task Force 136 during the U.S. naval blockade of Cuba, October 24–November 20, 1962.

White, Lincoln – U.S. State Department spokesman.

Woodward, Robert E. – U.S. assistant secretary of state for inter-American affairs from July 1961 until March 1962.

Yepishev, Gen. Aleksei – Head of the Main Political Directorate of the Soviet armed forces.

Zorin, Valerian – USSR permanent representative to the United Nations.

Bibliography

BOOKS, PAMPHLETS, ARTICLES

Alekseev, Aleksandr. "The Caribbean Crisis" in *Ekho Planety* 33, Moscow: November 1988.

Arboleya Cervera, Jesús. *La Contrarrevolución Cubana* [The Cuban Counterrevolution]. Havana: Editorial de Ciencias Sociales, 1997.

Beschloss, Michael R. *The Crisis Years: Kennedy and Khrushchev, 1960–1963.* New York: Edward Burlingame, 1991.

Blight, James G., and David A. Welch. *On the Brink: Americans and Soviets Reexamine the Cuban Missile Crisis.* First edition. New York: Hill and Wang, 1989.

——— *On the Brink: Americans and Soviets Reexamine the Cuban Missile Crisis.* Second edition. New York: Noonday Press, 1990.

Blight, James G., Bruce J. Allyn, and David A. Welch. *Cuba on the Brink: Castro, the Missile Crisis, and the Soviet Collapse.* New York: Pantheon Books, 1993.

Brugioni, Dino A. *Eyeball to Eyeball: The Inside Story of the Cuban Missile Crisis.* New York: Random House, 1991.

Castro Ruz, Fidel. "Discurso en el III Congreso Nacional de Consejos Municipales de Educación" [Speech at the Third National Congress of the Municipal Education Councils]. September 10, 1962. *Obra Revolucionaria,* no. 26. Havana: Editorial Nacional de Cuba, 1962.

——— "Discurso en el Congreso de la Asociación Nacional de Agricultores Pequeños" [Speech at the Congress of the National Association of Small Farmers], May 17, 1961. *Obra Revolucionaria,* no. 21. Havana: Imprenta Nacional de Cuba, 1961.

——— "Discurso en el XXX aniversario de la Victoria de Playa Girón" [Speech on the thirtieth anniversary of the victory at Playa Girón]. *Granma* special supplement. April 19, 1991.

——— "Informe al pueblo de Cuba sobre las conversaciones con el Secretario General de la ONU" [Report to the people of Cuba on the discussions with the UN secretary-general]. *Obra Revolucionaria,* no. 32, November 2, 1962.

——— *El Partido Marxista Leninista y la Revolución Cubana* [The Marxist-Leninist Party and the Cuban Revolution]. Presentation to the People's University, December 1, 1961. Havana, 1962.

——— *Primer Congreso del Partido Comunista de Cuba. Informe Central* [First Congress of the Communist Party of Cuba. Main Report]. Havana: DOR

(Departamento de Orientación Revolucionaria—Department of Revolutionary Orientation), 1975.

———— *La Revolución de Octubre y la Revolución Cubana: Discursos 1959–1976*. [The October Revolution and the Cuban Revolution: Speeches 1959–76]. Havana: DOR, 1977.

———— "Mensaje a Jrushov del 26 de octubre de 1962" [Message to Khrushchev on October 26, 1962]. Havana: *Granma*, November 23, 1990.

———— *Misiles en el Caribe* [Missiles in the Caribbean]. Interview with Fidel Castro by Maria Shriver of NBC television. Havana: Editora Política, 1993.

Castro Ruz, Raúl. *Defensa de Cuba* [Defense of Cuba]. People's University, 2d term, Havana, 1960.

———— "Discurso en conmemoración del III aniversario de la desaparición física del comandante Camilo Cienfuegos" [Speech commemorating the third anniversary of the physical disappearance of commander Camilo Cienfuegos]. Santiago de Cuba, October 28, 1962.

Cazañas Reyes, José. "Ni un minuto de tregua" [Not a minute's truce]. Interview with Raúl Menéndez Tomassevich. *Verde Olivo*, special issue, December 1986.

Chang, Laurence, and Peter Kornbluh, editors. *The Cuban Missile Crisis, 1962: A National Security Archive Documents Reader*. New York: The New Press, 1992.

Chang, Laurence, Donna Rich, and Chris Wallace. *A Chronology of the Cuban Missile Crisis*. Washington, D.C.: National Security Archive, 1987.

Con la razón histórica y la moral de Baraguá. 1962 Crisis de Octubre [With the historic justice and moral force of Baraguá. 1962 October Crisis]. Pamphlet. Havana: Editora Política, 1990.

Diez Acosta, Tomás. *Peligros y principios* [Dangers and principles]. Havana: Ediciones *Verde Olivo*, 1992.

———— *La guerra encubierta contra Cuba* [The covert war against Cuba]. Havana: Editora Política, 1997.

———— *La Crisis de los Misiles, 1962* [The Missile Crisis, 1962]. Havana: Ediciones *Verde Olivo*, 1997.

Dirección de Información Militar. *Aspectos militares de la Crisis de Octubre de 1962* [Military aspects of the October Crisis of 1962]. Havana: Editora Militar, 1967.

Dorticós Torrado, Osvaldo. "Discurso en la Asamblea General de la ONU el 8 de octubre de 1962" [Speech at the UN General Assembly October 8, 1962]. *Obra Revolucionaria*, no 26. Havana: Imprenta Nacional de Cuba, October 1962.

Edel Morales, Alberto. *El mecanismo de respuesta de la Revolución contra el bandidismo* [The Revolution's response mechanism against banditry]. Unpublished essay. Trinidad: Archive of the National Museum of the Struggle against Banditry, no date.

Etzold, Thomas H., and John Lewis Gaddis, editors. *Containment: Documents on American Policy and Strategy, 1945–1950*. New York: Columbia University Press, 1978.

Fursenko, Aleksandr, and Timothy J. Naftali. *One Hell of a Gamble: Khrushchev, Castro, and Kennedy, 1958–1964.* New York: W.W. Norton, 1997.

Garthoff, Raymond L. *Reflections on the Cuban Missile Crisis.* Revised edition. Washington, D.C.: Brookings Institute, 1989.

Glennon P. John, Ronald D. Landa. *Foreign Relations of the United States.* Washington, D.C.: United States Government Printing Office, 1991.

Gribkov, Gen. Anatoli I., and Gen. William Y. Smith. *Operation Anadyr: U.S. and Soviet Generals Recount the Cuban Missile Crisis.* Chicago, Berlin, Tokyo, and Moscow: Edition Q, Inc., 1994.

Gromyko, A. A. "The Caribbean Crisis: What Has Been Revealed Now and Was Hidden Then," in *Izvestia*, April 15, 1985.

Group of authors. *Valentía y Fraternidad* [Courage and brotherhood]. Havana: Editorial de Ciencias Sociales, 1983.

Group of authors from the Raúl Roa Institute of International Relations. *De Eisenhower a Reagan* [From Eisenhower to Reagan]. Havana: Editorial de Ciencias Sociales, 1987.

Guevara de la Serna, Ernesto. August 8, 1961, speech in *Ernesto Che Guevara, Obras 1957–1967*, Vol. 2. Havana: Casa de las Américas, 1970.

Hinckle, Warren, and William W. Turner, *The Fish Is Red: The Story of the Secret War against Castro.* Harper & Row, New York, 1981.

Kennedy, John F. *To Turn the Tide.* Hamish Hamilton, 1962.

Kennedy, Robert F. *Thirteen Days: A Memoir of the Cuban Missile Crisis.* New York: W.W. Norton, 1969.

Khrushchev, Nikita S. *Khrushchev Remembers.* Translated and edited by Strobe Talbott. Boston: Little, Brown, 1970.

——— *Khrushchev Remembers: The Glasnost Tapes.* Translated and edited by Jerrold L. Schecter with Vyacheslav V. Luchkov. Boston: Little, Brown, 1990.

Kissinger, Henry. *Mis memorias.* Buenos Aires: Editorial Atlántida S.A., 1979.

Kissinger, Henry. *The White House Years.* Boston: Little, Brown, 1979.

Lechuga, Carlos M. *Itinerario de una farsa* [Itinerary of a farce]. Havana: Editorial Pueblo y Educación, 1991.

——— *En el ojo de la tormenta* [In the eye of the storm]. Havana: SI-Mar SA., and Melbourne, Australia: Ocean Press, 1995.

——— "Carta al Secretario General de las Naciones Unidas" [Letter to the secretary-general of the United Nations]. New York, January 7, 1963. *Política Internacional*, no. 1, January–March 1963.

León Cotayo, Nicanor. *El bloqueo a Cuba* [The blockade of Cuba]. Havana: Editorial de Ciencias Sociales, 1983.

McNamara, Robert. "Secretario de Defensa en el Auditorio del Departamento de Estado, el miércoles 6 de febrero de 1963" [The Secretary of Defense in the Auditorium of the State Department, Wednesday, February 6, 1963]. Havana: Ediciones COR (Comisión de Orientación Revolucionaria—Revolutionary Orientation Commission), February 14, 1963.

Mendoza Díaz, Juan, M. Iserme Carrillo, L.B. Pérez Gallardo, and I. Pérez

Gutiérrez. *Demanda del Pueblo de Cuba al Gobierno de Estados Unidos por daños humanos* [Lawsuit by the People of Cuba v. the U.S. Government for Human Damages]. Havana: Editora Política, 1999.

Ministerio de Justicia. Laws 923 and 924. *Gaceta Oficial,* January 5, 1961.

Miró Cardona, José. *Renuncia ante el Consejo Revolucionario de Cuba* [Resignation from the Cuban Revolutionary Council]. Miami, 1963.

National Security Archive and Chadwyck-Healey, Inc. *The Cuban Missile Crisis.* Catalogue. Vols. 1 and 2. Washington D.C., 1990.

Novas Fernández, Luis. *Estudio Histórico-Militar de la Lucha Contra Bandidos en Cuba.* [Historical-Military Study of the Struggle against Bandits in Cuba]. Unpublished. *Library of the Institute of Cuban History.*

Posición de Cuba ante la Crisis del Caribe [Cuba's position on the Caribbean Crisis]. Havana: Ediciones COR, December 1962.

Prados, John. *Presidents' Secret Wars.* New York: William Morrow, 1986.

Sociedad Cubana de Derecho Internacional, *Agresiones de Estados Unidos a Cuba revolucionaria* [U.S. aggressions against revolutionary Cuba]. Havana: Editorial de Ciencias Sociales, 1989.

Schlesinger, Arthur M., Jr. *A Thousand Days: John F. Kennedy in the White House.* Boston: Houghton Mifflin, 1965.

Schlesinger, Arthur M. *Robert Kennedy and His Times.* Boston: Houghton Mifflin, 1978.

Sorensen, Theodore C. *Kennedy, el hombre, el presidente.* Barcelona, Mexico City: Ediciones Grijalbo S.A., 1966.

Sorensen, Theodore C. *Kennedy.* New York: Harper & Row, 1965, 1988.

Statsenko, Igor. "Sobre algunos aspectos político-militares de la Crisis del Caribe" [On certain political-military aspects of the Caribbean Crisis]. *América Latina,* no. 3. Moscow: Editorial Progreso, 1978.

"A Strategy of Flexible Response" in *Military Review,* March 1967.

Suárez Amador, José. *La Lucha Contra Bandidos en Cuba* [The Struggle against Bandits in Cuba]. Havana: Letras Cubanas, 1981.

Taylor, Maxwell D. *Swords and Plowshares.* New York: Norton, 1972.

Tello, Manuel. *México: una posición internacional* [Mexico: an international position]. Mexico City: Editorial Joaquín Muztiz, S.A., 1972.

United Nations. *Foreign Relations of the United States. 1946. Vol. 1, General.* Washington D.C.: United States Government Printing Office, 1972.

Un pueblo invencible [An invincible people]. Collection of documents on the October 1962 Crisis. Havana: Editorial José Martí, 1992.

U. S. Senate. *Alleged Assassination Plots Involving Foreign Leaders: An Interim Report of the Select Committee to Study Governmental Operations with Respect to Intelligence Activities* [the Church Committee report]. Washington D.C.: United States Government Printing Office, 1975.

U.S. Department of State. *Foreign Relations of the United States, 1961–1963, volume X, Cuba, 1961–1962.* Washington, D.C.: United States Government Printing Office, 1997.

——— *Foreign Relations of the United States, 1961–1963, volume XI, Cuban Missile Crisis and Aftermath.* Washington, D.C.: United States Government Printing Office, 1996.

U.S. Policy Toward Cuba. Washington, D.C.: Library of Congress, September 1962.

Wise, David, and Thomas B. Ross. *The Invisible Government.* New York: Random House, 1964.

PERIODICALS

Bohemia, no. 36, September 7, 1962.

Bulletin of the Department of State. Washington D.C. November 19, 1973.

Cables by international press agencies, September 13, 1962. Published by the COR, 1962.

Cables by U.S. news agencies from August, September, and October, 1962. Published by the Comisión de Orientaciones Revolucionarias [Commission of Revolutionary Orientation—COR], 1962.

Granma, November 23, 1990.

New Times (Moscow), nos. 4, 5, and 6, 1989.

New York Times, September 8, 1962.

Noticias de Hoy, September 12, 1962.

———, September 20, 1962.

———, October 9, 1962.

———, October 10, 1962.

———, October 23, 1962.

———, October 24, 1962.

———, October 25, 1962.

———, October 26, 1962.

———, October 28, 1962.

Política Internacional, no. 1. January–April 1963.

Revolución, August 30, 1962.

———, October 12, 1962.

U.S. News & World Report, September 24, 1962.

INTERVIEWS *

Aragonés Navarro, Emilio, interview conducted January 17, 1989.

Beloborodov, N.K., interviews conducted May and September 1990.

Burlov, A.M., interviews conducted December 1989 and September 1990.

Escalona, Dermidio, interview conducted September 1990.

Garbuz, Leonid S., interviews conducted December 1989 and May 1990.

---

* These interviews can be found in the October Crisis collection of the archives of the Institute of Cuban History.

Kovalenko, Aleksandr, interviews conducted May and September 1990.
La'O Estrada, Walfrido, account given directly to author.
Lemus, Franco, interview conducted 1989.
Maslov, Aleksei F., interview conducted March 1990.
Oropeza, Pedro, interview conducted 1989.
Santamaría Cuadrado, Aldo, interview conducted 1989.
Shishenko, I.V., interviews conducted December 1989 and September 1990.
Tikhonov, Aleksandr, interviews conducted December 1989 and September 1990.

Index

Abashvili, Vice Adm. Georgio S., 107, 309

Acheson, Dean, 141, 145, 309

Achilles, Theodore C., 34, 309

Adenauer, Konrad, 189

Adzhubei, Aleksei, 55

Ageyev, Maj. Gen. Pyotr V., 94, 309

Agrarian reform, 13, 236, 245

Akindinov, Maj. Gen. Pavel V., 106, 108, 309

Aleksandrovsk, 114, 160

Alekseev, Aleksandr, 127, 309; and missile proposal, 93, 95–96, 100

Alliance for Progress, 49, 50, 77, 228

Almeida, Juan, 62, 158, 309

Amory, Robert, 76, 309

ANAP (National Association of Small Farmers), 72–73, 110

Anderson, Adm. George W., 144, 147, 162, 177, 309

Anderson, Maj. Rudolf, 152, 175, 279, 280, 309

Antiaircraft Defense and Revolutionary Air Force (DAAFAR), 66

Aragonés, Emilio, 101–2, 128–29, 207, 309

Arbenz, Jacobo, 227

Arévalo, Juan José, 253

Argentina, 53, 130, 149

Ascunce Domenech, Manuel, 60

Assassination attempts, U.S.-organized, 12, 26, 40, 41, 45, 47–48, 85

Baian Pinto, Luis, 170

Ball, George W., 76, 136, 309

Baltic fleet, Soviet, 104

Bandilovsky, Lt. Col. A.Z., 118, 309

Bands, counterrevolutionary, 26, 41, 59–60, 70, 74; battle against, 62, 70–74

Barnes, C. Tracy, 39, 48, 309

Barroso Gómez, Octavio, 46–47

Batista, Fulgencio, 226

Bavier, 112

Bay of Pigs. *See* Playa Girón

Beloborodov, Lt. Gen. N.K., 113–14, 309–10

Benítez, Conrado, 59

Berlin, West, 139–40, 145

Bernal, John D., 156

Biryuzov, Marshal Sergei, 93–94, 95, 96, 100, 101, 102–3, 310

Bissell, Richard, 76, 310

Blockade, U.S. naval, 26, 251–52; called "quarantine," 141, 146, 251; discussions in ExComm on, 137, 139, 140–41, 142, 144, 146; endangers world shipping, 163, 218, 229; illegality of, 184, 238–39, 262, 263, 273; lifting of, 188, 189, 190, 285; proclamation of, 146, 153, 165, 224, 233, 249; Soviet eluding of, 160

Bolívar, Simón, 217

Bolivia, 52, 162

Bolshakov, Georgi, 133, 310

Bolshoi Theater, 159

Brazil, 51, 52, 53, 162, 170

Brezhnev, Leonid, 99, 310

Britain, 112, 126, 133

Bundy, McGeorge, 76, 80, 86, 136, 141, 310

Burke, Adm. Arleigh, 29, 34, 36, 86, 310

Burlatsky, Fyodor M., 94, 310
Burlov, Col. Anatoly M., 302, 310
Burton, Dan, 58
Butski, Aleksei S., 107, 310

Cabell, Gen. Charles, 76, 310
Capehart, Homer E., 130
Casas Regueiro, Senén, 63
Castilla Mas, Belarmino, 63, 310
Castillo de Armas, Carlos, 227
Castro, Fidel, 72, 110, 156–57, 160,
    182–83, 246–47, 310; on accepting
    missiles, 96, 99, 101–3; assassina-
    tion attempts on, 40, 41, 45, 47–48,
    85; correspondence with Khru-
    shchev, 160, 171–72, 181–82; and
    Cuba-USSR mutual defense pact,
    127–28, 207–12; on defending so-
    cialist camp, 101; on "excessive"
    confidence in USSR, 102; on FAR
    capability, 68–69; letters to U Thant,
    170, 175, 188, 189–90; on "inspec-
    tion" of Cuba, 161, 183–84, 186,
    247, 262–65, 269, 270, 272–73, 278;
    on missile secrecy, 103, 121–22,
    133–34; and nuclear "first strike"
    slander, 172, 182; Oct. 23 speech,
    160–61, 224–55; on "offensive" and
    "defensive" weapons, 133–34, 240,
    246; order to fire on spy planes,
    122–23, 165, 170, 174–75, 188; on
    Soviet errors, 121–22, 133–34,
    178–79, 181–83, 186; on unilateral
    missile withdrawal, 178–79; on
    United Nations, 265, 266, 278,
    281; on U.S. invasion of Cuba,
    131–32; and U Thant meetings,
    183–84, 256–84
Castro, Raúl, 63, 310; assassination
    attempts on, 40; during October
    Crisis, 158; and missile proposal,
    65, 100, 101, 103–4
Catholic Church hierarchy, 46
Central Intelligence Agency (CIA), 227,

273, 283; and Bay of Pigs defeat,
    35–36, 37, 60; covert actions against
    Cuba, 37–48, 76, 79, 84–85, 187,
    217, 245; and Operation Mon-
    goose, 76–80. See also McCone,
    John
Central Organization of Cuban Work-
    ers (CTC), 59
Cherkesov, Lt. Col. I.I., 118, 310
Chile, 52, 162
Cline, Ray, 98–99, 135, 310
Coerr, Wymberley, 76, 310
Cold War, 28, 55, 57, 146, 199, 203;
    Cuba-U.S. conflict and, 13, 25,
    200–201
Colombia, 52
Commander in Chief of the Atlantic
    Command (CINCLANT), 84, 91
Committees for the Defense of the
    Revolution, 69
Communist Party, U.S., 15. See also
    ORI
Communist Party of Cuba, 72
Congo, 247, 265, 266
Cuba: agrarian reform, 13, 236, 245;
    basis of foreign policy, 215; his-
    tory of U.S. domination, 225–26;
    literacy campaign, 13, 59–60, 236;
    mobilization during crisis, 157,
    167–68, 190, 231; revolution's
    measures, 13–14, 59–60, 236, 245;
    U.S. movement in solidarity with,
    15–16; as world example, 30, 34,
    37, 50; world solidarity with, 199,
    222. See also Revolutionary Armed
    Forces (FAR); Soviet missiles in
    Cuba
Cuban government positions: defense
    of sovereignty, 26, 132, 133, 134,
    161, 175, 186, 191, 198, 204, 220,
    243, 263–64, 277, 282; on disar-
    mament, 161, 200, 239–40, 248–
    49; on inspection, 161, 163, 179,
    183–84, 191, 193, 198, 199–200,

247–48, 269, 270, 286, 289–90;
November 25 statement, 190–92,
285–91; reply to Joint Resolution
of U.S. Congress, 132–33, 213–23,
232, 240, 241, 242; on right to obtain weaponry, 129, 131, 132, 133,
134, 167, 191, 219, 220–21, 241,
242–43, 246, 287–88, 289; on Soviet decision to withdraw missiles,
178–79; on spy flights, 122–23,
165, 170, 174–75, 179–80, 181,
188, 217; willingness to negotiate
with U.S., 60, 132–33, 161, 175,
242, 246. *See also* Five points to
end crisis
Cuban Missile Crisis. *See* October
Crisis
Cuba-Soviet differences, 13, 26, 197,
199–200, 202; on announcing missiles publicly, 13, 125, 131–34,
156; on inspection of Cuban territory, 179, 186; on unilateral missile withdrawal, 179, 181–83, 186
Cuba-Soviet mutual defense pact,
127–28, 207–12
Cuba Study Group. *See* Taylor Commission
Cuban Revolutionary Council, 42, 83,
87

Dankevich, Col. Gen. Pavel B., 106,
108, 109, 310
Davidkov, Col. Gen. Victor Y., 107,
310
Death penalty, 73
Defense Intelligence Agency (DIA),
84
DeGaulle, Charles, 189
del Valle, Sergio, 296, 310
Dementyev, Maj. Gen. Aleksei A.,
106, 108, 109, 310–11
Dennison, Adm. Robert L., 147, 311
Department of State Security (DSE),
41, 44–45, 69–70

Derkachev, Col. Mikhail I., 301, 311
Díaz, Dalia Jorge, 47
Díaz, Higinio, 41, 310
Diez Acosta, Tomás, 9–10, 11
Dillon, Douglas, 50, 136, 248, 310
Disarmament, 161, 200, 239–40, 248–
49
Dobrynin, Anatoly, 131, 311; meeting
with John Kennedy, 144–45; meet-
ings with Robert Kennedy, 162,
173, 176
Dominican Republic, 226
Donovan, James, 60
Dorticós, Osvaldo, 47, 101–2, 131,
311; UN address, 243, 264; at U
Thant meetings, 183, 267–68
Drake, Sir Francis, 250
Dulles, Allen, 29, 36, 311
Dumping, 49
Duncan, Gen. George T., 152

Ecuador, 52
Egypt, 265, 266
Eisenhower, Dwight, 28, 48, 49, 61,
144, 311
Eisenhower, Milton, 60, 311
Embargo, U.S. economic, 26, 30–31,
55, 82, 202, 217, 220, 227, 228, 244;
demand to end, 179, 180, 197, 289;
text of regulation, 56–57
Enterprise, 149
Escambray. *See* Bands, counterrevolutionary
Esterline, Jacob D., 48, 311
ExComm (Executive Committee of
the National Security Council):
composition of, 135–36; deliberations by, 137–38, 139–44, 162; secrecy of, 135, 136

Fair Play for Cuba Committee, 15
FAR. *See* Revolutionary Armed Forces
(FAR)
Farmers, 14, 72–73, 110

Fernández Mell, Oscar, 64, 311
Five points to end crisis, 179–80, 192, 193, 289; as only road to peace, 198, 268, 277, 280–81, 289; U.S. refusal to discuss, 194, 196
France, 126, 133, 166
Frondizi, Arturo, 52, 53–54, 311
Fundamental Law, 73

Gálvez Rodríguez, William, 64, 311
Garbuz, Maj. Gen. Leonid S., 106, 108, 119, 120, 121, 311
García Frías, Guillermo, 64, 311
García Incháustegui, Mario, 157, 163, 167, 311
García Martínez, Calixto, 63, 311
Germany, Nazi, 172, 237, 266
Germany, West, 112, 126, 133, 218
Gilpatric, Roswell, 80, 136, 188–89, 311
Goldwater, Sen. Barry, 130
González, Reynold, 47
Goodwin, Richard N., 35, 42, 50, 51, 311; and Operation Mongoose, 76, 79
Gordon, Lincoln, 170
Goulart, João, 53, 170, 311
Grechko, Maj. Gen. Stepan M., 106–7, 108, 312
Grechko, Marshal Andrei, 99, 311
Gribkov, Gen. Anatoly I., 105, 107, 121, 124, 158, 312
Gromyko, Andrei, 312; on decision to install missiles, 95, 96; meeting with Kennedy, 138–39, 145, 168
Guantánamo, U.S. naval base, 197, 217, 281; Cuba's defenses at, 64; demand for withdrawal, 180, 200, 289; and October 1962, 146, 148, 156, 233–34, 234–35; provocations around, 32, 40, 41, 89; in U.S. invasion plans, 90
Guatemala, 227
Guevara, Ernesto Che, 12, 26, 101–2,

312; during October Crisis, 158; at Punta del Este, 50–51; on outcome of crisis, 204; delivers draft agreement to Khrushchev, 128–29, 207

Haiti, 226
Harvey, William K., 84
Hayward, Rear Adm. John T., 149, 312
Helms-Burton Act, 57
Helms, Jesse, 58, 202
Helms, Richard M., 82, 312
Hitler, Adolf, 237
Hoover, Herbert, 144
Hungary, 55
Hurwitch, Robert A., 56, 76, 312

IL-28 bombers, 65, 116, 117; U.S. demands withdrawal of, 186, 187, 188, 189; withdrawal of, 186, 190, 285
Independence, 149
Indirgirka, 114
INRA (National Institute of Agrarian Reform), 110
Inspection: Cuba's rejection of, 161, 163; as pretext for U.S. attack, 190; Soviet agreement to, 186, 187, 198, 260, 272, 286; U.S. demands for, 179, 183–84, 185; U Thant urges Cuba accept, 181, 183–84, 260–62, 264–65, 272
Interagency Task Force, 29–35, 76–77
Isle of Pines, 64
Italy, U.S. missiles in, 13, 94, 169, 173, 196
Ivanov, Col. Gen. Semyon P., 99–100, 312

JM/WAVE, 84
Johnson, Gen. Max S., 89–90, 312
Johnson, Lyndon, 136, 312
Johnson, U. Alexis, 76, 80, 136, 312
Joint Chiefs of Staff: and Bay of Pigs, 36; and Cuba invasion, 14, 87–88;

and naval blockade, 84, 147, 165
Joint Resolution. *See* U.S. anti-Cuba actions, joint congressional resolution
Juárez, Benito, 217
JUCEI (Boards of Coordination, Implementation, and Inspection), 72
July 26 Movement, 72

Keating, Sen. Kenneth, 130
Kennedy, John F., 35, 36, 130, 131, 166, 213, 312; appeal to world opinion by, 134, 156; and Bay of Pigs, 28–29, 33, 35–36, 215, 243–44, 288; considers invasion of Cuba, 14, 86–87; and covert actions, 37, 42, 76, 79, 80; and Cuban exiles, 88, 197; on Cuban "subversion," 130, 190, 286–87; determination to crush Cuban Revolution, 12, 60–61, 82, 288; and economic embargo, 56–57, 82, 244; and ExComm, 135–36, 139, 141; on inspection, 185, 190, 194–95; letters to Khrushchev, 158, 169, 173–74, 176; meeting with Gromyko, 138–39, 145, 168; meetings with Soviet officials, 55, 138–39, 145, 168, 194; military options considered during crisis, 14, 86–87, 124, 139, 140, 141; and naval blockade, 140, 141, 153, 162, 189, 233, 249, 251–52; Nov. 20 news conference, 190, 285–86, 287; Oct. 22 speech, 142, 145–46, 157, 232–37; on "offensive" weapons in Cuba, 130, 145, 190, 195, 196; and Operation Mongoose, 77, 78–79, 86; pressure on Latin American governments, 48, 49, 52–54; and spy flights, 151, 169, 195; and U Thant mediation, 167, 168, 257, 258; on withdrawal of missiles, 13, 185, 189, 190, 196
Kennedy, Robert F., 36, 60, 80, 312;

and ExComm, 136, 143, 144; meetings with Dobrynin, 162, 173, 176; and Operation Mongoose, 12, 75–76, 78–79, 81, 82; "top priority" to crush Cuba, 82
Khrushchev, Nikita, 107, 158–59, 195–96, 312; agrees to inspection, 198, 260, 272; on Baltic fleet, 104, 129; Castro's assessment of, 122; correspondence with Castro, 160, 171–72, 181–82; and "offensive" and "defensive" weapons, 133–34, 240; and IL-28s, 190; letters to Kennedy, 159–60, 172–73, 173–74, 176, 177, 195; and negotiations to end crisis, 166–67, 169, 172–73; reasons for installing missiles, 94–100; on "producing missiles like sausages," 108; on secrecy of missile installation, 97, 103–4, 109, 125, 129; and Soviet Troop Force, 108–9, 110–11; and withdrawal of missiles, 13, 176, 178–79, 181–82, 260, 272
Khrushchev, Rada, 159
Khrushchev, Sergei, 108
King, Col. J.C., 76, 312
Kohler, Foy D., 158, 159, 312
Komsomol, 113
Kornienko, Georgi, 173, 312
Kosygin, Aleksei, 99, 312–13
Kovalenko, Col. Aleksandr, 111–12, 113, 118, 313
Kozlov, Frol R., 95, 96, 99, 313
Kubitschek, Juscelino, 52–53
Kuznetsov, Vasily V., 183, 185, 187, 197, 313

La Coubre, 229–30, 245
Lansdale, Gen. Edward G., 313; and Operation Mongoose, 76, 79, 80–82, 85–86
Lantigua Ortega, Pedro, 60
La'O Estrada, Walfrido, 313

Laos, 265, 266, 267

Latin America: Cuba's example for, 30, 34, 37; revolutionary struggle in, 239, 287; support for Cuba in, 52–53, 77, 142; tradition of resistance to foreign intervention, 216–17, 218; U.S. anti-Cuba efforts in, 26, 33, 43, 48, 51–54, 55–56, 161–62, 217–18, 239; U.S. exploitation of, 49; U.S. interventions in, 226. *See also* Alliance for Progress

Lebanon, 265, 266

Lechuga, Carlos, 52, 54–55, 183, 187, 192, 278, 279, 313

LeMay, Gen. Curtis, 177, 313

Lemnitzer, Gen. Lyman, 80

Lemus, Capt. Franco, 313

Leninski, 113

Lincoln, Abraham, 250

Literacy campaign, 13, 59–60, 236

Lobo, Julio, 45

Loginov, Evgenii, 110, 313

Loufti, Omar, 183, 313

Lucha Contra Bandidos (LCB), 62, 71–74

Lumumba, Patrice, 247, 265

Maceo, Antonio, 204

McCloy, John J., 185, 193–94, 313

McCone, John A., 77–78, 80, 126, 313; during October Crisis, 136, 141, 143, 162

MacMillan, Harold, 189

McNamara, Robert, 34, 35, 80, 86, 88, 98, 196, 313; during October Crisis, 136, 139, 143, 144, 162, 190, 249

Mafia, U.S., 80, 85

Malinovsky, Marshal Rodion Ya., 94–95, 97, 99, 103, 104, 107, 108, 313; during October Crisis, 158, 159, 175

Martí, José, 217

Martin, Edwin, 136, 139–40, 313

Martínez Andrade, Juan Alberto, 74

Maslov, Sgt. Aleksei F., 112, 113, 313

Menéndez Tomassevich, Raúl, 62, 313

Mexico, 51, 52, 54, 162, 226–27

Mikoyan, Anastas, 313; on installing missiles, 94, 95, 96, 99–100; talks with U.S. officials, 185, 192, 193–95; trip to Cuba, 185, 186

Mikoyan, Sergo, 94, 186, 313

Military Industrial Organization, 67

Ministry of the Interior, 69

Miró Cardona, José, 42, 55, 87, 314

Missile superiority, U.S., 98–99

Missiles. *See* Soviet missiles in Cuba

Mobutu, Joseph, 247

Monroe Doctrine, 141, 202

Montesino, Benito, 51

Morejón Quintana, Pedro, 59–60

Morgan, Henry, 250

National Security Council, 33–35, 87–88. *See also* ExComm

Nicaragua, 226

Nitze, Paul, 29, 76, 136, 314

Nonaligned Movement, 164, 183

North Atlantic Treaty Organization (NATO), 58, 155, 196

NSC 5412. *See* Special Group

Nuclear war, 25, 95, 155, 166, 175, 181; consequences for humanity of, 200, 252, 254; U.S. preparations for, 151–52, 154, 166

OAS Inter-American Economic and Social Council, 49, 50–51

October Crisis: alleged Cuban irresponsibility in, 172, 175, 181–82; peace not achieved, 191–92, 198, 200, 289; root cause of, 13, 25, 200–201, 225–30; U.S. portrayals of, 13, 25; U.S. responsible for, 11, 124, 159, 168, 171; worldwide demonstrations during, 15–16, 156–57, 251. *See also* Soviet missiles in Cuba

October Crisis, negotiations to end:

189, 192, 194, 197; exclusion of Cuba from, 27, 185, 194, 202; no Cuban obstacles to, 26–27, 181, 189, 269; results of, 191–92, 197–98, 200; and U.S. no-invasion "promise," 169, 172, 174, 179, 184, 192–93, 270–71, 283

Operation Anadyr, 65, 106. *See also* Soviet missiles in Cuba

Operation Jaula [Cage], 70

Operation Liborio, 45–48

Operation Mongoose, 12; Cuba Project, 82–83; organization of, 76–80; secrecy of, 79

Operation Patty, 40–41, 45

Operation Peter Pan. *See* "Parental Custody Act"

Organization of American States (OAS); and anti-Cuba campaign, 32, 33, 46, 48–55, 87, 131; Cuba's expulsion from, 54–55, 82, 218, 228, 288; 1961 Punta del Este conference, 49–51; support for naval blockade by, 142–43, 146, 161–62, 163–64, 225, 233, 234, 235

ORI (Integrated Revolutionary Organizations), 72, 101–2, 110, 128

Oropeza, Capt. Pedro E., 301, 314

Orozco Crespo, Miguel A., 187

Panama Canal, 186–87

"Parental Custody Act," 46, 47

Parrott, Thomas A., 47–48, 314

Peace: Cuba's position on, 132, 175, 184, 191–92, 198, 208, 215, 222–23, 249, 252, 254, 266, 267, 290–91; not achieved during October Crisis, 191–92, 198, 200, 289; Washington as threat to, 92, 95, 156, 166, 220, 222, 230, 232, 268, 289

Pelipenko, Maj. Gen. Nikolai R., 107, 108, 314

People's Defense, 66–67, 167–68

Peru, 51, 52, 53, 130

Petrenko, Gen. Pavel M., 106, 314

Phillips, David A., 45

Platt Amendment, 225

Playa Girón, 12, 60, 95, 228; Cuba's victory at, 13, 62; impact of U.S. defeat, 13, 25; Kennedy and, 28–29, 35–36, 37, 60, 215, 221, 243–44, 288; release of captured mercenaries, 60, 197; Washington's assessment of, 12, 33, 36, 37, 42–43, 75

Pliyev, Gen. Issa Alexandrovich, 106, 107–8, 109, 314; during October Crisis, 158–59, 170–71, 175

Popular Socialist Party (PSP), 72

Potelin, Sgt. Victor, 112, 113, 314

Powell, Gen. Herbert B., 152, 314

Powers, Gen. Thomas, 165–66, 314

Prado Ugarteche, Manuel, 53

Prados, John, 126

Presidents' Secret Wars (Prados), 126

Protests against U.S. war moves, 15–16, 156–57, 251

Pujals Mederos, José, 44–45, 46, 314

Quadros, Jânio, 53

Quarantine. *See* Blockade, U.S. naval

Quiñones, Manuel de Jesús, 164, 314

Radio-Technical Troops, 66

Rashidov, Sharaf, 93, 96, 100, 314

Red Cross, International, 183, 187, 270, 271

Religion, freedom of, 236

Reuther, Walter, 60, 314

Revolutionary Armed Forces (FAR), Cuba: air force, 65–66; antiaircraft defenses, 65–66, 164–65; anti-landing defenses, 61, 68; artillery, 68; Border Battalion, 64; Central Army, 62–63; combat alarm order, 157, 224, 231; command structure, 157–58; Eastern Army, 63, 64; G2 (Department of Information), 69;

leadership in, 66, 67, 69; military schools, 67–68; navy, 65–66; October 1962 mobilization, 156–57, 165, 167–68, 190, 231; process of organization, 61–62; size of, 61–62, 62–63, 63–64; strategy to confront U.S. invasion, 61, 68, 164; structure of, 62–64, 67; Western Army, 64

Revolutionary Directorate, 72

Revolutionary Police, 69

Rikhye, Gen. Indar Jit, 183, 314

Rio Treaty (Inter-American Treaty of Reciprocal Assistance), 48, 51, 53, 83, 137, 193, 232, 234

Rivero, Rear Adm. Horacio, 149, 314

Roa, Raúl, 157, 183, 314

Roca, Blas, 101–2, 314

Rodríguez, Carlos Rafael, 315

Roosevelt, Eleanor, 60, 315

Rusk, Dean, 80, 136, 144–45, 195, 315; and foreign ministers meeting, 161, 218

Russell, Bertrand, 156

Salinger, Pierre, 157, 250

Santamaría, Aldo, 315

Schlesinger, Arthur, Jr., 42, 315

Second Logistic Command, 153

Seleznyov, Maj. Gen. Victor P., 107, 315

Semykin, Col. Victor, 111, 112

Sen Cedré, Delfín, 60

Shishenko, Col. Ivan, 111, 113–14, 302, 315

Sidorov, Lt. Col. L.S., 118, 315

Silvester, Arthur, 195, 315

Smith, Gen. William Y., 293, 315

Socialist Workers Party, 15

Solovev, Lt. Col. Y.A., 118, 315

Somalia, 265

Sorensen, Theodore, 127, 136, 137, 139, 144, 315

Soviet missiles in Cuba: authorization to use, 107, 123, 172; concealment measures, 109, 111–12, 113, 121–23, 125; Cuba's acceptance of, 11–12, 26, 101–3; and Cuba's image in Latin America, 102; danger of U.S. discovery, 103, 104, 121–22, 125, 129; as deterrent, 96–97, 102, 108; making operational, 118–19, 119–21; military vulnerability of, 165; not needed for Cuba's defense, 12, 101, 102; nuclear capability, 115, 116, 117, 120–21, 123–24; as pretext for October Crisis, 26; proposal to Cuba on, 93–94, 100–103; public announcement plans, 104, 129; Soviet denial of, 133–34, 138–39; Soviet reasons for, 13, 94–100, 108, 109; Soviet political mishandling of, 26; Soviet secrecy around, 97, 101, 103–4, 105, 109, 111, 156; transporting, 104, 105, 113–14, 119, 126, 160; U.S. detection of, 121, 123, 135

Soviet missiles in Cuba, types: FKR cruise missiles, 116, 123; Luna, 114–15, 123; R-12, 118, 119, 120, 123; R-13, 117, 123; R-14, 118–19, 120–21; R-15, 116; SA-75, 115; Sopka, 116–17

Soviet missiles in Cuba, withdrawal, 118–19, 185, 187, 269; Cuban reaction to, 178–79, 182; unilateral announcement of, 13, 103–4, 128–29, 176, 179, 181–82, 187, 200; and U.S. missiles in Turkey and Italy, 169, 173, 176, 196; and U.S. noinvasion pledge, 169, 172, 174, 179, 261, 270–71

Soviet Troop Force (STF) in Cuba: air force units, 116, 117; antiaircraft defense forces, 115–16, 117; combat readiness of, 124, 158–59, 160, 171; command structure, 106–7, 108; communications regiment, 117; Cuban cooperation with, 110,

113, 114, 128, 210; and Cuban sovereignty, 128, 209; goal of, 127, 208–9; IL-28 bombers, 117, 190; infantry units, 114, 115; motorized regiments, 115; naval forces, 116, 117; size of, 12, 26, 105, 106, 123, 124; stationing of, 114–20; tank battalions, 115, 117; transport to Cuba of, 109, 110–14, 121. *See also* Soviet missiles in Cuba

Soviet Union: disappearance of, 203; German invasion of, 1941, 172; military aid to Cuba, 14, 61, 64–65, 182–83, 222; military mobilization, 155, 158–59, 190; and peace, 109, 159, 166–67, 168, 195, 254; ringed by U.S. missiles, 12, 94–95, 97, 104, 133, 155; and U.S. naval blockade, 167; U.S. threats against, 151. *See also* Cuba-Soviet differences; Soviet missiles in Cuba

Spanish civil war, 96

Special Group, 43–44, 78, 79–80; and Operation Mongoose, 80–81, 82, 85–86

Spy flights, U.S., 85, 146, 151, 160, 169, 188, 234; claimed as right, 188–89, 192, 279, 287; Cuba to fire on, 122–23, 165, 170, 174–75, 187, 188; illegality of, 122, 180, 279, 280

"Statsenko Division," 118, 124, 315

Statsenko, Maj. Gen. Igor D., 118

Stevenson, Adlai, 131, 136, 185, 193–94, 197, 315; in UN debates, 163, 168, 228

Strategic Air Command (SAC), 151, 155, 165–66

Student Peace Union, 15

Sugar quota, 183, 217, 227

Sweeney, Walter, 143, 150, 315

Tavares de Sa, Hernane, 183, 315

Taylor Commission (Cuba Study Group),

35–38

Taylor, Gen. Maxwell, 29, 35, 36, 47, 79, 315; in October 1962, 136, 139, 143; and Special Group, 80, 86

Taylor, Vice Adm. Edmund Battelle, 149, 315

Tello, Manuel, 52

Thompson, Llewellyn, 136, 315

Thyraud de Vosjoli, Philippe, 126, 316

Torricelli Act, 57, 202

Torricelli, Robert, 57

Tractors for Freedom Committee, 60

Trade relations, unequal, 49

Truman, Harry, 144

Tshombe, Moise, 247

Turbay Ayala, Julio César, 52

Turkey, U.S. missiles in, 94, 104, 133, 155, 169, 173, 176, 196

Tyree, Rear Adm. John A., 149, 316

U-2 spy craft, 85, 151; photos of missile sites, 12, 135; shootdown of, 122–23, 175, 181, 185, 279, 280

U Thant, 166, 167, 185, 187, 192, 256–84, 267, 269, 316; and U-2 shootdown, 185, 279–80; mediation efforts requested, 164, 169, 257; on U.S. naval blockade, 184, 273, 275, 280; on U.S. politics, 273–74, 283; on U.S. spy flights, 184, 273, 275, 279, 280; on UN military missions, 267, 270; urges Castro postpone speech, 274, 275; urges Cuba accept inspection, 181, 183–84, 260–62, 264–65, 272

U.S. anti-Cuba actions: agents inside Cuba, 38, 39–40, 41, 44, 45, 46–47, 76, 83; air strikes considered, 137, 139, 143–44; attacks on Cuban trade, 218; biological warfare, 81; budget of, 44, 82; covert action programs, 38–42, 43–44, 44–47; and Cuban "subversion," 31–32, 33, 43, 56, 130, 190, 192–93, 213,

214, 240, 286–87, 288; debate over methods, 33, 34–35, 42–43, 75; diplomatic isolation, 26, 33, 48, 51–54, 161, 217–18, 220, 228; economic warfare, 26, 30–31, 55, 82, 202, 217, 218, 220, 227, 228, 229, 244, 288; encouraging internal uprising, 32, 77, 81; failure of, 14, 36, 37, 75, 226, 227, 228, 229, 230; and Interagency Task Force Plan, 29–35; invasion threats, 283; joint congressional resolution, 130–31, 213–23, 240; media campaign, 43, 126, 128, 129, 161; as number-one U.S. priority, 82; overall goals, 28, 214; "psychological" warfare, 26, 30, 33, 39, 45, 46, 76, 81, 83, 85, 227; counterrevolutionary Cuban exiles and, 33, 42, 87–88; root cause of, 13, 200–201, 202, 225–30, 245; sabotage and terror attacks, 12, 26, 31, 41, 44, 45–46, 81, 83, 85, 86, 217, 220, 244, 245, 288; and Taylor Commission, 35–38; and underestimation of Cuba, 75. *See also* Assassination attempts; Blockade, U.S. naval; Embargo, U.S. economic; Operation Mongoose; Spy flights, U.S.

U.S. Department of Commerce, 38, 48, 57

U.S. Department of Defense, 78, 79, 142, 186, 249–50

U.S. Department of Justice, 29, 142

U.S. Department of State, 33, 38, 48, 56, 79, 142

U.S. Department of the Treasury, 38, 48

U.S. Information Agency, 38

U.S. invasion of Cuba, 12, 25, 137; casualty estimates in, 14; consideration of, 29, 31–32, 34–35, 137; and Cuba's defense capabilities, 14, 61, 68, 246, 247, 252; means world war, 171, 222; as goal of Operation Mongoose, 83–84; as only way to overthrow revolution, 12, 84, 86; plans for, 12; scenario for, 86–92; search for pretexts, 31, 32, 40, 41, 77, 81, 86, 88–89; as suicide, 131–32; as war on Soviet Union, 171

U.S. military deployment, October 1962: air force, 150–52; Atlantic Command, 147, 149–50, 152, 162; casualties during, 152; nuclear weapons in Europe, 166; number of troops involved, 150, 151, 153; U.S. Army units, 152–53

U.S. military exercises: Demolex, 89; Jupiter Spring, 98; Landphibex 1/62, 89; Phibriglex 62 (October 1962), 147–48; Sweep Clear II, 147; Swift Strike II, 89; Unitas III, 147

U.S. military, defense conditions: DEFCON-2, 151, 154, 165; DEFCON-3, 147, 153; DEFCON-5, 153

U.S. News & World Report, 90

U.S.-Soviet relations, 55

Uncertain Trumpet, The (Taylor), 35

United Nations, 137, 144, 146, 193, 281; Charter of, 54–55, 139, 163, 191, 198, 209, 214, 215, 232–33, 234; debates during crisis, 157, 162–63, 166, 167–68, 257, 261; and imperialist interventions, 265–66, 267. *See also* U Thant

United States: anti-Cuba campaign in, 214, 237, 274; impact of October Crisis within, 14–15, 161; 1962 elections, 97, 129, 130, 278; protest actions during October Crisis, 15–16

Uruguay, 54, 161

Ushakov, Lt. Gen. Sergei P., 94, 316

Veciana Blanch, Antonio, 45, 47

Venezuela, 130, 149

Vieques, 89, 148, 231–32
Vietnam War, 14, 16, 202
Volkogonov, Gen. Dimitri, 160

War, causes of, 267, 268. *See also* Peace
Ward, Vice Adm. Alfred G., 149, 316
Warsaw Pact, 155, 159, 190
Weapons—"offensive" and "defensive," 130, 141, 145, 187, 188, 192; Cuba's objection to use of terms,

134, 240, 246
White, Lincoln, 188, 316
Woodward, Robert F., 144, 316
Worker-farmer alliance, 14
World Peace Council, 156

Yepishev, Gen. Aleksei, 99–100, 316
Young Socialist Alliance, 15
Youth, 70

Zorin, Valerian, 163–64, 168–69, 316

From the Escambray to the Congo

In the Whirlwind of the Cuban Revolution

INTERVIEW WITH VÍCTOR DREKE
In this participant's account, Víctor Dreke describes how easy it became after the Cuban Revolution to take down the rope segregating blacks from whites at town dances, yet how enormous was the battle to transform social relations underlying all the ropes inherited from capitalism and Yankee domination. He recounts the determination, internationalism, and creative joy with which working people have defended their revolutionary course against U.S. imperialism from Cuba's own Escambray mountains, to the Americas, Africa, and beyond. $17.00

Che Guevara Speaks

ERNESTO CHE GUEVARA
"A faithful reflection of Che as he was, or, better, as he developed"—from the preface by Joseph Hansen. Includes major portions of Guevara's speech to the 1961 OAS-sponsored conference in Punta del Este, Uruguay, in response to Washington's drive to strangle the revolution economically and isolate it from the rest of the continent. $14.95

To Speak the Truth

Why Washington's 'Cold War' against Cuba Doesn't End

FIDEL CASTRO,
ERNESTO CHE GUEVARA
In historic speeches before the United Nations and UN bodies, Guevara and Castro address the workers of the world, explaining why the U.S. government so hates the example set by the socialist revolution in Cuba and why Washington's effort to destroy it will fail. $16.95

Dynamics of the Cuban Revolution

A Marxist Appreciation

JOSEPH HANSEN

How did the Cuban revolution come about? Why does it represent, as Hansen puts it, an "unbearable challenge" to U.S. imperialism? What political obstacles has it overcome? Written as the revolution advanced from its earliest days. $22.95

The Second Declaration of Havana

With the First Declaration of Havana

Two manifestos of the Cuban people to the oppressed and exploited throughout the Americas. The first declaration, proclaimed September 1960, calls for "the right of the peasants to the land; the right of the workers to the fruit of their labor; and the right of nations to nationalize the imperialist monopolies." The second declaration, February 1962, asks: "What does the Cuban revolution teach? That revolution is possible." $4.50

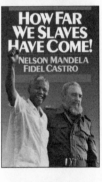

How Far We Slaves Have Come!

South Africa and Cuba in Today's World

NELSON MANDELA, FIDEL CASTRO

Speaking together in Cuba in 1991, Mandela and Castro discuss the unique relationship and example of the struggles of the South African and Cuban peoples. $9.95

Che Guevara and the Imperialist Reality

MARY-ALICE WATERS

"The world of capitalist disorder—the imperialist reality of the 21st century—would not be strange to Che," Waters writes. "Far from being dismayed by the odds we face, he would have examined the world with scientific precision and charted a course to win." $3.50

The Cuban Revolution in the world

Capitalism's World Disorder

WORKING-CLASS POLITICS AT THE MILLENNIUM
Jack Barnes

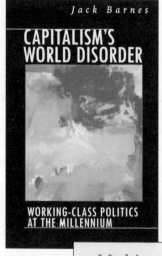

Today's spreading economic and social crises and acts of imperialist aggression are not the product of something gone wrong, Barnes explains, but of the lawful workings of capitalism. Yet the future can be changed by the united struggle and selfless action of workers and farmers conscious of their power to transform the world.

That was true during the October 1962 Cuban "missile" crisis, as well, Barnes points out, when "there were thousands of people in the United States who worked round the clock to stop Washington from invading Cuba." Also in Spanish and French. $24.95

Making History

INTERVIEWS WITH FOUR GENERALS OF
CUBA'S REVOLUTIONARY ARMED FORCES
*Néstor López Cuba, Enrique Carreras,
José Ramón Fernández, Harry Villegas*

Through the stories of four outstanding Cuban generals, each with close to half a century of revolutionary activity, we can see the class dynamics that have shaped our entire epoch. We can understand how the people of Cuba, as they struggle to build a new society, have for more than forty years held Washington at bay. Among other episodes in Cuba's revolutionary history, each of the generals describes his participation in the mobilization responding to the October 1962 crisis. $15.95

Playa Girón/Bay of Pigs

WASHINGTON'S FIRST MILITARY DEFEAT IN THE AMERICAS

Fidel Castro, José Ramón Fernández

In less than 72 hours of combat in April 1961, Cuba's revolutionary armed forces defeated an invasion by 1,500 mercenaries organized by Washington. In the process, the Cuban people set an example for workers, farmers, and youth throughout the world that with political consciousness, class solidarity, unflinching courage, and revolutionary leadership, it is possible to stand up to enormous might and seemingly insurmountable odds—and win. Essential background to the events that unfolded during the "missile" crisis a year and a half later. Also in Spanish. $23.95

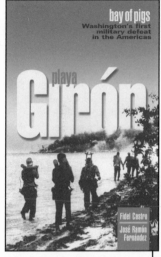

Cuba and the Coming American Revolution

Jack Barnes

After the defeat of the U.S.-organized mercenary assault in April 1961, followed by the "missile" crisis of October 1962, "the U.S. rulers never again attempted an invasion of Cuba." Barnes explains why.

This is a book about the class struggle in the United States, where the revolutionary capacities of working people are today as utterly discounted by the ruling powers as were those of the Cuban toilers. And just as wrongly. Also in Spanish and French. $13

The Changing Face of U.S. Politics
WORKING-CLASS POLITICS AND THE TRADE UNIONS
Jack Barnes

Building the kind of party the working class needs to prepare for coming class battles through which they will revolutionize themselves, their unions, and all of society. A handbook for workers, farmers, and youth repelled by the class inequalities, economic instability, racism, women's oppression, cop violence, and wars endemic to capitalism, and who are seeking the road toward effective action to overturn that exploitative system and join in reconstructing the world on new, socialist foundations. Also in French and Spanish. $23

The Communist Manifesto
Karl Marx and Frederick Engels

Founding document of the modern communist workers movement. In English and Spanish. $3.95

Their Trotsky and Ours
Jack Barnes

History shows that small revolutionary organizations will face not only the test of wars and repression, but also potentially shattering opportunities that emerge unexpectedly when strikes and social struggles explode. As that happens, communist parties recruit, fuse with other workers organizations, and grow into mass proletarian parties contesting to lead workers and farmers to power. This assumes that their cadres have absorbed a world communist program, are proletarian in life and work, and have forged a leadership with an acute sense of what to do next. *Their Trotsky and Ours* is about building such parties. Also in French and Spanish. $15

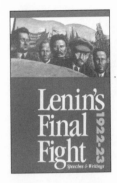

Pathfinder Was Born with the October Revolution
MARY-ALICE WATERS

Pathfinder Press traces its continuity to those who launched the worldwide effort to defend and emulate the first socialist revolution—the October 1917 revolution in Russia. From the writings of Marx, Engels, Lenin, and Trotsky, to the words of Malcolm X, Fidel Castro, and Che Guevara, to those of James P. Cannon, Farrell Dobbs, and leaders of the communist movement in the U.S. today, Pathfinder books aim to "advance the understanding, confidence, and combativity of working people." $3.00

Black Music, White Business
Illuminating the History and Political Economy of Jazz
FRANK KOFSKY

Probes the conflicts between the artistry of Black musicians and the control by largely white-owned businesses of jazz distribution—the recording companies, booking agencies, festivals, clubs, and magazines. $15.95

The Long View of History
GEORGE NOVACK

Why the struggle of working people for an end to oppression and exploitation is a realistic perspective built on sound scientific foundations, and why revolutionary change is fundamental to social and cultural progress. $5.00

The History of the Russian Revolution
LEON TROTSKY

The social, economic, and political dynamics of the first socialist revolution as told by one of its central leaders. "The history of a revolution is for us first of all a history of the forcible entrance of the masses into the realm of rulership over their own destiny," Trotsky writes. Unabridged edition, 3 vols. in one. $35.95

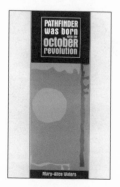
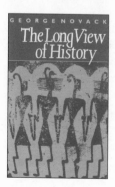

Fighting Racism in World War II

C.L.R. JAMES, GEORGE BREITMAN, EDGAR KEEMER, AND OTHERS

An account of struggles against lynch-mob terror and racist discrimination in U.S. war industries, the armed forces, and society as a whole from 1939 to 1945, taken from the pages of the socialist newsweekly, the *Militant*. These struggles helped lay the basis for the mass civil rights movement of the subsequent two decades. $21.95

Problems of Women's Liberation

EVELYN REED

Explores the social and economic roots of women's oppression from prehistoric society to modern capitalism and points the road forward to emancipation. $12.95

History of American Trotskyism 1928-38

Report of a Participant

JAMES P. CANNON

In twelve talks given in 1942, Cannon recounts the early efforts by communists in the U.S. to build a new kind of proletarian party. It carries the story from the first steps forward by vanguard workers politically responding to the victory of the October 1917 Russian Revolution up to the eve of World War II, when the communist organization in the U.S. takes the name Socialist Workers Party. With a new preface by Jack Barnes. Also in French and Spanish. $22

Teamster Rebellion

FARRELL DOBBS

The 1934 strikes that built the industrial union movement in Minneapolis and helped pave the way for the CIO, recounted by a central leader of that battle. The first in a four-volume series on the class-struggle leadership of the strikes and organizing drives that transformed the Teamsters union in much of the Midwest into a fighting social movement and pointed the road toward independent labor political action. $16.95

Write for a free catalog.

New International
A MAGAZINE OF MARXIST POLITICS AND THEORY

U.S. IMPERIALISM HAS LOST THE COLD WAR. That's what the Socialist Workers Party concluded at the opening of the 1990s, in the wake of the collapse of regimes and parties across Eastern Europe and in the USSR that claimed to be communist. Contrary to imperialism's hopes, the working class in those countries had not been crushed. It remains an intractable obstacle to reimposing and stabilizing capitalist relations, one that will have to be confronted by the exploiters in class battles—in a hot war.

Three issues of the Marxist magazine *New International* analyze the propertied rulers' failed expectations and chart a course for revolutionaries in response to rising worker and farmer resistance to the economic and social instability, spreading wars, and rightist currents bred by the world market system. They explain why the historic odds in favor of the working class have increased, not diminished, at the opening of the 21st century.

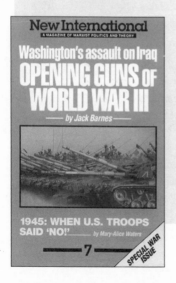

U.S. Imperialism Has Lost the Cold War

JACK BARNES

"It is only from fighters, from revolutionists of action, that communists will be forged in the course of struggle. And it is only from within the working class that the mass political vanguard of these fighters can come. The lesson from over 150 years of political struggle by the modern workers movement is that, more and more, to become and remain a revolutionist means becoming a communist." In *New International* no. 11. **$14.00**

Imperialism's March toward Fascism and War

JACK BARNES

"There will be new Hitlers, new Mussolinis. That is inevitable. What is not inevitable is that they will triumph. The working-class vanguard will organize our class to fight back against the devastating toll we are made to pay for the capitalist crisis. The future of humanity will be decided in the contest between these contending class forces." In *New International* no. 10. **$14.00**

Opening Guns of World War III

JACK BARNES

"Washington's Gulf war and its outcome did not open up a new world order of stability and UN-overseen harmony. Instead, it was the first war since the close of World War II that grew primarily out of the intensified competition and accelerating instability of the crises-ridden old imperialist world order." In *New International* no. 7. **$12.00**

Che Guevara, Cuba, and the Road to Socialism

ARTICLES BY ERNESTO CHE GUEVARA,
CARLOS RAFAEL RODRÍGUEZ, CARLOS TABLADA,
MARY-ALICE WATERS, STEVE CLARK,
JACK BARNES

Exchanges from the early 1960s and today on the political perspectives defended by Guevara as he helped lead working people to advance the transformation of economic and social relations in Cuba. In *New International* no. 8. **$10.00**

The Second Assassination of Maurice Bishop

STEVE CLARK

The lead article in *New International* no. 6 reviews the accomplishments of the 1979-83 revolution in the Caribbean island of Grenada. Explains the roots of the 1983 coup that led to the murder of revolutionary leader Maurice Bishop, and to the destruction of the workers and farmers government by a Stalinist political faction within the governing New Jewel Movement. **$15.00**

The Rise and Fall of the Nicaraguan Revolution

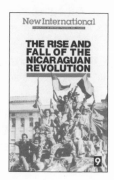

Based on ten years of socialist journalism from inside Nicaragua, this special issue of *New International* recounts the achievements and worldwide impact of the 1979 Nicaraguan revolution. It traces the political retreat of the Sandinista National Liberation Front leadership that led to the downfall of the workers and farmers government in the closing years of the 1980s. Documents of the Socialist Workers Party by Jack Barnes, Steve Clark, and Larry Seigle. In *New International* no. 9. **$14.00**

Distributed by Pathfinder